Arnold Feil • Franz Schubert

Arnold Feil

# FRANZ SCHUBERT

## Die schöne Müllerin • Winterreise
[The lovely miller maiden • Winter journey]

With an Essay, "Wilhelm Müller and Romanticism"
by Rolf Vollmann

Translated by Ann C. Sherwin

Reinhard G. Pauly, General Editor

**AMADEUS PRESS**
*Portland, Oregon*

All rights reserved © 1975 Philipp Reclam jun. GmbH & Co.
Siemensstrasse 32, Postfach 1349, D-7257 Ditizingen, West Germany

Translation © 1988 by Amadeus Press
All rights reserved
ISBN 0-931340-09-8

Printed in Singapore

AMADEUS PRESS
9999 S.W. Wilshire
Portland, Oregon 97225

**Library of Congress Cataloging-in-Publication Data**

Feil, Arnold.
   [Franz Schubert, Die schöne Müllerin, Winterreise. English]
   Franz Schubert, Die schöne Müllerin, Winterreise (The lovely
miller maiden, Winter journey) / Arnold Feil; with an essay Wilhelm
Müller and romanticism by Rolf Vollmann; translated by Ann C.
Sherwin; Reinhard G. Pauly, general editor.
     p.    cm.
   Translation of: Franz Schubert, Die schöne Müllerin, Winterreise.
   Bibliography: p.
   ISBN 0-931340-09-8
   1. Schubert, Franz, 1797–1828. Schöne Müllerin.  2. Schubert,
Franz, 1797–1828. Winterreise.  3. Müller, Wilhelm, 1794–1827.
I. Vollmann, Rolf. Wilhelm Müller and die Romantik. English.
1988.  II. Title.  III. Title: Lovely miller maiden. Winter journey.
ML410.S3F3313  1988
784.3'0092'4—dc19                            88-8111
                                              CIP
                                              MN

# Contents

# I. Foreword

In thinking about how I would explain the relationship of my text to its subject, Schubert's music, I turned to the observations of others who have undertaken the task of analyzing and describing music. Alban Berg once expressed better than anyone else what I would like to say here:

> This guidebook [to Arnold Schönberg's *Gurrelieder*] makes no claim to completeness. Such a goal would be impossible even if space limitations did not force me to write concisely and to withhold much of what should be said. I had to choose between a uniformly superficial treatment and one that went into detail only in certain cases. By adopting the latter, I had to forgo from the outset the formal polish and well-roundedness that characterize other guidebooks. I willingly ran the risk that the thoroughness of my discussions would not be proportional to the length and magnitude of the topic discussed. I feel all the more justified in this, considering that my guidebook differs in purpose from the ususal thematic analyses. It was not my intent to *accompany* this musical work with words, to find at least one decorative epithet for every mood or to point out intensifications and climaxes. On the other hand, *if I were to analyze,* I would not be content with citing themes, as if the essence of the music were not just as likely to be found in a progression of harmonies, a chord, or even a note; as if *results* and *developments* of a theme were not at least as important as the theme itself.
>
> Avoiding all poetry and psychology, I have tried instead to speak with cool objectivity about the various musical components wherever they occur. On one occasion I might deal with harmonic structure; on another with the construction of motifs, themes, melodies and transitions; with form and the combining of larger musical structures; contrapuntal composition, choral writing, voice leading; or, finally, with the nature of the instrumentation. I have tried to deal with each of these in depth at least once, citing examples from the work [ ...]. If I have succeeded, then this little book has achieved its purpose, and I needn't regret that where the immeasurable beauty of this music calls for reverent silence, I have sought and found words—theoretical though they may be.

It is difficult to present an objective and appropriate analysis of a musical composition derived from Beethoven obbligato accompaniment (see below, p. 20), which is also a song composition, without dismantling the piece. Such an analysis must elucidate the composition and the music—that is, a work of art—in a way that is helpful to both performer and listener. Not everyone sees the need for this kind of writing. An intelligent man, the music historian Alfred Einstein, once asserted that analysis was of no use to someone unfamiliar with a work, while anyone familiar with it did not need it. This may be true of analyses that do not aim for a final synthesis.

On the other hand, Theodor W. Adorno held that the key to the content of all art lies in its technique. So if content is of interest, then the technique employed must be revealed.

But regardless of the complexities of the task, music lovers and musicians must surely welcome guides to listening and understanding—to intelligent listening and meaningful interpretation. For who among us would presume to claim that he fully understands Schubert once and for all? Anyone who thinks in this way misunderstands music, for it does not really exist until it is sounded. But sound is always tied to a particular moment, while the urge to make music continually challenges the performer and the listener to *create* the work, which neither already *possess* in some imperishable form. In music-making, musicians and audiences are bound together, because only through their common activity, the common effort of both, as Sartre put it, can the work come into being.

This book is intended only as an aid to musicians and their audience. Such verbal explanations are no substitute for musical interpretation, for the sound itself. But they can provide a supplement, as it were, that prepares the way for musical understanding. Should this understanding then have a bearing on a performance, stimulating new or different interpretations, then my goal will have been attained. This book is primarily a contribution to musical interpretation and only secondarily to musical analysis, to put it in a nutshell.

I have tried to go beyond the usual concept of analysis, sometimes even of interpretation, which is often little more than a retelling of the musical text. Therefore, the reader should allow himself to become part of the process of creative expression. He must be willing to listen, think, understand, make music, and listen again. Then perhaps he will benefit from the experience. Anyone who simply expects understanding to come without making the effort to look at the sheet music, who resists the idea of listening to records with thoughtful reflection as well as pleasure, will probably be disappointed.

Finally, I must also disappoint those who expect nothing more than confirmation of what they already know or think they know—perhaps that the works are *good,* that this or that song is especially *beautiful,* and that Schubert was a good composer. After all, why should one write about the obvious? All of which brings me to another important point:

Any author writing about music in an intelligible way must presuppose a certain amount of musical experience on the reader's part. Only that which is seen, heard, grasped—in a word, jointly experienced—by writer and reader can be imparted or recognized; otherwise words and sentences exist only in a vacuum. This book is meant to convey something specific about a specific musical reality. This objective is possible only in so far as the reader is in touch with the reality of the music, either through direct or indirect experience. There is no way around it. The reader must follow the music as he reads this text, so that he has a clear idea of the sound. In so doing, he should resist the temptation to interpret immediately on his own, thus robbing himself of the opportunity to understand the points I am endeavoring to make. He should pass through our stations of interpretation offerred before proceeding to his own.

To help the reader follow my interpretive course, I have included numerous musical examples, which should always be referred to, for in all my descriptions attention is directed first and foremost to the rhythm—and rhythm exists only in the doing, only as an immediate action. Written symbols are no substitute for the actual realization of music. If one merely reads the text, contextual gaps will occur wherever an example has been ignored. These gaps can only be closed if the reader not only looks at the examples, but actually sings or plays them as suggested.

The next logical question is: Why was *rhythm* chosen as the focal point? No one would attribute lesser significance to melody, harmony or structure ("form," as is often said, which only creates confusion). But whereas much has been said about melody and harmony and their expressive qualities, as well as about "form," rhythm is seldom discussed, either specifically or in general—and meaningful discussion of rhythm is even rarer. Today's musical audiences have largely forgotten how to "listen rhythmically." Consequently, little note is taken of the rhythmic component in music, and descriptions are rarely any better. For this reason alone, I expect a thorough study and exposition of music from the standpoint of rhythm to produce new insights. But I had another, more important reason: Schubert's concept, inspired by a poem, seemingly relates to a *narrower* region of his *musical* imagination, mainly that of motion and its rhythmic correlate. Therefore, the musical parameter of rhythm seems to play a special role in his composing. Melodic and harmonic factors often simply emerge, as it were, while the arrangement of the whole, like its parts, is chiefly a matter of rhythm.[1]

One final question comes to mind: Why is the music still so relevant today? The answer is as difficult as the fact itself is indisputable. A more theoretical treatment would require careful consideration and complex research of a scholarly nature, for which this is not the place. On the other hand, anyone who hears the music can experience this relevance for himself. When the music speaks to him, it becomes a part of him. The purpose of this book is to pave the way to such experience

Much has been written about Schubert's songs, especially those of his cycles based on Wilhelm Müller's poems. But because musicology does not recognize a musical-literary genre for which a name such as "description of a work that leads to interpretation" might fit, I owe credit to essentially one book: Thrasybulos G. Georgiades, *Schubert. Musik und Lyrik*, Göttingen 1967.[2] Like Georgiades, I have tried to analyze musical structures as part of the interpretive process. Thus similarities or agreements in method and results, insofar as interpretations have or are results, are by no means coincidental.[3]

# II. Introduction

## 1. Song

October 19, 1814, has been called the "Birthday of German Song." On this day Franz Schubert is supposed to have composed "Gretchen am Spinnrade" [Gretchen at the spinning wheel] (Goethe; Op. 2 D 118)[3a], "the first significant single song he wrote."[4] We hear and read this kind of thing again and again—it's easily said and written. Even if it were universally accepted that Schubert composed the song on that particular day,[5] this birthday claim could not be seriously sustained, but it does contain a kernel of truth.

Of course everyone sings. German people have sung their lullabies, nursery rhymes, seasonal carols, work songs, dance tunes, and hymns for centuries just like everyone else—and in their native language, naturally. So German songs have been around for a long time. The tunes lived on through oral tradition, which simply means that people didn't learn them by reading the notes in song books but from their mother or father, at social gatherings, on the job, on the street, or in school. In any case, they learned them by rote or by singing along. These tunes were not part songs, not polyphonic compositions that had to be written down, nor were they "performed" as such. They simply passed from mouth to mouth. Consequently, the tunes were simple, particularly in the sense of having only one voice part, even though they were sometimes sung in two parts. The second part was never a product of musical composition, nor did it pretend to be. No, everyone simply "knew" the part. It was not genuine two-part music, in the polyphonic sense, for the added part usually paralleled the melody in lower thirds or sixths.

The music perpetuated in this way, which today we call folk music, was indeed the music of the folk, of all the men and women who comprised an ethnic group. It bound them together as did their dialect. On the other hand, art music— polyphonic music worked out in written form and intended for "performance" (i.e., composed music) was available only to the few whose social standing or profession allowed them to receive a musical education. From a statistical view, the bulk of all music can be classified as "oral music" and only a very small part as "composed music." Interestingly, though, almost all the music of the past that has survived is found in this relatively small body of composed music. The relationship between these two musical realms, even their "quantitative ratio," was upset and underwent far-reaching changes in the 18th century, with the dawn of the industrial age and the fundamental transformation it brought about in our society and our world. The people reacted immediately at their most sensitive point, where they were especially used to expressing themselves, where they were most inclined to vent their feelings: in their music. We know of this reaction only indirectly, though unequivocally: from the widespread lamentation of the day over the decline of the folksong; from the flurry to collect that which was about to be lost, especially through the efforts of Johann Gottfried Herder (1744–1803); and not least of all, from vigorous and unusual efforts by musicians and poets of the Berlin song schools, as they are called by music historians. Their spokesmen, Karl Wilhelm Ramler (1725–1798), Christian Gottfried Krause (1719–1770), Johann Georg Sulzer (1720–1779), and somewhat later, the musicians Johann Abraham Peter Schulz (1747–1800) and Johann Friedrich Reichardt (1752–1814), repeatedly emphasized in their essays and the prologues to the song collections they published the importance they attached to composing songs "in the folk manner"—a clear indication that a major cultural change was taking place.

> Germans everywhere are now studying music, but in many big cities people want to hear nothing but opera arias. Yet rarely is a light, jocular song encountered among these arias, a song that can issue effortlessly from any mouth and be sung without piano or other accompaniment. If our composers would compose their songs by singing, without using a piano and without thinking they need to add a bass, then singing would soon become a more popular pastime in our nation, spreading merriment and camaraderie everywhere.
>
> It is already evident that the people of our land no longer drink simply to become intoxicated nor no longer eat excessively. In our major cities, proper parties are beginning to be held. We live sociably. And what is more natural on such occasions than to sing? But on such occasions people simply don't want to sing serious songs, for in coming together they seek a break from their serious daily concerns. The songs they wish to sing are charming, delicate, simple—not so poetic that the pretty songstress can't understand them, but not so light and flowing that those with any wits would not care to read them.[6]

In this introduction from the popular and highly acclaimed first song collection of the Berlin Song School (*Oden mit Melodien* [Odes with melodies], Berlin 1753), the editors Ramler and Krause describe what amounts to a new urban middle class, a class that lives convivially and wishes to entertain itself in a new fashion. They acknowledge that this society seems to want to hear nothing but opera arias, meaning the opera hits of the current season, but that in reality it needs music that it apparently doesn't have, or no longer has. It needs songs that are easy for everyone to sing, yet not simplistic.

What these songs are to be like is clearly stated elsewhere, almost programmatically formulated, in fact, by Reichardt in the foreword to his *Frohe Lieder für deutsche Männer* [Joyful songs for German men] (Berlin 1781), an "experiment with songs in the folk manner, to be sung without accompaniment at ordinary social gatherings."[7]

> Song tunes that anyone with ear and voice can at once join in singing must be able to stand alone, without any accompaniment. They must be so well-suited to the text, with a simple melodic line, straightforward motion, exact correlation at section breaks, etc., that once one learns the tune, one cannot conceive of it without the words, or the words without the tune. The melody must be everything with the words and nothing by itself. Thus Herder's preference for the German word *Weise* [tune, with its connotation of "fashion" or "manner"] is more fitting than the usual term *Melodie*.

Such a melody will always have true unison character (to explain it to the artist succinctly) —that is, harmony is neither needed nor permitted.

This is what all songs were like in the days when our ancestral tradition was still rich in song, before the introduction of consonant harmony, and even after its introduction in the church, its place of origin, to which it was limited for years. But once songs were embellished with harmony, our ear began to demand it on every occasion; so our melodies have become superficial, serving only as clothing for the harmony.

How wonderful it was back in the days before this studied music-making was widespread, when a happy-go-lucky soul did not feel compelled to understand why he felt as he did, but simply rejoiced in his happy feelings. Can anyone today simply sit and experience such euphoria from most of our songs?

The reader can probably name a hundred old folk melodies that don't have this unison character, that lend themselves very easily to a second part and probably even invite it. But these are not genuine folk melodies; they are hunting horn pieces or country dances, in which the words are of secondary importance.

Yet even these two-part pieces have no intervals in their natural form other than alternating thirds, fifths, and octaves; because the natural-tone wind instruments from which they are derived can only play such intervals in tune. When the open-minded artist recognizes this fact and then recalls the musical system he has learned, he can once more experience that first delightful revelation, upon hearing those corresponding intervals. He can then think again of the happy hours he spent working out all those intricacies that were whimsically added, whereupon whole new worlds opened before him.

One more word about folk songs. The true artist, as he begins to understand the tortured paths of his art, turns to folk songs as the mariner turns to the North Star. It is by studying them that he draws the greatest benefit.

Only melodies such as the Swiss "Es hätt' e' Buur e' Töchterli" [There was a farmer who had a daughter] are genuine, original folk melodies. They excite and stir the feelings of every listener.

It would be hard to come up with a more accurate description of true folk music, as contrasted to art music—the latter being "propped up" by the "system of consonant harmony," that is, multi-part or polyphonic composition. The oral music tradition can hardly be characterized better—even though it is presented as a guide for composers who have learned and now practice their craft of art music, the other, if not opposite, realm of music.

This is an outright paradox. How can a composer, an artist, sing "more in the folk style than in the art style," or "somehow create an illusion of familiarity" without sinking into banality? How does a song achieve this illusion, "the appearance of the spontaneous, the artless, the familiar, in a word: *the folk idiom*," if the composer is schooled in the art system?[8] One cannot make something that must seem spontaneous. One cannot compose while disregarding composition—that is, musical style—which is an historic reality. Simplicity and the illusion of familiarity are no more easily realized than complexity and innovation. We know of only a few fortunate cases in which something truly fine and at the same time simple has been achieved, where the art is artfully concealed. Nearly every undertaking claiming to be simple is really simplistic or worse yet has slipped into banality.

This then was the situation of song and song composition in the second half of the 18th century: There was a new and strongly felt need to create music for the urban middle class, to replace the disappearing oral musical tradition. This undertaking resulted in an incredible growth in the production of songs. Of the approximately 900 song collections published in the 18th century, 37 had appeared by the year 1750; roughly 200 by 1775; and the rest, over 600 collections, in the remaining years. However, the products, the composed songs, generally fell short of good musical standards. They were only imitations of something truly genuine and could not be what they were supposed to be: genuine. Secondly, the compositional skill they displayed was behind the times.[9] And lastly, despite a conscious effort to follow the simple, unison, unaccompanied song, songs with a simple piano or guitar accompaniment had became popular. The "system" of composition could no longer be ignored. Obviously these songs were no solution to the new music problem that historical circumstances posed. It is not surprising that the entire song output of those decades has been largely forgotten, with only a few exceptions, such as the marvelous "Der Mond ist aufgegangen" [The moon has risen] by Johann Abraham Peter Schulz, based on Matthias Claudius' poem. Nor is it any wonder that the division of composed music into light and serious forms arose out of this very situation.[10]

However, this unique historical situation also afforded composers the opportunity to pursue a new direction. That opportunity lay in accepting as art music new songs with simple accompaniment, thus to put an end to the tyranny of popular appeal in composition. This new art song was based on the consistent use of polyphonic musical technique with all its accomplishments. After all, art music did recognize the genre "song," and not just the polyphonic, but certainly the unison song with simple accompaniment as well, though not in the "folk style!" However, this new genre stood at the sidelines for some years and was only marginally popular. It was Franz Schubert, himself a product of the new urban middle class, who united the seemingly incompatible: western polyphony and song. It was he who succeeded in maneuvering this new form to a central position in musical thinking and creativity, and who realized "lyric poetry as musical structure."[11] He single handedly opened a new realm for European music. In this light we can better understand the meaning underlying the assertion quoted at the beginning of this chapter: that Schubert gave birth to the German Song.

## 2. Franz Schubert's Song

Schubert was born in Vienna January 31, 1797, the only composer of the Viennese classical school to be born in the city. Only a few years earlier, his parents had moved from the country to the city, where they became acquainted and were married in 1785. His grandparents were farmers in Neudorf near Mährisch-Schönberg and craftspeople in Zuckmantel, Austrian Silesia. His father, Franz Schubert, Sr., was a schoolteacher in Lichtental, and after 1786 in Himmelpfortgrund, both suburbs of Vienna. Despite their extremely crowded quarters and limited means, there was much singing and music-making in the teacher's family. The children began receiving instruction in several instruments at an early age, but there was never any talk of any of them becoming a professional musician. Though always known and yet repeatedly overlooked, Schubert did not start life, either by education or vocation, as a musician. He was a teacher in an elementary school, a position from which he resigned in 1818. Schubert found himself in quite different circumstances than his musical colleagues when he turned to music and composition.

> He had no friend nor master standing beside him, who could have guided him in these efforts [larger works], advising, warning, correcting. He had some lessons with Salieri early on but the latter was too old and belonged to a totally different school and artistic era. Salieri could not act as a master for a youth who was inspired by and imbued with Beethoven's genius. [12]

When Leopold von Sonnleithner, a close friend, describes Schubert's musical education in these terms, he of course underestimates what Antonio Salieri (1750–1825) could and did teach the young composer: namely, the craft of composition, especially Italian song composition. [13] But this was simply not Schubert's principal interest, and certainly, the reference here to Beethoven is of great significance. One other thing distinguished Schubert from other musicians: he did not compose for others, so to speak—at least not initially. He later did so but in a different sense than his colleagues. In his early career there was no public demand for the genre in which he was mainly interested, the song. No commissions for composing songs were offered. Songs were seldom included in public performances. They were largely sung in private circles or in concerts of a more private nature, so-called "evening entertainment" gatherings. When songs were occasionally included in large concerts, misgivings were immediately voiced. A reviewer of the musical "academy," held on May 6, 1827 in the Great University Hall, reports:

> No. 3. "Im Freien" [In the open], poem by Seidl, set to music and accompanied on the piano by Mr. Schubert, sung by Mr. Tietze. Beautiful though the composition and performance were, the reviewer must say that, in his opinion, this is too large a place for performing a song of which even the most delicate shading must not be lost. It would be much more effective in a smaller chamber. [14]

Schubert's friend Spaun expressed a similar view in his *Aufzeichnungen über meinen Verkehr mit Franz Schubert* [Notes of my acquaintance with Franz Schubert] (1858) [15]:

> Neither are his songs suitable for the concert hall, for grand productions. The audience possess a feeling for the poem and enjoy the beautiful song with him. In short, it requires an audience vastly different from the one that fills theaters and concert halls.

Schubert's audience was not that of the great concert or the generally popular musical genres. It was a circle of friends and the middle class from which they came. Musically speaking, this society was no longer "folk," in the sense discussed earlier. It no longer felt comfortable or secure in an oral music tradition. Nor did the audience for Schubert's songs feel comfortable in the courts of the higher nobility, where art and music had been cultivated almost exclusively before the great social revolution. Schubert's middle class audience had created their own circle, in which they "kept musical company." They sang, arranged parlor games, acted out plays, and made music in their homes. Even after Schubert had raised the song to the level of other musical genres and many of his songs had found their way into the concert hall, his point of departure was still the home—though it was not *Hausmusik* [home music] as Reichardt and Zelter may have envisioned it. The musical society in which Schubert lived and for which he composed was about to inherit the legacy of the arts from the higher nobility, and thus it was anything but unpretentious. Indeed, what occurred here was what later came to be called the "cultivation of the arts." These were no vagabond bohemians, these people who met in the theater, at concerts, and often in coffee houses afterwards, who flocked to evening home readings and musical gatherings—"Schubertiaden," as they called them. They were artists—some by profession, most of them dilettantes in the better sense; and Schubert, Moritz von Schwind, and Franz Grillparzer were not the only creatively active ones among them. They worked more or less in collaboration, just as they shared the same role models, the heroes whom they admired. Among their musical heroes, Beethoven headed the list.

The "Rede am Grabe Beethovens" [Oration at Beethoven's grave], which Grillparzer, Schubert's friend, had written, closed with these words:

> And if ever in your life the power of his creations overwhelms you like the coming storm, if your tears flow in the midst of a generation yet unborn, remember this hour and think: we were there when they buried him, and we wept when he died.[16]

Schubert was one of the torchbearers who walked along beside the coffin. Although no one knows whether Schubert ever spoke a word to Beethoven, it is certain that "the youth who was inspired by and imbued with Beethoven's genius" followed and learned from the work of his model; that, living in the same time period and place as Beethoven, he consciously took advantage of his good fortune. In 1822, Schubert published his Opus 10 (eight variations on a French song, for piano, four hands, in E minor, from the year 1818, D624) and dedicated it to Beethoven. We can safely assume that he had had some contact with the master, but we have no certain knowledge of it. On March 31, 1824, Schubert wrote a long letter to his friend Leopold Kupelwieser, the first part of which reveals his great discouragement:

> As for songs, I have done little that is new. Instead I tried my hand at several instrumental pieces. I composed two quartets for violins, viola and cello [A minor, D 804; D minor, D 810] and an octet [F major, D 803], and I intend to write another quartet [not carried out]. In this manner, I hope to prepare my way to the large symphony.
>     The latest news in Vienna is that Beethoven is giving a concert [on May 7, 1824], in which his new symphony [No. 9, D minor, Op. 125], three pieces from the new mass [Kyrie, Credo and Agnus Dei from the *Missa solemnis*, Op. 123], and a new overture [C major, *Die Weihe des*

*Hauses* (The consecration of the house), Op. 124] will be performed. God willing, I intend to give a similar concert in the coming year.[17]

It was probably shortly before the performance of the Ninth Symphony in this concert that Beethoven changed the trombone parts in the second and fourth movements. The new parts, in Beethoven's handwriting, later turned up in Schubert's possession. He had apparently either received them as a gift or taken them as a memento. More important than such personal pieces of evidence, however, is this: in order to "prepare [his] way to the large symphony," whereby he could hardly have meant a particular symphony, but rather the genre, Schubert wrote string quartets and a larger chamber music work for string and wind players, using Beethoven as his model. But rather than choosing one of the master's late works, whose genesis and publication he had witnessed, as a model for his octet, he chose the Septet Op. 20 from the years 1799/1800. Certainly he must have been influenced by the fact that, in the Septet, Beethoven had created a new model in the genre of chamber music for string and wind players, a work that had proved extremely successful. But the determining factor has to have been the insight it offered into the process of musical composition. In this early example, Beethoven's technique of formal construction was fully transparent; here Schubert no doubt believed he could best learn, through imitation, what he needed in the way of compositional technique. In a letter dated March 6, 1824, to Franz von Schober, another of Schubert's friends, Moritz von Schwind describes how intensively Schubert went about this work:

> Schubert is superhuman in his diligence. A new quartet is being performed Sunday at the home of Schuphanzig, who is very enthusiastic and is said to have rehearsed especially diligently. For some time now, he [Schubert] has been writing an octet with great zeal. If anyone goes to his house during the day, he says, "Hello, how are you? Fine," and then continues writing, whereupon the caller withdraws. He has already set two of Müller's poems to music very beautifully. I spend nearly every evening at his home.[18]

The task at which we find Schubert here, in Beethoven's presence so to speak, can perhaps be described as applying the practical knowledge and technique of western polyphonic composition to the genre that interested him most. Since persistent attempts at pure unaccompanied unison were doomed to failure for the reasons already noted,[19] the song in the second half of the 18th century had developed a homophony of sorts, in which the melody was dominant and any accompaniment was totally subordinate, serving merely as support or filler. In these songs, multi-part composition was essentially reduced to an upper voice, because the other voices had ceased to be independent. The harmonic sequence of the supporting chords, even when broken into simple accompanying configurations for the instrumentalist, no longer resulted in polyphonic composition, strictly speaking. When nothing is left but what "the judicious composer or even the practiced ear adds mentally when singing in unison," when multi-part music is reduced to mere homophony, then we can no longer speak of it as musical composition, as the characteristic product of western art. The challenge, therefore, was to compose music in the polyphonic tradition as song—in other words, to develop *one* setting that combined a lyrical voice part with an instrumental part.

Of course Mozart and Beethoven were also aware of this problem, but the few songs they wrote contributed little toward its solution. They were unable to bring about a change in the 18th-century tradition of the genre. Reichardt was certainly justified in his complaint of 1796 (in the foreword to his collection *Lieder geselliger Freude* [Songs for social pleasure]) that he had found no acceptable compositions by Haydn and Mozart; that he could not comprehend 'how these superb men should have made so little use of our best poets, on the one hand, and on the other hardly dealt with the song in its true form at all."[20] In Haydn's and Mozart's work, as well as Beethoven's, the genre continues to stand at the periphery. Beethoven's catalog of works lists roughly 70 songs, but the fact that barely a handful of them are known speaks for itself—and Beethoven himself made no secret of it: "I simply do not like to write songs!"[21]

Thus Schubert can hardly have admired Mozart and Beethoven for their song composition; no help was to be found here. In experimenting with the instrumental technique he had observed and absorbed over many years from the classical school, in his efforts to develop a new compositional technique especially applicable to the song, he had to do without examples from his heroes. He had to look elsewhere for models that he could adapt and transform. These he found in the ballads of Johann Rudolf Zumsteeg (1760–1802), director of the court music in Stuttgart. Zumsteeg's ballads had found wide acceptance shortly after 1800, although—or because—they went contrary to the prevailing ideal of the strophic song, the simple, traditional song.[22] Zumsteeg had "through-composed" ballads with action-filled texts—that is, he created a different musical setting for each stanza. And it was this practice that fascinated young Schubert. Zumsteeg's songs [*Gesänge*] —I hesitate to use the traditional term *Lied* for his early works—display the broad sweep of his efforts to focus on scene and plot rather than on melodies that "anyone with a voice can easily learn," that could pass from mouth to mouth. It was "involvement in the particulars" of the text that was of greatest interest to Zumsteeg. He tried to demand and generate this focus in his listeners, even though this ran contrary to the esthetics of song prevailing at the time. The most eminent advocate of the latter was Goethe, whom Schubert highly admired. After reading the following, one need no longer wonder that Goethe was not pleased with songs like Schubert's 'Erlkönig' [Erlking] (Op. 1, 1815, D 328). In February 1801, Goethe records in his *Tag- und Jahreshefte* [Diaries and yearbooks]:

> Ehlers was suited to many acting and singing roles and gave pleasing performances. Especially in the latter capacity, he was most welcome at social gatherings, where, accompanied on the guitar, he would present ballads and other such songs in matchless form, rendering the words with utmost precision. He was untiring in his attention to the most accurate expression, which required that the singer be able to express through a *single* melody the diversity of meanings in the individual stanzas, thus filling the roles of lyric and epic poet at the same time. Absorbed in this endeavor, he didn't mind my asking him to repeat the same song meticulously, in all its fine nuances, for several hours in the evening, indeed until late into the night; for through successful application, he became convinced of the failure of so-called through-composing of songs, whereby the overall lyrical character is completely wanting, overwhelmed by a false interest in the particular which it demands and generates.

At first, Schubert depended heavily on Zumsteeg's through-composed models, whether by direct imitation, following what lay before him section by section, as in one of his first songs, "Hagars Klage" [Hagar's lament], 1811, D5; or by free imitation that bore Zumsteeg's mark, as in "Leichenfantasie" [Funeral fantasy], 1811, D 7. He then fully adopted Zumsteeg's method of composition and used it superbly for Schiller's ballad "Der Taucher" [The diver]. He worked on the first version (D 77) from September 17, 1813 to April 5, 1814 and completed the second version (D 111) in August 1814, only to make fundamental changes in it once again in the spring of 1815. This is one of many examples illustrating how Schubert often worked long, hard, and persistently not only to shape a particular song but also to develop his compositional technique.

Now the label "genialer Wurf" [brilliantly tossed off], once applied to "Gretchen am Spinnrade," and its designation as the "first significant single song that he wrote" as noted earlier, appear in a different light. For the first time, the new musical style which Schubert had developed after years of striving for what was essentially a new definition of "song," had met with success in a completed work. With this song, a new musical concept had broken through and gained acceptance, a concept whose importance for the 19th century cannot be overestimated.

From this point of view, many of the commonly held notions about Schubert and his "song art" appear inaccurate. We often find references to "Schubert oder die Melodie" [Schubert: the melody], which incorrectly implies that the only significant element in Schubert's music is beautiful melody. Some would-be experts have called his music "homophonic," but this label is inadequate. One also notes the oft-repeated criticism by other would-be experts that Schubert hadn't mastered counterpoint. [23] Certainly "Der Lindenbaum" [The linden tree] has become a folk song. But rarely is it mentioned that Schubert's setting contains this passage in the middle section: "Der Hut flog mir vom Kopfe, ich wendete mich nicht" [My hat flew off my head, I did not turn around], and that this thoroughly unmelodious part simply could not be carried over into the folk song. Shouldn't we ask if anything else of Schubert's has become a folk song? Certainly not "Das Wandern ist des Müllers Lust" [Traveling is the miller's joy]! After all, who could sing Schubert's song without the piano accompaniment and get any pleasure from it? The familiar folk tune [sung to the same text—ed.] is more suitable for that.

No, I think it is something else that characterizes Schubert other than his superb melodies. In an April 1930 Vienna radio broadcast, Alban Berg, pupil of Arnold Schönberg and composer of the operas *Wozzeck* and *Lulu*, participated in a dialogue with an opponent of atonality. Among the composers Berg invoked in defense of his "richly crimped and serrated melodic style" was Schubert, "this melodist par excellence" [Berg's words]. He then went on to cite "Letzte Hoffnung," [Last hope], "Wasserflut," [Flood of tears], and "Der stürmische Morgen" [The stormy morning] from *Winterreise* to support his assertion. These examples may seem far-fetched, but the fact that Alban Berg sought to rest his argument on Schubert at all, and particularly on his late works, surely says something about the breadth of Schubert's musical practice.

Another fact bears on this matter: In early November 1828, a few days before his death (Nov. 19, 1828), Schubert and a friend, Wolfgang Josef Lanz, arranged to take instruction in counterpoint, a fundamental discipline of musical composition, using Friedrich Wilhelm Marpurg's *Abhandlung von der Fuge* [Treatise on the fugue], Berlin 1753/54. Their instructor was to be Simon Sechter (1788–1867), a theory teacher well known in Vienna at that time, who later became Anton Bruckner's teacher. This strange decision of Schubert's has never been fully understood. What could this genius, "creator of immortal melodies," hope to learn from the pedestrian Sechter? Craftsmanship! Specifically, an aspect of musical craftsmanship to which he now wanted to devote special attention in his work. In the passages usually cited in defense of Schubert's contrapuntal competence, the label most frequently used to describe his compositional style is the one which Beethoven designated as his own: "obligates Accompagnement." (An example is found in the second movement of the 1824 Octet for Strings and Winds, especially the G-flat major episode, measure 25 ff.[24])

When on December 15, 1800, Beethoven offered his Septet (Op. 20) to Hofmeister, a publisher in Leipzig, he added the following note: "ein Septett per il violino, viola, violoncello, contra basso, clarinett, corno, fagotto, —tutti obligati (ich kann gar nichts unobligates schreiben, weil ich schon mit einem obligaten Accompagnement auf die Welt gekommen bin.)" [a septet for the violin, viola, cello, double bass, clarinet, horn, bassoon—all obbligato (I cannot write anything non-obbligato, because I came into the world with an obbligato accompaniment.)] So in the very work to which Schubert would turn for help 25 years later in order to prepare his way to greater works,[25] Beethoven used "obligates Accompagnement" to describe his compositional style. How are we to understand this term?

The parts of Beethoven's composition are not contrapuntal in the traditional sense, i.e. each is not as independent as possible, as in a fugue. Save for certain sections such as the second theme in the first-movement form of a sonata, the lower parts are not subordinate to and dependent on the melody, as accompaniment. Rather, all the parts share in a new "musical task": the motivic work, the treatment of the musical material in the overall framework, the building of the structure. In this respect, the parts are obbligato, despite a certain melodic dominance of the upper voice in the accompaniment and in the composition as a whole.

Schubert took this style, especially as it was employed in the instrumental music of the Viennese classical school, and applied it to the song—adapting it to the genre, of course, and modifying it as necessary. And in so doing, Schubert redefined the genre. "Song"—or "piano song" (Klavierlied), as it was now called because of the new style—was not just melody with more or less differentiated accompaniment. From that time on, through the 19th and first quarter of the 20th century, song was the genre (aside from opera) in the western vocal polyphonic tradition. Schubert's mark on the genre was so profound, that it spread to other countries; together with the word Lied, the German name for the genre, it was incorporated into the national music styles that flowered in the 19th century.

One other matter remains to attend to again. The individual art song is not the only thing we call "song." Our folk and religious songs belong in the genre now as before; although we don't often think of them in this context, we still refer to many of the poems of Goethe and Schiller as songs ("Das Lied von der Glocke" [The song of the bell])as well as those of Wilhelm Müller and Heinrich Heine (Buch der Lieder [Book of songs]); and it was not mere coincidence that Bertolt Brecht entitled many of his poems "song." The intent is clear: The texts are supposed to be sung, or they are modeled after texts that are, or once were, sung. Here, the "illusion of familiarity" shines through again, that illusion that was once connected to the way the text was expressed musically and perhaps still is in Bertolt Brecht's songs. Many of these "songs" are effective only when sung, even though their texts are important qua text and were not created to be set to music. The literary and the musical "songs" are related through the element in which the text is, was or should be rendered: the "melody." This is why the part of the song that supports the text has always dominated, despite all ties to the accompaniment, despite its fusion into a single musical form from Schubert's time on. We distinguish it from the other parts of the composition with a special designation. It is "the melody," even in those cases in which it cannot be separated from the composition as a whole, where it cannot successfully convey the text by itself, as in the Schubertian piano song. History and tradition come into play here: The German word *Weise* [way; melody] refers to the manner or way in which a song—a text meant for singing—has been rendered over the years. Such a "Weise" is old enough that, even if integrated into polyphonic composition, it can "turn its back on it", as Georgiades expressed it. Since Schubert, "melody" and "accompaniment," though we tend to speak of them separately, are no longer separable; and yet each retains its individuality, its original independence. The new song form of Schubert holds vocal and instrumental elements apart yet at the same time binds them together.

## 3. The Origin of Schubert's Song Cycles

In the winter of 1816/17 in Berlin,

at the home of privy councillor von Stägemann, a youthful circle of talented people had formed around his wife and their daughter, and the members would assign one another poetic tasks. One of the members was the poet Wilhelm Müller (1794–1827), who rapidly gained fame, only to be quickly snatched from life. [By virtue of his "Griechenlieder" (Greek songs), he became the poetic spokesman for philhellenism in Germany.] It was here that he wrote the first of the beautiful songs that eventually spread through all of Germany—some as hiking songs, some bearing other labels. Under the title "Rose, die Müllerin" [Rose, the miller maiden], a dramatic task had been proposed, which could only be realized by a series or chain of songs: Rose, the lovely miller maid, is loved by the miller, the young gardener, and the hunter. In a light, flirtatious spirit, she indicates her preference for the last, but not without having previously encouraged the first and raised his hopes.

These roles were now assigned in the circle. The spirited daughter of the house, who was blessed with an extraordinary poetic talent, agreed to play the miller maid; Wilhelm Müller was to be the miller; the painter Hensel, who later became Fanny Mendelssohn's husband, would represent the hunter. Each had to express himself in song, after which the exact situation was explained in more detail. The game had great appeal. The music was to be Ludwig Berger's responsibility, who sought to make the play into an integrated whole. The circumstances were to develop step by step, each clearly leading to the next. Therefore Berger asked W. Müller to write a few more transitional poems to tie the series together, while he wanted others removed. The poet was ready and willing. Thus it was Berger who led Müller to rework the theme in so many variations that it eventually resulted in an entire song book.[26]

is account from the biography of the musician Ludwig Berger (1777–1839), by Ludwig Rellstab (1799–1860), another poet whose work was used by ert for some of his songs. According to Rellstab, *Die Schöne Müllerin* issued from a circle of middle-class artist friends who, as a social activity, put together a play in songs. Not only did several persons play the parts, but they also wrote them. Wilhelm Müller's version, a cycle of 23 poems proposed by Berger, then emerged in the years 1818–1820, some of the poems appearing in magazines and almanacs prior to the publication of the entire cycle. It is evident from the departures in the final version that Müller took pains to revise his poems again and again. The song cycle appeared in Dessau in November 1820, although the title page is dated 1821, in the collection *Sieben und siebzig Gedichte aus den hinterlassenen Papieren eines reisenden Waldhornisten. Herausgegeben von Wilhelm Müller* [Seventy-seven poems from the papers left by a traveling French horn player. Edited by Wilhelm Müller]. *Die schöne Müllerin* opens this collection.

> The fresh sincerity of the verses is due to their confessional-autobiographical nature. Behind the songs lies the story of Wilhelm Müller's affection for Luise Hensel, the devout text writer of the religious songs "Müde bin ich, geh zur Ruh' " [I am weary, go to rest] and "Immer muss ich wieder lesen" [Ever must I read again]. Clemens Brentano, who also competed for Luise's hand as earnestly but not as shyly as Wilhelm Müller, is hidden in the song cycle in the character of the hunter.[27]

The origin, preservation, and publication of Schubert's song cycle *Die schöne Müllerin* (D 795), is recounted by Walther Dürr in his most recent research findings incorporated in *Franz Schubert. Neue Ausgabe sämtlicher Werke, Serie IV: Lieder. Band 2:*

> On November 30, 1823, Schubert wrote to Franz von Schober: "Since the opera, I have composed nothing but a few miller songs. The miller songs will appear in four booklets, with vignettes by Schwind. I might add that I hope to regain my health, and this newfound treasure will make me forget many a sorrow. . . ." (*Dokumente*, p. 207—See Note 14)
>
> The opera referred to here has to be *Fierabras* (D 796), composed between May 25 and October 2, 1823, for in a letter to Schober written from Steyr on August 14, Schubert advised that he was working on the opera. There was another work to which Schubert referred simply as "the opera" in writing to his friend: *Alfonso und Estrella* (D 732), composed on a libretto of Schober's, but it was completed in February 1822. Thus we can infer that Schubert began composing the "miller songs" in October 1823, after finishing *Fierabras,* and that by November 30 they were sufficiently close to completion that he could arrange with the publisher not only the publication of the cycle but even the way it would appear: in four booklets (actually it appeared in five).
>
> There is further support for not dating the beginning of the composition any earlier: According to Josef von Spaun, Schubert composed the "miller songs" "im Spitale" [in the hospital] (*Erinnerungen* [Memoirs], p. 423; see Note 12). Now it is true that Leopold Kupelwieser wrote to Schober as early as July 26, 1823, that Schubert was ill (*Dokumente*, p. 196).

But Schubert cannot have been in the hospital at that time, because he was on his way to Upper Austria, arriving in Linz on July 28. Kupelwieser's choice of words rules out the possibility of an earlier illness: He heard "yesterday" that Schubert was ill. The report was news to him and also to Schober—at least Kupelwieser assumes so. Therefore Schubert can hardly have been in the "General Hospital" in May. It is much more likely to have been in October, after Schubert's return from his trip. It is also during this period that references to his illness appear most frequently.

According to one of Benedikt Randhartinger's stories, Schubert found the texts of the "miller songs" at his house. "One day," reports Schubert's biographer Kreissle, "Schubert visited Count Seczenyi's private secretary, Mr. Benedict Randhartinger. . . . Scarcely had he entered the room, when the secretary was summoned by the count. . . . Franz stepped up to the desk, found a volume of poems lying there, . . . tucked the book under his arm and left without waiting for Randhartinger to return. Soon after his return, the latter missed his poetry collection, and on the following day, he went to Schubert to retrieve the book. Franz excused himself for his high-handed action by speaking of the interest that the poems had aroused in him; and as proof that his borrowing of the book had not been fruitless, he presented the astonished secretary with the musical settings for the first 'miller songs,' some of which he had completed during the night." There is little credibility in the details of the report. Randhartinger did not become secretary to Graf Széchényi until 1825, long after the origin of the "miller songs" (compare *Erinnerungen,* p. 234). Since Randhartinger was often inclined to embellish his experiences with Schubert through anecdotes, it is of course conceivable that he actually did lend him Wilhelm Müller's *Sieben und siebzig Gedichte aus den hinterlassenen Papieren eines reisenden Waldhornisten,* but that he could no longer recall the exact time of the songs' origin when he invented this story.

The first two booklets of the cycle appeared in February and March 1824; but there was a long wait before the next three came out in August. Schubert, who was spending the summer in Zseliz, at the home of the Esterházy family, had grown impatient. "Before anything else," he wrote to Schwind in August, "I lay it upon your conscience to spur Leidesdorf to action. . . . Progress with the miller songs is just as slow—one booklet is published every three months." (*Dokumente,* p. 255) His impatience is understandable, in view of the fact that Father Schubert wrote his son at the end of June that Ferdinand had done the proofreading in his stead. But once the booklets finally appeared, their success apparently did not fulfill Schubert's expectations. An echo of this disappointment is discernible in Schober's letter of December 2, 1824, to Schubert: "So you are having problems with Leidesdorf? I'm very sorry about that; and your miller songs have also brought no great acclaim?" (*Dokumente,* p. 265)

In 1829, Anton Diabelli & Co. acquired the rights to the cycle and republished it a year later. This new edition contains numerous musical changes which, as Josef Gänsbacher reported in 1864, can largely be traced back to Johann Michael Vogl.[27a] The changes are of various kinds. Melodic phrases are ornamented; the declamation, especially in recitative sections, is sharpened, and many accents are shifted; performance symbols, especially fermatas, are added. Such changes resemble those often encountered in Vogl,[28] so they might actually be traceable to him. Other changes, like the deletion of difficult leaps in the voice part (as in "Mein!") seem curious in this context. Presumably they can be attributed to the publisher. A comparison of the versions published by Diabelli with those of a few hand-written copies in Franziska Tremier's song album (such as "Trockne Blumen" [Wilted flowers] and "Der Müller und der Bach" [The miller and the brook]) seems to support this hypothesis. For the most part, the copies, probably made in 1828, hand down the same changes as the later Diabelli edition, but in many cases they go beyond the latter. Since Franziska Tremier's song album also contains an additional song [»An Emma" (To Emma), D 113], with changes that undoubtedly go back to Vogl, the album copies probably accurately transmit his original changes for *Die schöne Müllerin*. The publisher took from it—and no doubt occasionally from Schubert's original text as well—only what he believed would appeal to his broader public.[29]

Schubert's autograph is lost. Save for the copies mentioned, our only source is the original edition, which is not completely reliable because Schubert did not proofread it himself: *Die schöne Müllerin. Ein Cyclus von Liedern gedichtet von Wilhelm Müller . . . 25. Werk . . . 1. Heft . . . Wien, Sauer & Leidesdorf* [The lovely miller maiden. A cycle of songs with words by Wilhelm Müller . . . Op. 25 . . . Vol. 1 . . . Vienna, S. & L.] (Plate No. S & L 502; announced in the official *Wiener Zeitung* February 17, 1824).

The first 12 poems of Wilhelm Müller's *Die Winterreise* appeared in the collection *Urania. Taschenbuch auf das Jahr 1823* [Urania. Pocketbook (i.e. almanac) for the year 1823]. This pocketbook was probably the text from which Schubert worked for the first part of his composition. Ten more poems from the cycle appeared in 1823 in *Deutsche Blätter für Poesie, Litteratur . . .* [German pages for poetry and literature . . .] in Breslau in the following order (the position in Schubert's sequence is indicated at right):

| | |
|---|---|
| Der greise Kopf [The gray head] | 14 |
| Letzte Hoffnung [Last hope] | 16 |
| Die Krähe [The raven] | 15 |
| Im Dorfe [In the village] | 17 |
| Der stürmische Morgen [The stormy morning] | 18 |
| Die Nebensonnen [Rival suns] | 23 |
| Der Wegweiser [The sign post] | 20 |
| Das Wirtshaus [The inn] | 21 |
| Mut! [Courage] | 22 |
| Der Leiermann [The organ-grinder] | 24 |

One can see that the order is considerably different from Schubert's. "Die Post" [The mail coach] and "Täuschung" [Deception] are missing. Schubert did not use this edition for his second part, turning instead to the complete publication of the cycle in the second volume of *Gedichte aus den hinterlassenen Papieren eines reisenden Waldhornisten. Herausgegeben von Wilhelm Müller* ("dem Meister des deutschen Gesanges Carl Maria von Weber als Pfand seiner Freundschaft und

Verehrung gewidmet von dem Herausgeber" [dedicated by the editor to the master of German song, Carl Maria von Weber, as a token of his friendship and admiration]). This collection appeared in Dessau in 1824. The sequence of the poems in this edition is (position in Schubert's version at right):

| | |
|---|---|
| Gute Nacht [Farewell] | 1 |
| Die Wetterfahne [The weather-vane] | 2 |
| Gefrorene Tränen [Frozen tears] | 3 |
| Erstarrung [Numbness] | 4 |
| Der Lindenbaum [The linden tree] | 5 |
| Die Post [The mail coach] | 13 |
| Wasserflut [Flood of tears] | 6 |
| Auf dem Flusse [On the river] | 7 |
| Rückblick [Glance back] | 8 |
| Der greise Kopf [The gray head] | 14 |
| Die Krähe [The raven] | 15 |
| Letzte Hoffnung [Last hope] | 16 |
| Im Dorfe [In the village] | 17 |
| Der stürmische Morgen [The stormy morning] | 18 |
| Täuschung [Deception] | 19 |
| Der Wegweiser [The sign post] | 20 |
| Das Wirtshaus [The inn] | 21 |
| Irrlicht [Will-o'-the-wisp] | 9 |
| Rast [Rest] | 10 |
| Die Nebensonnen [Rival suns] | 23 |
| Frühlingstraum [Spring dream] | 11 |
| Einsamkeit [Solitude] | 12 |
| Mut! [Courage] | 22 |
| Der Leiermann [The organ-grinder] | 24 |

The added poems are interspersed among those already published in the *Urania* pocketbook, yet—taken by themselves—they are almost in the same sequence as in Schubert's second part. The only change Schubert made was to reverse "Die Nebensonnen" (No.23) and "Mut!" (No. 22), in order to end the cycle the way he envisioned it musically, with "Die Nebensonnen" (See below, p. 123). So Schubert first set to music the twelve poems that had appeared in the *Urania* pocketbook, and at the end of his manuscript wrote *fine* (the end)! Then, when he had Müller's complete cycle before him, he composed music for the other 12 poems, one by one, as 'Fortsetzung der Winterreise von Wilh. Müller" [Continuation of Wilh. Müller's winter journey] and again numbered them 1 through 12 in his manuscript.

Schubert's autograph, which is in the possession of the Pierpont Morgan Library, New York: The Mary Flagler Cary Collection, is a combination of various drafts. Nine songs in Part One: "Die Wetterfahne," "Gefrorne Tränen," "Erstarrung," "Der Lindenbaum," "Wasserflut," "Auf dem Flusse," "Irrlicht," "Rast," "Frühlingstraum," and the first page of 'Einsamkeit' are preserved in Schubert's working draft—and with many revealing corrections.[30] For "Gute Nacht," "Rückblick," the other two pages of 'Einsamkeit," and the entire second part, from 'Die Post' to 'Der Leiermann", we have only a "fair copy" in Schubert's hand—that is, a copy made from the working manuscript in its final form. In addition, an earlier, shorter version of 'Mut' in private possession has come down to us, and part of an earlier and, in places, different version of "Die Nebensonnen", in the archive of the Gesellschaft der Musikfreunde [Society of the Friends of Music] in Vienna. A copyist's version for the engraver has been preserved in the Wiener Stadt-bibliothek [Vienna City Library], which contains numerous corrections in Schubert's hand. So to make a long story short, the autograph and the first printed versions differ.[31] (These differences are noted in the texts reproduced in Chapter VI, insofar as they pertain to the text.) The first page of the autograph (see facsimile, p. 86) is dated "Febr. 1827"; the page on which the "Continuation of Wilh. Müller's Winter Journey" begins with "Die Post" is dated "Oct. 1827." These dates probably indicate not when the composition was begun, but when the fair copy was made. We do know that the earlier version we have of "Die Nebensonnen" originated in Graz in September 1827, for the autograph was originally in the possession of Schubert's host there, Dr. Karl Pachler. On the other hand, Schubert did not give the publisher the manuscript (or the copyist's version?) for the second part until September 1828—unless he had given it to Haslinger *again;* that is to say, Haslinger may have had it in hand once and then returned it.

Schubert's friend Josef von Spaun recounts the origin of *Winterreise* (*Erinnerungen,* p. 160ff):

Schubert had been gloomier for some time and seemed exhausted. When I asked what was happening to him, he only said, "You will soon hear it and understand." One day he said to me, "Come to Schober's house today, and I will sing you a cycle of eerie songs. I am eager to know what you think of them. They have affected me more than any of my other songs." He sang *Winterreise* all the way through for us, his voice filled with emotion. We were completely stunned by the somber mood of these songs, and Schober said he liked only one of the songs, "Der Linden-baum". Schubert's only reply was, "I like these songs best of all, and you will come to like them too." And he was right. We soon became enthusiastic about the effect of the melancholy songs, which Vogl per-formed masterfully. Surely there are no more beautiful German songs than these, and they were really his swan song. His health was shattered from then on, yet his condition was not yet so obvious as to arouse con-cern. Many believed, and still believe, that Schubert was an impassive fellow whom nothing could shake. But those who knew him better know how deeply his creations affected him and how he bore them in pain. Anyone who has ever seen him in the morning, hard at composing, with flushed face and shining eyes—yes, even his speech was different, like a somnambulant,—will never forget the picture. (After all, how could he have written these songs without being profoundly gripped by them!) In the afternoons, of course, he was a different person again, but he was still sensitive and felt deeply. He just preferred not to show his feelings, but to keep them locked within. . . . I have no doubt whatsoever that the agitated state in which he composed his most beautiful songs, especially his *Winterreise,* contributed to his early death.

Joseph von Spaun reports in another place (*Erinnerungen,* p. 36):

On November 11 [1828], he had to take to his bed. Although dangerously ill, he felt no pain and complained only of weakness. Now and then he would fall into delirium, during which time he sang continuously. He used his few lucid intervals to revise the second part of *Winterreise*. . . .On November 19, at three o'clock in the afternoon, he breathed his last.

Another friend of Schubert, the poet Johann Mayrhofer, relates the following (*Erinnerungen,* p. 20):

It now seems appropriate to mention two poems by Wilhelm Müller that form a larger cycle and allow a deeper look into the composer's heart. . . .Although it is somber in parts, especially at the end, [*Die schöne Müllerin*] offers much that is refreshing, tender, and delightful. Not so in *Winterreise*, the choice of which clearly shows that the composer had become more sober. He had been seriously ill for a long time, he had had depressing experiences, and life's rosy color had vanished; winter had come for him. The poet's irony, rooting itself in misery, appealed to him; he expressed it in cutting tones. I was seized with pain.

*Winterreise* (D 911) was published in Vienna by Tobias Haslinger as Op. 89 in two sections (Plate No. T. H. 5101–5112 and T. H. 5113–5124; on both title pages: 5101–5112). The publisher advertised them—as was customary then—in the official *Wiener Zeitung,* the first part on January 14, 1828, the second on December 30, 1828, only a few weeks after Schubert's death. Their reception was strong and very favorable.

Of the departures from the autograph in the first edition, the most surprising are the transpositions of individual songs. "Wasserflut" is transposed from F-sharp minor in the manuscript to E minor in print, "Rast" from D minor to C minor, "Einsamkeit" from D minor to B minor, "Mut" from A minor to G minor, "Der Leiermann" from B minor to A minor. Weren't the keys chosen, one may ask, in keeping with an overall plan, which would be destroyed by these changes? Wouldn't a transposition of the whole cycle have been decidedly preferable to a transposition of individual songs? Certainly. Then, one will ask, doesn't each song have or require its particular key? Why would Schubert himself undertake such a glaring departure from the key characteristics of his songs? Finally there is this question: Might the transposition cause the piano part to fall into registers of such a different sound quality that the character of the whole would be changed?

The answer to these questions is to be found on an autograph copy [now lost] of "Des Müllers Blumen" from *Die schöne Müllerin,* which sets the song in G major instead of A major. A note in Schubert's hand reads: "NB Die Begleitung dieses Liedes kann füglich um eine Oktave höher gespielt werden. Franz Schubert." [The accompaniment of this song can, if necessary be played one octave higher. Franz Schubert.] As certainly as Schubert had certain keys and key relationships in mind in his cycles, e.g. the tritonal relationship of the last song to the first in *Die schöne Müllerin,* his songs are just as certainly transposable, with only a few exceptions, [32] because true to their roots in the song genre, they are not bound to any particular voice range or register. *Lied* or song, from the time of its origin, meant "for everyone to sing;" and so for the voice and its accompaniment, this requires adapting to the voice range in the tuning of the instrument (as with lutes and violins), in the register, in the dynamics, in the figuration (such as its density); in short: in the whole mode of playing. Even though the musical composition and the tuning of the instrument cannot be changed for Schubert's songs, this certainly does not mean that they should be sung only if the range they are written in "suits" the singer. A singer is more likely to disregard the designated key than to sing outside his normal voice range. In this case, the power of lively music-making in the ancient tradition prevails over that of western polyphonic style and tonality. Songs are songs, even at the mature level of European musical development reflected in Schubert's works.

The cycle known as *Schwanengesang* [Swan song] (D 957) was not intended by Schubert to form a cycle. After Schubert's death, publisher Tobias Haslinger collected 14 songs from his late period and advertised the publication in January 1829 as follows:

> Prepublication notice for *Franz Schubert's Schwanen-Gesang* with piano accompaniment. Dedicated to his patrons and friends. *Last work . . .The last flowers* of his noble talent are offered to the numerous friends of his classic muse under the above title. These are the musical poems he wrote in August 1828, shortly before his passing. Works that proclaim him beyond a doubt as a richly gifted master, so that one could almost believe that this superb genius, who vanished in the prime of life, has arisen again in a brilliant display of all his fullness and power to leave a most precious parting gift to those he held dear. . . . (*Dokumente*, p. 573)

The edition appeared at Easter 1829. Although *Schwanengesang* as a whole is not a true cycle, it contains two smaller "cycles." Schubert often created such groupings for publication, combining songs by a single poet or on a specific theme, and he probably had the same intention for these. One of the "cycles" is based on poems by Ludwig Rellstab (*Lebensmut* [Courage], Fragment, D 937, and 'Herbst' [Autumn], D 945, may also belong here); the other, on poems by Heinrich Heine (which he had already offered to publisher Probst in Leipzig on October 2, 1828).

# III. Individual Songs from the Two Cycles

> Suddenly there was a firmness in it, an almost cold firmness such as I had never heard before. If you would allow me an observation—perhaps surprising, coming from an old man who has torn so many artists to pieces—it was as if I were hearing Schubert for the first time; and whoever was playing it—I couldn't have told you whether it was a man or woman—had not just learned something but had understood something as well—and it very seldom happens that nonprofessionals comprehend that sort of thing. That wasn't someone playing the piano. It was—it was *music happening* . . .
>
> Heinrich Boell,
> *Gruppenbild mit Dame*
> [Group portrait with lady]

In examining Schubert's song cycles, in our effort to interpret the songs through structural analysis, we will be looking primarily at rhythm and meter, as pointed out in the foreword, because this is generally the most important single element in Schubert's compositional practice. Furthermore, Schubert's work can be approached more easily and understood more fully from this aspect than from any other. Hence the limitation is not really restrictive. I hope to show that, from this viewpoint, we can perceive something of what is termed "substance"—to complete Adorno's statement previously quoted. Clearly such an analysis must be not only careful and thorough, but sensitive as well. Such an approach nearly always requires more thoroughness over a longer time span than can be expected of a reader who is more interested in the finished work than in problems of compositional technique. But becoming and being go hand in hand, even in art, so we must pursue the former in order to grasp the latter.

I hope the reader will make the effort, first of all, to follow three detailed song interpretations. Then when he reads the less-detailed discussions and interpretations that follow, he will be able to see and appreciate what lies behind them, where they are aimed, and what they should suggest to him. Not every musical work can be described this clearly, but these three songs were selected because in them even the musical layman can gain insight into the art or technique hidden behind what he experiences spontaneously in listening. [34]

## 1. "Im Dorfe" [In the village] from *Winterreise*

The principal difference between the two stanzas of Wilhelm Müller's poem (see below p. 149) is that the first contains an objective description of a sleeping village on a winter night: "Es bellen die Hunde . . ." [The dogs are barking . . .], whereas in the second stanza a subject appears and speaks, beginning abruptly

with the imperative: "Bellt mich nur fort . . .!" [Drive me away with your barking!]
Arriving at the village with its sleeping inhabitants, the subject feels rejected. The
traveler must move on.

Schubert sets this two-part poem to music as a three-part song, with the third
part corresponding to the first. The middle section, idyllically directed more
toward the sleeping villagers, stands in contrast to the other two. If we try to pin-
point the contrasts, we notice a number of things immediately: The tonality is now
that of the inherently mild, soothing subdominant; the voice and piano parts inter-
mingle "lyrically" and move together; the voice part declaims in shorter phrases,
underscored by the repetition of "Je nun" [Oh, well] and "und hoffen" [and hope];
and above all, the restless sixteenth-note figure, which characterizes the piano part
in the first and third sections, has disappeared.

But are these simple and powerful contrasts all there is to the tension inherent
in the song? Does contrasting the middle section to the outer two get to the heart of
the matter? We cannot answer this question without at least trying to explain the
musical events (the composition, the lay-out, the "technique") of all three parts.
Only such a close comparison can reveal whether the contrast we observed was
important to the composer. Schubert could have had another element in mind as
worthy of emphasis, such as the mood of the winter night in the sleeping village
where the dogs are barking. At any rate, wherever this song is discussed, we hear it
said that the sixteenth-note figure in the piano accompaniment was inspired by the
rattling of the chains or the barking of the dogs—that is, by an atmospheric element in the poem. So I repeat the question: Is this really important? There is no
denying that the sixteenth-note figure has significance for the composition, but we
must look more closely before concluding that it serves primarily to set the mood
of the poem, lyrically speaking.

If we attend to the piano introduction, simply listening, and then consider its
function in the whole, we recognize at once that this is not an introduction in the
usual sense, written only to get the song started, to prepare for the singer's
entrance, a prelude that could just as well be omitted.[35] A separation of "introduction" and "song itself" is out of the question here. It may not even be correct to say
that the introduction carries over into the song, but let us set this matter aside for
now. What we hear is a compact sequence of chord repetitions over an almost trill-
like figure in the bass that leads into an open position of the same chord. The music
then breaks off abruptly, followed by a long rest until the same sequence resumes
in the second measure. In the following measures, an additional harmonic component comes into play, the natural progression of which seems to be the step from
the fifth degree of the scale to the first, from the dominant to the tonic, and thus a
repetition of the opening measures in the piano beginning with measure 7. The
harmony, however, makes a lesser impression than the insistence, if not stubborn-
ness, of the continuous sequence: restless chord repetition/long rest, restless
chord repetition/long rest.

And again the question arises, what do we actually hear? What is it that strikes
us? An examination of the actual notes and Schubert's description of them will
help us express this in words. First let us consider his tempo mark: "Etwas
langsam" [somewhat slowly]. Originally Schubert specifed only "slowly;" "somewhat" was added later, apparently when "slowly" appeared to him to be too slow.
Just what does "somewhat slowly" mean? you may ask; better yet, what is it in this
piano part that goes "somewhat slowly?" Even at a slow tempo, the eighth-note

chords in the prescribed 12/8 time follow in quick succession, and the sixteenth notes still more quickly. When played, you will find that "slow" refers only to the even up-and-down motion of the whole—a breathing rhythm, we might say—in half-measures, not in twelve eighth-note beats. If one tries "conducting" it as it is to be played here, as the music "has to go," one gets a quiet motion of downbeats and upbeats in half-measures, whereby the entrance always occurs on the stress or downbeat. The accent mark over the chord at the middle of each opening measure was merely Schubert's way of calling attention to a minimal melodic element, the leap of the upper note in the right piano hand, and the change from closed to open position, and vice versa; of chords in the middle of the measure. He certainly did not mean to introduce any stress pattern other than that noted in the time signature. The motion takes off from the downbeat, from beat one, then rises in the long rest in the second half of the measure, only to descend again on the first beat of the next measure, on the onset of the alarmingly restless chord sequence, which constitutes the sharpest contrast to the restful motion in the pulse of this piece. This contrast is certainly of greater significance for the composition than the one we first observed between the middle and outer sections of the song. But there is yet another contrasting element to consider.

Experiment by playing the introduction, whether on the piano or a recording, and then start singing the voice part, but without looking at the music! —whenever you wish to begin, in whatever way seems natural—that is, as the musical flow of the "introduction" suggests. I suspect that everyone will begin as shown in Example 1. If one then continues playing and singing, not until reaching "träumen sich manches" will one notice that one is singing incorrectly because the wrong starting point was chosen; but up to this point, the voice and piano parts seem to go together.

Example 1

What do we learn from the experiment? Schubert has the voice enter in a way the listener does *not* expect and does *not* find natural, not as the "introduction" suggests, but differently (Example 2). Any reader who carried out the experiment and "naturally" began in the wrong place will recognize Schubert's intention and realize how difficult it is to sing this part correctly, that is, to begin correctly. The difficulty is rooted in the conflict, which is *reality* in the musical composition. Through the almost stereotype repetition of the down-up motion in the piano introduction, the impression of proceeding in full measures is so firmly implanted

Example 2

in the listener's mind that it seems as if the entry of the voice part *must* follow this pattern. But when the singer does *not* follow it—and Schubert intends that he not follow it—then a motion tendency develops that is directly counter to that of the piano part. This divergence can be shown graphically.

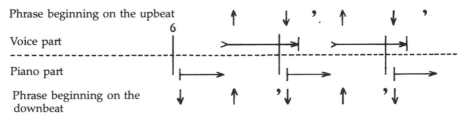

Example 3

An attempt to put into words what has just been experienced musically might go something like this: Both voice and piano are bound to the restful rhythm of the "somewhat slow" tempo. They are components of the motion but have differing, contradictory roles. Thus we receive the impression that within the single structure there are two different planes on which the various elements move in opposition.

The conflict between the voice part, always entering on an upbeat (on the long upbeat of a half-measure, at that!), and piano part, with its persistent downbeat entry, lasts throughout the entire first section. The contradiction is not resolved but only leads, in measures 17–18, to a compromise of sorts. The right piano hand moves from the sixteenth-note figure, now in the upper staff, into a kind of melodic cadence, whereby it seems to meet the voice part.

In measures 18 and 19, between the first and second part of the song, a rhythmic calm sets in, an apparent outcome of the compromise. Here the motion, with its components, seems to be reduced to zero—if such a bold metaphor is permissible. The sixteenth notes in the first and the eighth notes in the second of the two measures are not subdivided. They continue emptily, so to speak, clearing the way for the introduction of a new structure, so that it can actually be experienced as new. From the constant d in measures 18–19 (the tonic note for the first part and the main key of the song), a surprising G major bursts forth in the middle section; likewise a 6/8 time pattern unfolds as piano and voice move together expressing a "contented" feeling. No new time signature is noted—it was not customary in Schubert's time—but the change takes place nevertheless. In this relatively short-winded 6/8 time, in comparison to the 12/8 time of the first section, the voice almost seems to rock in melody and the piano to revel in the simple accompaniment, having given up its resistance. In terms of musical technique, this means dissolution of the tie between piano and voice parts in an obbligato accompaniment in favor of a homophonic style in which the "accompaniment" merely gives expression to the harmonies implied in the voice part.

The first thing we noted in our examination of this song was its division into three parts, a structure that musical form theory usually designates with the formula A-B-A'. If our closer look at parts A and B had revealed only that they were different, then we could expect the third to be a recapitulation of the first, with perhaps minimal deviations. But the difference we observed involved the musical structure and was such that a recapitulation, even with variations, is out of the question. Only a resolution of the conflicts that have been set up can provide a satisfying conclusion, and it must be worked out in painstaking musical detail. The inherent tension between the voice and piano parts, which are bound together in the obbligato style, cannot be so easily resolved as in that "compromise" of measure 17, if we are to take seriously what we have just heard and analyzed. The contrast in the middle section turned out to be founded not only on a change of mood, but on differences in style (song-like accompaniment to a lyrical voice part), motion (6/8 instead of 12/8 time) and structure (departure from the "two-plane" division). The result was powerful. So when the third part begins to bring back the structural tension we remember from the first part, the listener is forced to wonder, consciously or unconsciously, how the song could possibly reach a satisfying conclusion.

Whereas the poet avoids a conciliatory conclusion in his poem, Schubert seeks to resolve the conflict in the song by fusing the various elements. For the sake of unity, he must carry these conflicting gestures (illustrated in Example 3) to a common conclusion. This calls for decisive intervention in the structure of the composition—a willful act, so to speak, which forces a decision. Here is how Schubert accomplishes this: In measure 37, at the first "Was will ich unter den Schläfern säumen?" he surprises us by having the voice enter at a place in the measure (third-from-last eighth note) and at a moment in the motion (middle of an upbeat) in which neither voice nor piano has entered before. It is as if the traveler were tearing himself loose from the scene, as if in contemplating the sleeping village he finally fully recognized his situation and now suddenly wanted to change it. For the first time (aside from the middle section) the piano part does not persist with its stereotypical sixteenth-note figure; for the first time it defers to the voice part; for the first time voice and piano parts unite within the obbligato accompaniment, moving together in a gesture of grandeur. This gesture comes so unexpectedly, it is ripped so forcefully from the structure which previously prevailed, that it cancels the rhythmic order and interrupts the continuity of motion at the same time. Not only does Schubert drop the subdivision of the measure into eighth notes, he also changes the rhythmic pattern from an even number of beats to an odd; in place of the even 12/8 time comprised of eighth-note values, he switches to an uneven (triple meter) 18/8 time subdivided in dotted-quarter-note values. The "somewhat slow" motion turns from two ♩. (12/8) to three ♩. (18/8).

Example 4

I should no doubt digress for a moment to answer a question the reader is sure to raise: "Time change? There is no time change noted in my edition!" In Schubert's day, musical rhythm was still subject to the rule of recurring equivalents at constant intervals. This means, for example, that in the sequence

| heavy-light | heavy-light | downbeat-upbeat | downbeat-upbeat |

i.e. in 2/4 time (also in our slow 12/8 time, in which a half-measure equals one beat—we are not concerned here with triple meter or 4/4 time), the stresses on beat one recur at constant intervals because between the ones there is always a two, an unstressed beat. This strict rule of musical rhythm developed to its full extent in the 18th century, with meters that are still used today. Schubert was one of the first to break with it, and our song is an example. However, conventional notation still allowed no exception. It was not customary to write in a time change. So if Schubert wanted to change the rhythm temporarily from that indicated in the time signature, in order to realize a particular rhythmic texture, he was forced to circumvent the immovable bar lines and use other signs to indicate the new rhythm (for it is the bar line that actually makes the stresspoint of the measure visible). To indicate stresses that do not coincide with those of the noted time, he uses the accent mark, the dynamic signs *fp* or *fz,* or even accents *plus* one of these signs; to prepare for them, he uses crescendo marks or the word *crescendo* alone.

So far, so good. But not every accent or *fp* preceded by a crescendo signifies a change in meter from that of the time signature. Some indicate a particular rhythmic constellation that remains within the noted time. In printed editions, even during Schubert's lifetime, his accent marks—and the accent was his favorite mark, used thousands of times—were usually reproduced as short decrescendo marks, so that a dynamic swelling and fading was also suggested to the reader in places where Schubert meant only to indicate a special rhythmic intention that deviated from the noted time. Nevertheless, his intention is usually recognizable, at least for those who look and listen closely.

Viewed in a vacuum, the crescendo mark at the end of measure 37 or 42 in the piano part of our song makes no sense on an eighth note followed by a rest. But in conjunction with the corresponding marks in the next measure, it becomes a signal for altered meter, the special rhythmic structure of this passage, discernible despite the immovable bar lines. If the reader is ever in doubt as to what is meant, as to whether printed decrescendo marks should be read as accents or as instructions to decrescendo in other Schubert passages, try being led by the music (do not actively conduct!) in simple conducting motions that interpret the sound meaningfully, that make it *visible*.[36] Using this device one will immediately know what is meant. In our example, a declamation corresponding to the noted time is virtually impossible:

↑ ↓ ↑ ↓ ↑ ↓
"was |will ich unter den|Schläfern säu-|men?"

But if the bar lines are disregarded and Schubert's accent marks heeded instead, a different rhythm and a meaningful declamation emerges:

↑ ↓ → ↑ ↓ ↓
"was |will ich unter den Schläfern |säu-|men?"

The last "säu-men" [tarry] is surprising, of course—but to understand it, we must return to the description of our song.

The act of beginning the 3 ♩. phrase "was will ich unter den Schläfern säumen?" on an upbeat affects all levels or planes of the structure. When all planes suddenly converge to change the structure and diverge from the established form, one realizes just how deeply this gesture must affect the course of the whole.

To strengthen its impact, Schubert repeats the critical passage, but not without further clarifying his intention: As if the intrusion were not drastic enough the first time, as if there is not enough energy to resolve the painful conflict, as if the traveler's decision to break away were not sufficiently resolute, the old rhythm and motion break through in the second 3 ♩. measure with the stereotype figure in the piano part; and along with it comes the difference in the motion, again (measure 40: "säu-men? Ich bin zu Ende"). Directly after beat one of the measure, the downbeat, the 3 ♩. rhythm is suddenly interrupted by a new downbeat before the respective upbeat can occur, before a beat two can intervene. In reintroducing the old

Example 5

structure, Schubert cancels the effect of the break (measures 37–39) with a single blow. Like the break itself, the undoing of it has a powerful effect. The juxtaposition of two downbeats runs counter to the usual practice of musical rhythm that requires constant intervals between stressed and unstressed beats. The listener perceives this as the intrusion of "free" motion, non-musical in origin, into the established musical framework. All the rhythmic elements, as well as the structure that ties them together, become manifest here, allowing the listener to experience the musical event as reality, as musical motion.

Thus the listener discovers that the resolution of the conflict has failed on the first attempt, requiring a more aggressive intrusion. Not until the second attempt does the far-reaching gesture of *two* complete 3 ♩. measures (beginning with measure 43 and the repeated "was will ich") force the disparate elements together, neutralizing the opposition and effecting a resolution. It is at this point that the traveler finally breaks away (Example 6).

For such a critical moment in the composition, the composer uses all the devices available, including melody and harmony, to achieve his goal. And now we hear the entire work, even though we have described and analyzed it from only one standpoint, that of rhythm—or what might be better termed motion. We hear the whole even though we may focus on one thing or another at any given time. Who could fail to hear the drastic melodic change from the g' in measure 37 to g'-sharp of "was . . ." in measure 42 as an expression of someone writhing in pain? It is

Example 6

an intensification in which the senses are almost driven beyond their limits, not only crying for resolution but seeming to bring it about by the very act of expression. Who can escape the effect of the color contrast between the B-flat major/G minor of measure 37 and the D major of the following measure, whereby the "will ich" seems bathed in light? Moreover, there are few instances in classical music literature where one can hear a complete harmonic cadence—and *experience* it, both as release from tension and as complete harmonic conclusion—as clearly as in the cadence of measures 43–46, where all appoggiaturas can be savored to the fullest. This effect is due to the fact that although the same cadence has already been heard in measures 38–40 and the earlier occurrence was also harmonically complete, it was suddenly interrupted and broken off. Furthermore, in the first part, and in the third up to the first turning point, the harmony changed from measure to measure but remained constant within a given measure, so that its progressions were barely noticeable; but here, in two measures, the harmony cadences with a rapid chord progression, so that the change suddenly becomes manifest and a rhythmic urgency is created. It could be said that the composition at this point is determined by a "harmonic rhythm."

Now, at the conclusion, peace finally arrives, marked by the slower motion in the second cadence, with the 3 ♩. measures and the seemingly endless a' (a whole 3 ♩. measure) in the voice part. All elements seem to reflect this: for the first time, the D major chord in the right piano hand is in root position; for the first time, the chord does not change in the second half of the measure; the stereotypical sixteenth-note figure in the left hand has lost its restless drive; the F-sharp in the bass of the third measure from the end, although it reminds us of the phrases that began on an upbeat and thereby of the discrepancies in the structure, now brings only friendly reminiscence. The conflict that characterizes the song is neutralized within the composition and ultimately removed.

Let us now turn to the question of "Im Dorfe" in relation to the problems of song composition in general dealt with in the previous chapter. Our song is not a strophic song. Is it through-composed? Goethe criticizes "so-called through-composition," saying that in it "the overall lyrical character is completely wanting, overwhelmed by a false interest in the particular which it demands and generates." Clearly, our song is *not* through-composed, for interest in many different details— obviously this is what Goethe means—is neither demanded nor generated; rather the whole song seems to be composed around one point. The traveler, enchained and rejected at the same time, escapes his inner conflict by tearing himself away. It is around this conflict that Schubert's song is laid out. It culminates in the moment of breaking loose, in an eventful moment. The song is the musical realization of an event or action, but more in the sense of a deed than of ongoing action; it centers around a specific detail of the traveler's action, giving it appropriate musical expression. The "overall lyrical character" is significant, in that the tension, between voice and piano parts, which forces its own resolution, originates in this character. But Schubert does not see this tension as mere circumstance. He neither conveys an "overall lyrical character" nor "demands and generates interest in the particular"; nor does he paint a "mood" or describe a "state of mind." Instead he develops the tension as musical event, as reality in the narrower sense, and he accomplishes this through the special structure of his composition.

When Schubert composes music for lyric poetry, of course he approaches the poem from a particular viewpoint. But it is not from the "focal point" of which E. T. A. Hoffmann, the poet, speaks when he describes Goethe's "overall lyric character" in his own way:

> Inspired by the song's deep meaning, the composer must draw all elements of feeling as if to a focal point, from whence the melody shines forth [melody is equivalent to composition here]. These sounds in turn ... symbolize all the various elements of inner feeling contained in the poet's song.[37]

Hoffmann is thinking of the atmosphere in which the musician should immerse the whole, so that associations hidden behind the words of the poem can appear in the musical medium and develop into a prevailing mood, thereby becoming perceptible through the senses.

Anyone seeking this kind of musical setting of poetry in Schubert's songs will find less than he expected and will immediately concede that other composers, such as Robert Schumann, Johannes Brahms, and later Hugo Wolf and Richard Strauss, have written more beautiful songs. But actual musical experience should cause one to stop and think: More beautiful? It can only be a matter of "different!" In songs such as Schumann's "Mondnacht" [Moonlit night] (words by Eichendorff, Op. 35, 1840), or "Traum durch die Dämmerung" [Dream through the twilight] by Richard Strauss (words by Otto Julius Bierbaum, Op. 29, 1894/85), which are comparable to our "Im Dorfe" in terms of text, much more of the atmosphere of a night or the mood of a soul, much more "color" has been recreated than in Schubert's song. The result is an entirely different musical product. That these songs differ from Schubert's in this respect is indisputable. But no one would seriously claim that it makes them more beautiful. Schubert has a different intention than Schumann or Richard Strauss, and therein lies the difference. It is sparked not by what Goethe called the overall lyrical character, nor by Hoffmann's focal point, to which all elements of feeling are drawn and from which Schumann and Strauss make their songs "shine forth." Schubert's intention is realized at the point where the lyric element can be transformed into musical motion and the latter composed as musical structure.

Granted, it is seldom that the structure of a musical work can be exposed and described this explicitly, as if it were a kind of "construction."[38] But our song, "Im Dorfe", is by no means unique in this regard. The realization of motion concepts as music can be seen even more clearly in another song from *Winterreise:* "Rückblick" [Glance back].

## 2. "Rückblick" from *Winterreise*

Is "Rückblick" (Text, see p. 145) the right title for this song? Shouldn't it be "Flucht" [Flight] instead? At any rate, Schubert uses only the two hindsight stanzas, "Wie anders hast du mich empfangen . . . da war's geschehn um dich, Gesell!" [How differently you received me . . . then all was lost for you, fellow] , to contrast with what seems, in the first stanza, to be the definitive concept: flight—a panicky, rushing, breathless fleeing. Of course the last stanza does not support this idea. It reveals that the traveler does not really want to flee at all; he would like to look back, to turn back one more time and "vor ihrem Hause stille stehn" [stand still before her house] . If, as we claim, Schubert means to draw the poem to a focal point and let it shine forth from there as music, if he conjures up associations of motion for the listener, then ties them together with musical structures (consummated in the act of listening) through compositional devices, if this is how Schubert intends to interpret the poem's content, then he must recreate the intense motion of breathless fleeing as well as the calm of standing still. Within the song unit, he must develop both moods equally and build a transition from the former to the latter. How does Schubert accomplish this? That he succeeds is something we experience whenever we sing, play, or hear the song, and we know that what we hear is founded not merely on beautiful sensation, but on a musical reality.

The composer can render the lines of this poem in either 3/4 or 2/4 time. Different words are stressed in each case. If one wishes to avoid the less meaningful emphasis "unter *beiden* Sohlen" [under *both* soles], in favor of "unter beiden *Sohlen*" [under both *soles*], then one must choose 3/4 time:

Example 7

Of course then the less attractive stress "Atem *holen*" [*catch* my breath] comes along with it, which could be avoided by a declamation in 2/4 time:

Example 8

Schubert decides in favor of 3/4 time and establishes the uneven meter (inherently more striking than even meter) so firmly that the introduction seems to pound out the beats, above which the voice part can unfold all the more freely. With the monotony of the quarter notes in the introduction, a certain unrest seizes the listener; but this regularity is what makes the quarter notes leave their rhythmic imprint. Then, with the entry of the voice part, Schubert disturbs the regularity and degree of the motion. He interrupts the clearly marked 3/4 time using the compositional device of an irregular time structure in order to create the image of breathlessly rushing, stumblingly fleeing motion as musical reality.

How Schubert manages to bring the poetic lines into a regular rhythm in 3/4 time is shown in the third and fourth stanzas, which form the middle section of the song: "Wie anders has du mich empfangen, ... da war's geschehn um dich, Gesell." But in the first and last sections, he holds to no real rhythmic pattern. In one instance, the course of the melody determines declamation in that melodic high points serve to underscore syllables and words, thereby setting rhythmic stress points (Example 9). In his notation, Schubert further underscores the vertex

Example 9

Example 10

and main stress point with a crescendo, followed by an accent mark in the voice part, which is not at all customary.[39] In another place, the melody steps aside and the harmonic sequence—a compelling cadence—governs the declamation (Example 10). In still another place, declamation is determined by the fact that the melodic and dynamic accents of the voice part coincide with those of the piano part. In the following examples, the accent marks above the text pertain to the voice part, and those under the text, to the piano part:

                                >                    >

Measures 21 and 24: "Die Krähen warfen Bäll und Schlossen" [The crows threw snowballs and hailstones)]
           >                   >

This is not the case elsewhere. In the difference between the repetitions of the line "auf meinen Hut von jedem Haus," one can observe how Schubert has deliberately shifted the stresses back and forth between voice and piano parts:

                             >                 >

Measure 21 ff: "Die Krähen warfen Bäll und Schlossen [The crows threw snowballs and hailstones]

           >            >

auf meinen Hut von jedem Haus." [on my hat from every house.]
 >

                 >               >

Measure 24 ff: "Die Krähen warfen Bäll und Schlossen
                       >              >

           >            >

auf meinen Hut von jedem Haus."
     >

So in order for Schubert to indicate his intended declamation clearly through notation, he had to introduce rhythmic changes in the voice part and—independently—in the piano part. If we sing the voice part without the piano, then play the piano part without the voice, trying to detach ourselves from Schubert's original meter, if we disregard the given bar lines and arbitrarily reset them so that each one falls before a "natural" stress point, then a notation such as in Example 11 results.

If we take this notation seriously and try to carry it out with rhythmic precision, what emerges is *not* what we might expect, namely concurrent stresses in juxtaposition. Rather, the stresses in the two parts offset each other, so that a metric change is no longer apparent and a kind of "meterlessness" takes over. We can observe the same effect if we compare parallel text lines in their rhythmic-melodic trappings. Schubert has evidently avoided the very device that was supposed to distinguish and alone could justify a notational shift with the help of time changes: a distinct, though extraordinary, rhythm (compare the lines in Example 12). However, Schubert does not avoid parallelisms entirely; on the contrary, he indicates them but then deliberately exposes the parallel impressions as deceptive. In so doing, he virtually destroys them. (Compare 2a with 2b in Example 12.)

Thus our attempt to impose a metric pattern after the voice entry, corresponding to the musical sound, is bound to fail—even with the help of metric changes, and even with the shifting of stresses in the accompaniment against those in the voice part. Just as the constant quarter notes in the introduction are securely tied into a 3/4 time, they emphatically renounce this tie from the moment the voice enters. Although declamatory units form and rhythmic stresses emerge, the intervals are irregular and vary between voice and piano parts. Musical and

Example 11

linguistic metrics are canceled; measurement is abandoned.

    With the same energy as in the introduction, but in a completely different manner, Schubert resumes this pattern of constant quarter notes tied into 3/4 time in the middle section of the song. The fugitive's hesitation and the awakening of the precious memory are conveyed not only by the major mode, by the simple, periodically subdivided lyric melody with its straightforward piano accompaniment, and by the obvious agreement between the rhythmic-musical foreground and background, but also by a totally different kind of motion. Here too, it is primarily the motion that distinguishes the "Wie anders..." [How differently . . .].[40]

    Thus the basic motion of quarter-notes grouped in threes established in the introduction is expanded in the middle section. Then Schubert gently leads back to it toward the end of the song as well. Once again the restless, irregular motion flows into measured 3/4 time; however, it no longer scans hectically, as in the introduction, but only binds lightly. Naturally a considerable expenditure of effort in terms of melodic-rhythmic construction is required to bring this about. Two of the structural elements are described here. In the following examples, I have

Example 12. Parallel text lines: the rhythm as it appears in the notation is given above the text line, the rhythm as declaimed, below.

placed the bar lines to correspond to the music as it sounds—that is, each one falls before a stressed note.

In the first part of the song, the repositioning of the stresses

from: "Die Krähen . . . auf meinen Hut von jedem Haus."

to: "Die Krähen . . . auf meinen Hut von jedem Haus."

like the entire rhythmic construction of the stanza, conveys the concept of hasty, stumbling flight. For this, quarter-note values are grouped by twos or threes in the declamation units with no regularity. Not so in the parallel passage of the closing major section: "möcht ich zurücke wieder wanken, vor ihrem Hause stille stehn."

In both of these instances (measures 59 and 62), inserted between the two 2/4 units (Example 13) and the main stress point "vor *ihrem*" [before *her*] is a single accented quarter-note, which seems like a drastically truncated 2/4 unit (Example 14). Through the text declamation, with the help of melodic and harmonic devices, a definite rhythmic structure is created secondarily, that is, a time change is introduced, and the result is a text that seems to *speak*.

Example 13                                   Example 14

The gesture through which the melodic and rhythmic high point "vor *ih*rem Hause" [before *her* house] (measures 60 and 63) is reached does in fact have something violent about it, but the effect is intentional. Perniciousness *must* be conquered, unrestrained motion must be harnessed in the measure, and it must be in 3/4 time. On the first try, the gesture is not confident enough; the quarter beats continue to press on with full force. The second time, Schubert intervenes so drastically, summoning, as it were, all possible means, that the motion is finally tethered, at least in the voice part. The piano part in 3/4 time continues to resist subordination. The cadence is delayed (measure 65 = fifth measure from the end). Not until the second beat does the melodic line formed by the top notes of the right-hand chords sink to the tonic. So the rhythmic order remains uncertain (measure 65 ff), the harmony vacillates from one beat to the next between dominant and tonic, and the voice part is brought in again to lead the reluctant piano part gently but firmly into the serenity of paced motion.

Schubert uses the repetitions of the last line, "vor ihrem Hause stille stehn" (measure 60 ff), as an opportunity to express individual words important to the context with varying emphasis. Using both rhythmic and melodic means (even the melody wavers!), he makes full use of the advantages musical performance has over speech.

Measures 60–61: "vor *ih*rem [her] Hause stille stehn,"
Measures 63–65: "vor *ih*rem Hause stille *stehn* [stand],"
Measures 66–68: "vor ihrem Hause *stille* [quietly] stehn."

So the particular compositional structure insures a particular interpretation of the text, but deliberate declamation is by no means the only element that determines the structure. Schubert does not "set words to music" in the usual, literal sense of the word; nor does he "interpret" the text by elaborating details or by maintaining a certain mood throughout the piece. All this does play a role in his composition, but it is secondary, at best. Rather he transposes to music the mental image he has received from the poem. This image seems to be suggested primarily by movements that enable the song to unfold in time and space. The image of motion extracted from the text is then precipitated in musical form; Schubert obtains musical structures from this process; he realizes the image as music. Thus he creates the text anew as he composes—just as the poet created it originally. This kind of composition explains something every thoughtful listener is sure to experience, if he hasn't already, and which Arnold Schönberg (Yearbook, *Der blaue Reiter*, Munich 1912, p. 30 f) has expressed thus:

I was deeply ashamed a few years ago when I discovered that for a few very familiar Schubert songs, I had no idea what was going on in the poems on which they were based. But then after reading the poems, I found that I had gained nothing in my understanding of these songs, since they did not require me to change my perception of the musical performance in the least. On the contrary, I realized that without knowing the poem, I had grasped the content of the songs, the real content, perhaps even more fully than if I had clung to the surface of the actual word meanings.

So "the real content" (perhaps it would be more accurate to say the effective content) of the poem in Schubert's composition is the expression of a mental image inspired by the poem and embracing it, but *musically* oriented from its inception. Schönberg grasped the meaning of the poem just as clearly, if not more so, from the musical content as from the text. This means Schubert's music cannot have been written "according to" the text; instead text and music must be rooted in a common ground that existed "before" the text took shape. To put it differently, Schubert's music is based on an underlying basic concept, not the text words.

Since the hasty, stumbling flight portrayed in "Rückblick" must be rendered as irregular motion, which cannot be achieved through traditional rhythmic means, Schubert resorts to a special rhythmic structure. The first thing we notice about this structure is that the music is not unified by an even pulse throughout. Schubert dispenses with the measure as a ruler for organizing time. He does not lay the course in advance, marking off the field in segments. The constant alternation of downbeats and upbeats is lacking. He does away with the specifically musical aspect of the time divisions. There remains a formless continuum at the foundation, which in itself seems to represent the flow of time. The basic rhythmic motion is reduced to continuous quarter-note values and can no longer be perceived as motion; it has lost its momentum. The formless continuum in relation to the motion in the upper layer of the piece serves as rhythmically neutral ground, like foil from which figures are to be cut.

Another special rhythmic feature of this song is that in the first and third parts, the continuum of quarter-note values in the foundation is broken by freely disposed phrases. The piano introduction, the middle part, and the closing of the song are organized around 3/4 time and two-measure phrasing, elements of musical form; but the divisions in the first and third parts seem determined only by an intent to translate the concept of motion into action. The rhythmics of motion has overpowered and replaced the musical rhythmics.

Schubert establishes the precondition for such a structure by couching the song in a simple three-part arrangement and by proceeding from and returning to simple musical-rhythmic figures. Only because he uses musical rhythm in the introduction and returns to it in the middle part and conclusion can he venture to leave this ordered terrain in the first and third parts. The concept of motion suggested by the poem is given concrete expression, so to speak, through the special rhythmic structure of the song. Conversely, the structure effects the concept of motion; along with other compositional elements less significant for this piece, it lends unity to the work.

# 3. "Halt!" [Pause] from *Die schöne Müllerin*

In other songs as well, Schubert takes what might be termed the "unraveling in time,"the *modus eundi,* creating contrasts that make for a high level of musical reality. An example is "Halt!," the third song in *Die schöne Müllerin.* (Text, see page 133)

The miller lad, who is following the course of the brook in his travels, stops suddenly when he sees the mill, which is the sense Schubert wants to convey; Wilhelm Müller does not deal with the stop save in the title. He returns to thoughts which, in the preceding song, seemed to float away with the water sprites. But the question he asks himself is not: "Ei, Bächlein, liebes Bächlein, war es also gemeint?" [Ah, brooklet, dear brooklet, was it meant to be so?] Instead, the poem implies something like: "Shall I go to this mill, ask for work, and interrupt my happy travels for what may only be a deceptive happiness?" It is this question, not its answer, that is the subject of the poem and song. Not until the next song do we learn the miller lad's decision. There he tells us that he has understood the brook to say "Zur Müllerin hin!" [Go to the miller maiden!] and that he has heeded the call and found work "für die Hände, für's Herze vollauf genug!" [for my hands and my heart, quite enough!]. Meanwhile in "Halt!" the question is still new. It has taken the miller lad by surprise, and the listener wonders along with him whether it is really the mill calling, "Ei, willkommen!" [Welcome!]. Hinting at deception, the song, whose title includes an exclamation point, concludes with the strange question, "War es also gemeint?"

Understandably one has associated the piano introduction, particularly in the rolling figure at the beginning[41] but the entire piano part as well, with the revolving mill wheels, and the forte and sharp accentuation of this figure with the 'Rädergebraus" [roar of the wheels]. There is little to say to the contrary. Anyone sensing this movement is not hearing wrong. But it should not be left at that. What the rolling figure "means" or what kind of feeling it arouses is less important than what it achieves in the musical composition beyond the simple association at the beginning, what it contributes to the effect of the whole. This certainly is not determined only by the lines "durch Rauschen und Singen bricht Rädergebraus" [through the rushing and singing, the roar of the wheels can be heard]. Not until the end of the song does the figure actually make complete revolutions, justifying the association with the mill wheels in a strangely unsubstantial closing section. At the beginning it appears only at long intervals and obviously sets off sections. In each case it opens a small section of the composition, a group of measures. In Schubert's time, these sections were called "rhythms;" our introduction might have been described something like this: "The revolving figure initiates the first rhythm of four measures, the second rhythm of six measures, and from then on (until measure 22) rhythms of two measures each." Such a description would reveal that Schubert's contemporaries designated something else as "rhythm," because they heard it rhythmically: the systematic ordering and arrangement of the measures in the compositional framework. Because we rarely hear rhythmically in this way today, we no longer designate it as such. This being so, our revolving figure takes on special significance by virtue of the fact that it marks the first measure of each group or "rhythm" of several measures. Schubert accentuates this signification through other means as well. Who among us is not surprised in measure 5 by the dominant minor chord, because we naturally expect the tonic to follow the dominant seventh chord of measure 4? This surprising chord appears, forte and accented, in the revolving figure. The lead-in to the voice entry is different. Here Schubert expands the "rhythm of four measures" for the following group of measures (5–10) to six, and provides a perfect bass cadence in the transition (measures 10–11), so that the step from the dominant in measure 10 to the tonic in 11 (the first of the next group of measures) is forceful. The revolving figure has again signaled the beginning of a new "rhythm," and its position in the first measure of the "rhythm" is emphasized.

In this way, a rhythm is marked out in the composition. When the voice part enters, it must follow suit. Unlike the piano part, it enters on an upbeat, the upbeat of the second measure of each "rhythm." Like the piano part, it subdivides into two-measure phrases. (The schematic illustration in Example 15 may help to clarify this usage.) But in measure 23, when the voice part begins the second stanza, "Ei willkommen, ei willkommen, süsser Mühlengesang," [Welcome, welcome, sweet mill song], *not* on an upbeat but on a downbeat like the piano part, and in the *first* rather than the second measure of the "rhythm," in other words, too early, earlier than we expect. The effect is startling (Example 15): It is as if the "Ei willkommen" carried a musical exclamation point. It seems to cry out.

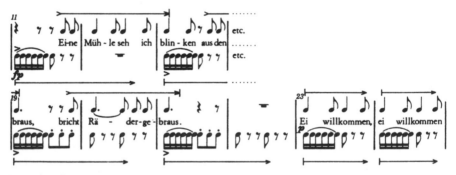

Example 15

But that is not all. Schubert wants to formulate the entire composition as a musical exclamation. Therefore he sets "Ei willkommen, ei willkommen, süsser Mühlengesang" in four-measure "rhythms" (the "rhythm of two measures" has prevailed since the voice entry), and within these he repeats the revolving figure three times: in the first, second and fourth measures. The figure has carried an 'inner weight' up to this point, in that it always signaled the first measure of a "rhythm." This weight is effective here in the altered constellation as well. The four measures of the exclamatory sentence form a group with the following rhythmic division:

| 23 | 24 | 25 | 26 |
|---|---|---|---|
| Ei willkommen, | ei willkommen, | süsser Mühlenge- | sang |
| stressed— | stressed— | unstressed— | stressed |

On the higher plane of the "rhythm of measures," especially with the repeat of these four measures (27–30), the revolving motion is intensified, forming a new kind of musical reality.

If the voice part were to fully adapt to the actual rhythm of these measures (stressed—stressed—unstressed—stressed), the result would be an unnatural stress on the last syllable: "süsser Mühlengesang" [sweet mill *song*]. To avoid this, Schubert directs the melody in the unstressed third measure of the "rhythm" (corresponding measures 25 and 29) in such a way that "süsser" [sweet] receives a moderate stress, because it falls on the very first beat, where the bass has a rest. This makes the unstressed eighth-note figure that follows pull strongly toward the last measure of the phrase (30). But then Schubert highlights *"Mühlengesang"* [*mill* song] by placing it at the high turning point of the melodic lines as well through the dynamics (——<——>——). The stress that would normally have fallen on the last syllable, "Mühlengesang," according to the rhythmic sequence of the four-measure group, is forestalled, as if the pattern stressed—stressed—unstressed—stressed relates largely to the piano part and only secondarily to the voice part. Although this impression is deceiving, it is created intentionally. "War es also gemeint?" [Was it meant to be so?] will be the question raised in the last stanza, but no answer will assure the inquirer that the friendly house, the bright sun, and the luring song of the mill are not deceiving. On the contrary, everything seems deceptive. Schubert realizes the uncertainty as musical structure. He summons all possible means to this end, but especially rhythm, as we have seen and will continue to see as the story unfolds.

The line "und die Fenster so blank" [and the windows, so shining] is set unmistakably—at least in the piano part—in a four-measure unit (34–37) and joined to the following one by the step from the dominant seventh to the tonic chord. However, the parallel line preceding it, "Und das Haus, wie so traulich" [and the house, oh how cozy] (measures 31–33)[42], lacks this clarity. The unit of only *three* measures is confusing, as is the surprising reentry (34) of the revolving figure in D minor, instead of the expected C major, so that the dominant seventh chord (33) remains unresolved and the continuation in measures 33/34 seems "wrong." This is Schubert's intention, of course. For then the next unit seems all the more "right"—the beginning (37/38) of the first and only episode that is supposed to shine forth unbroken and undeceiving, the only forte passage in the whole song: "Und die Sonne, wie helle vom Himmel sie scheint!" [And the sun, how brightly it shines from the heavens]. It is no wonder, one might say, that our revolving figure here is different from the preceding, and subsequent, occurrences and that the measures are grouped differently. One might express it this way, though the facts of the matter naturally call for an explanation in reverse order. The new effect is a result of the new grouping, which now uses the revolving bass figure in a different way. From measure 38 on, the voice and piano parts together form groups of two, which are connected in the simple periodic pattern 2×2. In each case, the revolving figure does not occur until the second measure. Here the composition finally appears to be "in order." At last a simple, accompanying foundation is laid in the piano part, even though the voice part swings out freely in the melody.

No matter how bright the sun, the question "Ei, Bächlein, liebes Bächlein, war es also gemeint?" keeps gnawing. For Schubert's composition, this means that the "security" just won musically must be relinquished again. It cannot be reinforced as the composition continues. The four-measure phrases of "Ei, Bächlein, liebes Bächlein . . ." do in fact deceive (measure 46 ff), for they are musically related, particularly in their rhythmic structure, to those of the line "Ei willkommen, ei willkommen, süsser Mühlengesang," which seemed to have an exclamation point—but now these same four-measure phrases contain an interrogative!

The deception continues in the link with the next song, "Danksagung an den Bach" [Thanksgiving to the brook]. The question "war es also gemeint?" from "Halt!" is repeated here, but the motion relates to that of the first two songs of the cycle, here somewhat slower. The deceptive question recalls the time before "Halt!" when no danger has yet threatened the traveler. In this context, we can detect a hint of mockery in "Danksagung an den Bach." We hear it clearly in the melodic phrase of "zur Müllerin hin, so lautet der Sinn" [to the miller maiden, that's what it seemed to say]. When sung by itself, the song lacks this touch, and therefore its beauty may cause the unsentimental listener some uneasiness. The textual link alone illustrates why actually none of the songs should be sung out of context; but now we know it from a musical standpoint as well. The very quality that can displease us when we hear "Danksagung an den Bach" sung by itself is an important feature in the overall context of the cycle: that touch of irony.

# IV. Die schöne Müllerin

> The cycle *Die schöne Müllerin* is discussed in detail too seldom, and *Winterreise* not at all. The unsettling *Winterreise*, probably the most beautiful music ever written to a German poem, would seem to merit extensive and elaborate discussion. Granted, it is difficult to write about such masterpieces, such melodic and poetic effusions, but it would be highly rewarding.
>
> Schubert's friend, Josef von Spaun

There is no easy answer to the question of whether, and to what extent, *Die schöne Müllerin* and *Winterreise* are cycles, musically speaking—that is, whether the songs form a musically coherent whole and, if so, in what it consists. Certainly unity is established first of all by the text. Because *Die schöne Müllerin* originated from a song drama, with roles distributed to be read, the poem cycle has a plot. A young, blond mill hand (says Wilhelm Müller in his prologue), following the brook as he travels, comes to a mill, where he asks for work and is hired by the master. He falls in love with the miller's daughter and wins her, but she is fickle and later bestows her favors on the hunter. Broken-hearted, the miller lad seeks death in the brook.

*Winterreise,* on the other hand, is made up of the individual, unrelated songs of a lad who has left the city out of unrequited love (the girl has chosen a rich man instead) and seems to seek death. His travels are like aimless wandering through a snow-shrouded landscape. Whereas the love story actually takes place in the first cycle, it has preceded the second. Accordingly, this cycle is only loosely coherent, while the first, because of its story development, is more compact.

In both cycles, the poems are held together by a single speaker, the traveler. In *Die schöne Müllerin,* the first two songs depict the miller lad actually traveling. When he sees the mill gleaming, he stops—"Halt!"—and now the action begins—on location, so to speak. But *Winterreise,* although pervaded by the motif of travel or departure, lacks a song like "Das Wandern" or "Wohin?"—that is, a hiking song, or one that at least appears to be. Here, only the *idea* of travel is suggested. Thus the musical element of motion is present in both cycles, but within a different sense.

"Das Wandern" ["Wandering" (in German, hiking, traveling by foot)] is the title of the first song in *Die schöne Müllerin*.[43] Can one hike to it? "Why not?" one might say. "It's a good song to sing while hiking, in both text and music." Indeed, Wilhelm Müller's poem has become *the* German hiking song—not in Schubert's setting, however, but in the old familiar melody of Carl Friedrich Zöllner[44] (compare Example 21). One can hike to this melody, as the eighth notes match the human stride or vice versa. One can walk in time to the eighth notes and, as indicated by the tempo mark, "munter" [merrily].[45]

Though it would seem self-evident that one should also be able to walk or hike to Schubert's "Das Wandern," this turns out to be impossible. Try it—not in a room, of course, nor in the mountains, but in a grassy valley with a brook that could drive a mill or has done so. In a good musical rendering, if keeping pace with the eighth notes of the 2/4 measure, one ends up jogging; or if by the quarters, then it becomes a solemn walk. If the reverse is done—rendering the song at a tempo to which one can hike—one ends up laughing and stumbling; it simply doesn't work. "Have I forgotten how to hike?" one may ask. "How can I sing and play a hiking song, if I don't know for sure how one moves when hiking?" But one can! Over the course of centuries, music, especially instrumental music, has developed not only typical dance forms, but other forms that suggest certain kinds of motion to the listener, even though it may be impossible to realize the motion in a given case. Although this musical motion cannot be fully realized in physical motion, it can to a certain degree be translated. If one can imagine it musically, one should be able to "realize it *musically*." Usually we experience such phenomena negatively. Who among us has not laughed during Beethoven's *Fidelio*[46] when a musically helpless stage director has had the guard come prancing in, when they are to march in step. Or who has not been annoyed in the scene "Non più andrai" ["Say goodbye now to pastime"] at the end of the first act of *Figaro,* when a conductor, insensitive to the action on stage, sets such a fast tempo that when it finally breaks into a march, Figaro is *unable* to march holding Cherubino's hand. The soldiers in *Fidelio* cannot march to Beethoven's music; Figaro and Cherubino must march to Mozart's. The tempos are considerably different, yet both cases involve marches—musical forms so typical that they are unquestionably associated with marching, even though the mental image can be transformed into reality in only one case.

So it is with Schubert. This "hiking song" of his is no fun to sing while hiking. Not that the melody isn't merry! But it has rests that one cannot bridge over in singing, much as one would like to, that cannot be omitted or circumvented, even though they are "only" rests. They are a substantive part of Schubert's melody. One cannot sing this melody without piano accompaniment, because the voice and piano parts are so intertwined in a single musical structure that one makes no sense without the other. The voice part is not purely melody, the piano part not purely accompaniment.

The tempo creates even more problems, as we have just seen in our experiment. Schubert stipulates "mässig geschwind" [moderately fast]. This means that the quarter notes—for these are the units that determine the tempo—are to be taken fast, but only moderately so. The correct tempo for practiced performers[47] is about $\quarternote = 90$. If the association with hiking is so strong, almost compulsive, despite the tempo problem, there must be reasons for it; and these can only be found in Schubert's composition, i.e. in the technique—in this case we might even say the mechanics—of his music.

The piano introduction, which also serves as an interlude between stanzas and as the closing, has always been praised as simple, even as amazingly simple. The constant sixteenth notes and the even stride of the eighth-note octaves in the bass seem to represent the revolving millwheel working tirelessly in the distance. A mood is established with superb finesse:

Schubert's melody reflects all the traveling miller lad's youthful vigor and love of singing; but beneath this light-hearted gaiety, a soft, wistful yearning propels him toward an unknown end. The music follows the quietest stirring of his thoughts. . . .[48]

This appearance is deceptive, however. In reality, the piano introduction is not at all simple but has a highly complicated structure, almost cunningly formed; and if anyone claims that it merely sets the mood, he has missed the point.

The introduction comprises four measures, ending not on beat one of the fourth measure, as is customary, but in the middle of the measure. The technical term "feminine cadence" describes this phenomenon only inadequately. The listener is not fully aware of the 2/4 time, i.e. the subordination of the second quarter note in each measure to the first (Example 16). The confident attack on the downbeat (beat one) and the ending on the upbeat (beat two) (Example 17), which actually contradict each other, prevent us from hearing any subordination of the beats, at least any whose repetition could be taken for granted. After all, what is there to make us subordinate the second half of the first measure to the first half or the second beat of measure 2 to the first beat of measure 3? In a proper 2/4 measure, this would be a perfectly natural interpretation. Yet the fact is that we do not hear a constant 2/4 rhythm. Instead, we hear what might be described as a 2/4 order that is "attacked" by a 1/4 sequence with a tremendous driving effect. This is also evident in the grouping of the measures.

Example 16

Example 17

The four introductory measures are subdivided 2 + 2 as usual, but not into an opening phrase and a complementary cadence. Except for the final chord, which cuts off the continuous sixteenth notes, the second phrase is identical to the first, a simple repetition of it. This would be nothing extraordinary, except that the point where the repeat begins (measure 3) shows up as a hiatus. The harmony on the last beat of the first phrase (beat two of measure 2) is followed immediately by the same harmony on the first beat of the second phrase (beat one of measure 3):

$$\begin{array}{cccc}
\xrightarrow{\hspace{2cm}} & \prime & \xleftarrow{\hspace{1cm}} & \\
1 & 2 & 3 & 4
\end{array}$$

Harmonic steps | I    I | V    I | I    I | V    I |

Therefore the prescribed 2/4 time cannot really function as such; instead the quarters themselves seem actively to push forward.

This effect is decidedly reinforced by an element of the composition which, oddly enough, we rarely find mentioned anywhere, much less described at length, obvious though it is to the ear and fundamental to the "mechanics" of the composition: the thirds and sixths of the right piano hand. They create a rhythm that compromises the uniformity of the sixteenth notes, as does the unconventional harmonic change from the fifth to the first degree—which is bound not only to the eighth notes of the bass, but, in a way, also to the thirds and sixths of the right piano hand (Example 18). Georgiades offers this imaginative suggestion: "The compositional structure can be illustrated by a hypothetical percussion instrumentation for the bass pulses and the rhythm of double stops [i.e., thirds and sixths in Example 18]:[49]

Example 18

Example 19
(according to Georgiades)

different
at the
beginning:

Example 20

If one tries this example—it is fun, by the way, though not as simple as one would expect—one will see at once that it is not the continuity of an uninterrupted eighth- and sixteenth-note sequence that creates the tirelessly driving effect. It is the compositional elements that compartmentalize, if not break, this continuity, forcing a new beginning again and again. This is most important: the piano part drives forward, not because it is uninterrupted, but because it keeps beginning anew. "Relentlessness" is the effect; the mechanical compositional structure, the cause. This quality is especially evident each time the voice concludes a stanza and the introduction/closing comes in again. A transition? Just the opposite: a self-powered attack that constantly seems to renew itself, even though the eighth and sixteenth notes in the accompaniment are continuous.

Also contributing to this effect are the different style of the lines 'Das muss ein schlechter Müller sein, dem niemals fiel das Wandern ein" [He must be a poor miller who hasn't felt the urge to travel] and the surprisingly wide swing of the harmonic change for the final words of the stanza, "das Wandern, das Wandern" (Example 20). The contrast in style strengthens the effect of the first part of the song. Another contrast in this "different" part of the song is the way it is subdivided. This is the only place where two identically structured lines are joined with rhyme:

> Das Wandern ist des Müllers Lust,
> Das Wandern!
> Das muss ein schlechter Müller sein,
> Dem niemals fiel das Wandern ein,
> Das Wandern.
>
> [To travel is the miller's joy, to travel!
> He must be a poor miller,
> who hasn't felt the urge to travel,
> to travel.]

The result is a lyrical section with a simple, lilting repeat, so that two four-measure phrases emerge naturally. This is completely unlike the first section, where the voice part consists of tightly self-contained three-measure phrases. Granted, the latter are predetermined by the text, but they would have been easy to circumvent. Schubert would have *had* to form four-measure phrases if he had had a hiking song in mind, as Carl Friedrich Zöllner did later. However, he was concerned not with creating "a song to sing while hiking" but with getting his cycle under way and awakening a vivid picture of traveling in the listener's mind through musical motion.

That he welcomed the repetitions of a strophic song for this purpose is obvious. In a strophic song, once the motion is started, it seems able to go on endlessly. Accordingly, 'Das Wandern" has no real ending; one is just as likely to want to continue beyond the fifth stanza as to sing fewer than five stanzas.[50]

But there is still another aspect to consider in a comparison of Schubert's setting with that of Zöllner. It is only fair to ask whether Zöllner's melody isn't more appropriate, perhaps even better than Schubert's. Indeed, a closer look reveals that it follows the text more closely. After all, the key word is 'Das Wandern" [traveling]. In a musical setting, all other words must be subordinate. And Zöllner's melody meets this requirement (Example 21). In the first line, 'Das Wandern" is emphasized and "des Müllers Lust" [the miller's joy] trails behind; in the second, 'Das Wandern" is stressed again, but this time "des Müllers Lust" is

Das Wan-dern ist des    Mül-lers Lust, das Wan-dern ist des    Mül-lers Lust, das    Wan - - dern.

Example 21

given equal emphasis, and is thereby marked as significant. Zöllner's melody is masterfully balanced. The same cannot be said of Schubert's melody. The melodic emphasis: "des *Müllers* Lust" seems almost ludicrous; and the stress: "Das *muss* ein schlechter Müller sein" [He *must* be a poor miller], seems all the more ridiculous, since this is hardly a happy line, melodically or in the sequence. Schubert obviously did not base his melody on the text of the first stanza. There is nothing unusual about this. In strophic songs, we frequently encounter melodies that were not designed for the first stanza, simply because the composer was inspired by another one, because his idea originated from a later stanza. In this case, Schubert apparently took his idea for the first part of the song from the first sentence of the third stanza, and the idea for the second part from the second sentence of the fourth stanza:

> Das sehn wir auch den Rädern ab,
> Den Rädern!
> [We pick this up from the wheels too, the wheels!]

> Sie tanzen mit den muntern Reihn
> Und wollen gar noch schneller sein,
> Die Steine.
> [They join in the merry dance
> And want to go even faster,
> The stones.]

One sees at once that text and melody correspond now—the melody seems made for the text. It fits rather poorly with the other stanzas, of course, even though, as we said, the key word occurs in the first stanza.

This raises another question, more deserving of consideration than this comparison[51] and critique, but seldom asked: Why doesn't it bother us that Schubert's melody is imperfect? Why do we seldom notice the imperfection at all?

Well, it is simply not worth noticing. Justifiable though our detailed criticism may be, the relation of melody to text in this song was obviously of secondary importance to Schubert. Other elements had to take precedence if his intention was to be realized. This is the first song of the cycle. Its title, "Das Wandern," conveys meaning and is therefore important. But what was clearly more important to Schubert than stressing the key word through the simple means of an emphatic musical setting, more important than creating the mood of a happy traveler through simple association with the word "Wandern," was that something be set in motion with this first song, that the listener not only be put in the right mood but moved in the concrete sense of the word. The musical structure demands vicarious participation by the listener to be effective. If the listener performs the activity demanded of him, he actually takes part in a music that indeed seems to move. Therefore the listener himself begins to move in a way that is different from—and more than—an emotional response.

Schubert's and Zöllner's settings differ in the musical methods used and in their musical realizations. Consequently, Schubert's composition affects us differently than Zöllner's. Because we sense this difference, whether we can express it in words or not, we can enjoy both Schubert's composition and Zöllner's song, appreciating each for its own sake. We are in no way compelled to compare and weigh. Our musical understanding tells us that the reason for the difference lies in the composers' intentions. Of course valid comparisons can only be made between compositions that are approximately equivalent in quality, and we must concede that Zöllner's song is also a masterpiece in its own way.

Example 21a

Once the music is set in motion in the first song, "Das Wandern," it seems to run on its own power. The second song, "Wohin?" runs too, though somewhat more leisurely. It seems to lack intentional movement, as if the music were letting the miller lad indulge in a certain pensiveness. The words that later signify the tragic ending occur here for the first time: "Tief unten" [deep down] and "hinunter" [downward]; yet we hardly suspect that the depths of the brook will later pull the lad down. Of course, to anyone who is familiar with the cycle or who, like the literates of Schubert's time, expects that these song dramas always end with the hero's death; to anyone who sings, plays, or hears this song full of ominous, unanswered questions, in which it is still not clear whether it is the water sprites who sing the last sentence to the journeyman, "Lass singen Gesell, lass rauschen und wandre fröhlich nach!" [Let the singing and roaring (of water) go on, lad, and follow merrily along!] or whether the fellow is talking to himself  to anyone who is aware of all this, the song sounds differently than the first, at least more restrained, not like a second hiking song, not merrily and gay, as it is often sung. Schubert carefully yields to this nuance of feeling without changing the basic style, and thereby connects this song to the first, tying it into the cycle. Despite variations in form (in the bass, overlapping quarter notes instead of eighth notes, and an open fifth instead of the octaves; in the right piano hand, sixteenth-note triplets), the element that simulated walking in the first song is retained: the 2/4 time, with eighth-note and sixteenth-note movement; but gone now are the self-renewing impulses and strophic construction; the music spreads abroad as if on an open plain.

The song is styled after a well-developed model from the instrumental music of the Viennese classical school, which combines the structures of the rondo and sonata[52]:

$$
\begin{array}{ccccccc}
& 11 & 15 & 23 & 53 & 62 & 73 \\
A & B & A & C & A & D & A'
\end{array}
$$

Stanzas      1      2      3+4+5      5      6

Here the travel is no longer "relentless." With the question "Wohin?" [whither?], the forward drive of "Das Wandern" is no longer so obvious. This second song has meaning only in relation to the first. For when it is sung by itself, and we often do hear it alone, the important musical constituents, variations of those in "Das Wandern," lose their point of reference; the piano part is reduced to an accompaniment without deeper meaning, because there is no binding force in the motion. Granted, it gains tone painting characteristics instead, but these could hardly have been Schubert's intention, considering the way in which the cycle is composed. At any rate, they were certainly not meant to stand out as they do when the song is heard alone.

If our observation is correct—that the music in our cycle is literally set in motion by the first song and continues automatically in the second—then the third song, "Halt!" is clearly in sharp contrast. It must express this contrast as musical structure and make it recognizable in the composition. And so it does (compare p. 45ff). Here we will only consider the song's position in the cycle and how it fulfills its function. There is some question as to whether Schubert means to bring the song cycle to a standstill at all with "Halt!" After all, the scene where the action will take place has been reached; in the fourth song, "Danksagung an den Bach" [Thanksgiving to the brook], the miller lad is working, the love story has begun— yet the idea of traveling is taken up once again. "Halt!" ends with the line "war es also gemeint?" [was it meant to be so?] and "Danksagung an den Bach" opens with the same line. This is one of the few instances in Wilhelm Müller's poems where one song is linked directly to another. That Schubert would pick up this link musically should by no means be taken for granted. First we should ask: does he pick it up at all? Certainly, but not in the way one would expect. Schubert skips over "Halt!" and reaches back to the *second* song. In "Danksagung an den Bach," he picks up the momentum that "Halt!" has interrupted, that of walking or hiking. At the beginning, this momentum was realized in a narrower sense: We heard "Das Wandern" as a musical device, as an impetus. Now, as the momentum resumes, everything that follows seems to reach across the intervening song in which the motion was halted and relate back to the beginning.

One can see and hear at once that the compositional style of "Danksagung an den Bach," with all its variations, is the same as that of the first two songs: 2/4 time; eighth-note beats in the bass and constant sixteenth notes in the right piano hand; a form that, in spite of its three distinct parts, impresses us as a strophic song with variations. The tempo is "Etwas langsam" [somewhat slow], befitting the situation: the miller lad is no longer traveling but is reflecting on his travels and destination.

As in the first song, the piano introduction, which also functions as a closing, is a four-measure phrase ending in the middle of the fourth measure and is divided into two half-phrases. But unlike the first song, the juncture between measures 2 and 3 does not seem like a hiatus. It is bridged by an association of the final chord of the opening half-phrase with the first chord of the closing half-phrase. The harmonic steps have a different relationship:

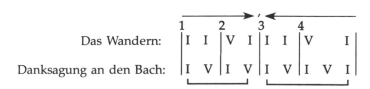

As in the first song, the fact that the introduction ends in the middle of the measure is significant. The voice part assumes the four-measure phrasing of the introduction. But instead of ending the phrase in the fourth measure, it carries it over from the fourth to the fifth. In an analogy to the introduction, the listener expects this (Example 22). By the repetition of the concluding question, "War es also gemeint?," the phrase that consisted of eight quarter-note values in the introduction is extended to ten quarters. Such an extension is found frequently in compositions of Schubert's day. It is of no rhythmic or metric significance, because the conclusion of the phrase falls in the middle of the measure equally often. But at the juncture "dein Singen, dein Klingen,/war es also gemeint?" [your singing, your ringing,/was it meant to be so?], Schubert extends the phrase one more quarter, so that the unit (measures 5–10) now contains not ten but eleven quarters and ends on the first beat of a measure. This modification of the composition, though simple in itself, is far-reaching in effect. Having been presented with a musical entity as succinct, unified, and perfect as this piano introduction to "Danksagung an den Bach," the listener has a very definite expectation at the moment the repetition is begun.

Example 22

*dein* | *Sin - gen, dein Klin-gen, war es* | *al - so ge-meint,*

*war es* | *al - so ge-meint?*

Corresponding to this is the parallel passage:

*das* | *möcht ich noch wis - sen, ob* | *sie dich ge-schickt,*

*ob* | *sie dich ge-schickt.*

The four-measure introduction is a rhythmic entity comparable to a line of verse. Just as we approach a new line in a poem with a clear expectation, based on the form of the previous line, an expectation that is necessary if the lines are to be connected at all into stanzas, so it is with music. When we have already heard a "rhythm of four measures," and a repetition of it is apparently about to begin, we expect the phrase to be the same—or, if it should be different, we at least expect another "rhythm" of *four* measures. If our expectation is not fulfilled, if the "rhythm of four measures" is changed, our receptive musical mind looks for causes, reasons, and explanations; listening, it looks for them by way of obvious associations. (Whether this is done consciously or unconsciously is immaterial; for in the attentive, receptive listener, the listening experience occurs automatically). Do not think I am overemphasizing this moment. One might argue that it hardly enters our consciousness, perhaps that it is totally undetectable, since the natural declamation of the text before the repeat of "War es also gemeint?" makes a somewhat larger break seem reasonable—even suggests it. Certainly! But that is precisely the point. We hear the miller lad *speak* suddenly—and freely, free of the constraints of the repeat, free of the limitations of simple periodicity "naturally" required for "simple singing" of a simple song stanza. We must ask whether it is really natural, in a "hiking song," to encounter a speaking subject, not just figuratively, but in a real sense. The next section will perhaps clarify what this means.

From the five stanzas of the poem, Schubert forms a three-part song. Especially because the introduction is repeated as interlude (measures 18–21) and closing, it strikes us as a strophic song with variations, the middle stanza being in a minor key, and the third shortened by half.

$$1 \quad 2 \quad 3 \quad 4 \quad 5$$

$$A \qquad A' \qquad \frac{A}{2}$$

In this form, text stanzas 2 and 4 correspond musically (Example 23). One will note that the first part actually contains an extra measure (measure 13) that would not

Example 23

be missed it if it were left out. To describe it in technical terms: a measure of the piano part, before it occurs in measure 14, is anticipated as measure 13; and in the voice part, a single note that exclaims "Gelt!" is inserted in the melody.[53] This is all it amounts to. But this measure has an effect that the listener neither expects nor wants in a simple song: the rhythm is disrupted, and the simple lyrical declamation seems to have been abandoned altogether. The line

˘  ‾  ˘  ˘  ‾  ˘
"Gelt, hab ich's verstanden"

which begins on an upbeat in the poem, corresponding to

˘  ˘  ‾  ˘  ˘  ‾  ˘
'Was ich such, hab ich funden"

is turned into a double-downbeat line, when an extra main stress is inserted before the main stress 'háb":

‾  ‾  ˘  ˘  ‾  ˘
"Gelt, hab ich's verstanden."

With this measure, the solid rhythmic structure is cracked, and out of the crack, the "Gelt!" comes through as a shout, as real speech; Schubert has given the colloquial interjection a musical exclamation point.[54] Both the composition and the content of the song hinge on this point. The interruption in the rhythmic structure, in the continuity of the motion, brings the traveler to life; he is physically present in the song, in that he *speaks*. An image becomes musical reality. The "tone mechanism"—the term art theorists of Schubert's day would have used[55]—of a unique rhythmic structure has its emotional equivalent in the physical concept of motion.

In "Das Wandern" and "Wohin?" physical motion appeared merely as motion itself, whereas here it is that of a physical being, the person we seemed to encounter for the first time in "Halt!" But "Halt!" was not a hiking song. Thus two elements that were introduced separately in each of the preceding songs are combined in "Danksagung an den Bach." This completes the introduction to the cycle, and now the real plot can begin. In all subsequent songs, it takes only a hint to remind us of elements in the introduction. For instance, the eighth notes in the bass of "Am Feierabend" [Leisure at evening] are clearly reminiscent of the "hiking" eighth notes of the 2/4 songs at the beginning, despite the 6/8 time, and even though they occur first on beats one and three, four and six, but later on one and two, four and five. Likewise "Mein!" [Mine!] (tempo as in "Das Wandern": "Mässig geschwind" [moderately fast]) and "Des Baches Wiegenlied" (tempo as in "Wohin?": "Mässig" [moderato]) are linked through their motion to the hiking songs at the beginning. However, because of their different mood, they belong in another, related category, and are therefore written in ¢ time.[56] From here on, wherever the device of recitative is used or even hinted at (the first time is in the very next song, "Am Feierabend"), speech in the song no longer seems strange. Travel and reflections on travel on the one hand and the presence of a speaker on the other hand, when realized as composition, are the elements that provide musical coherence and story development; through them, we recognize a "musical content."

Thus I repeat my view that the songs of our cycle are not only "arranged simply" but are musically coherent—though not in the sense that one normally expects. Related themes and motifs, melodic quotations, even echoes are hardly relevant here, nor can any special importance be attached to consistency of mood or similar features. Nevertheless we have recognized coherence, particularly at points where textual and musical content seem to converge.

Moreover, we have hit upon a second element of coherence. The first lay in the area of musical motion and its emotional equivalent; the second lies in the area of musical speech and its emotional equivalent. We discovered both elements when we examined the "tone mechanism" of the songs and tried to find parallels in our aural perception—if I may elaborate on this expression that was linked to the understanding of the analytical process even in Schubert's day. Now let us pursue the element of speech and discover how it is realized musically.

The song "Am Feierabend" has vigorous tone-painting qualities. The piano part turns wheels with its sixteenth notes, though for the moment they are not "roaring" but soft. This association does not emerge fully until the beginning is repeated forte after the middle section; here the millwheels really do "roar" as they begin to turn again. (It calls to mind the piano part in "Gretchen am Spinnrade," where similar musical devices are used. The spinning wheel seems to turn, then stops at the climax of the song, "und ach, sein Kuss!" [and oh, his kiss!], and must be restarted; but it starts up only hesitantly, as if unwilling.)

As I have already pointed out, Schubert goes beyond instrumental tone painting in linking the piano part to the songs at the beginning of the cycle, where the octaves in the bass and the sixteenth-note figure in the right piano hand correspond to the foot traveler's movements in the text. Songs 1, 2, 4 and "Am Feierabend" are related in compositional style. But I see the tone painting and motion as peripheral elements, and something else as the essence. Once the shout "Gelt" in "Danksagung an den Bach" has brought a speaking being on the scene, Schubert turns to the musical device of recitative; that is, he has a person speak in traditional musical manner.[57] But this person is not the "I" who has been speaking all along; rather, the miller lad quotes *others*: the "Meister" [master] and "das liebe Mädchen" [the dear maiden]. As if this were not already strange enough, Schubert chooses this place to introduce an element that has not yet come into play in the cycle: the element of feeling—painful feeling.

We are delighted again and again when the "dear maiden" says, "allen eine gute Nacht" [to all a good night], because this line is speech-like and comes as a surprise. The effect lies, first of all, in the interruption of the established pattern of declamation. Until now the lines began on an upbeat, following the natural rhythm of the text, but this line begins on a downbeat, so that the emphasis is not: "Allen| *eine* gute Nacht" but: | "*allen* eine gute Nacht." The effect is so greatly intensified, through melodic and harmonic devices, that the surprising anticipation of the second "allen . . ." *in the piano part* (measure 56) cuts the perceptive listener to the quick. Though it is harmonic and in itself a perfectly "harmless" variation of the simple cadence in the F-major/D-minor mode (in Schubert's day, such simple harmonic devices had not yet suffered from overuse), this anticipatory chord hurts. We hear it as a cutting dissonance and find its supposed resolution displeasing. One might well ask: What kind of pain is this? But here, too, a rhythmic-metric component comes into play. So far, the unstressed syllables that begin each line of text have been matched in the music as a "pick-up":

$$\smile \quad \smile \quad \_{\!\!\frown} \quad \smile \qquad \smile\smile \quad \_{\!\!\frown} \qquad \smile \quad \smile \, \_{\!\!\frown}\smile \quad \_{\!\!\frown} \, \smile$$
"und der Meister", "euer Werk", "und das liebe Mädchen"

$$\smile\smile \; \_{\!\!\frown}\smile \; \_{\!\!\frown}\smile \quad \_{\!\!\frown}$$
But because the corresponding syllable of "allen eine gute Nacht" falls on the *stressed* beat, it takes three measures, not two, to complete the line. Thus the "dear maiden's" words depart from the established pattern of two-measure phrases that we have come to expect.

The combined effect of these components now leads the listener to a conclusion that he was certainly entitled to assume, but which has not yet been expressed: that there is a relationship between the miller lad who is speaking and the "dear maiden" whom he quotes, and that this relationship will end painfully. With the anticipated chord (piano part, measure 56)—the effect of which can hardly be explained through harmonic interpretation alone—the inevitability of a tragic ending breaks through our consciousness. It breaks through at the moment Schubert uses recitative for the first time, when he brings a second person to the scene musically by having the maiden speak through the mouth of the miller lad.

So it is not just the repositioning of the stress of a syllable by musical means, the emphasis of "allen" (which in itself is hardly profound!), that gives the middle part and thus the entire song much of its individuality. It is the myriad of associations that the listener can and does make when he hears the song in the context of the cycle.

"Am Feierabend" shows that a "musical change of plan" for text stresses can be effective, but that the individuality of the song cannot be attributed to this alone. If one compares the text in the first part of the song with its repeat in the third part (the song has the form A-B-A'), one will note that one line is first declaimed beginning on a downbeat[58] (measure 16 ff):

"I dass die schöne | Müllerin . . ."

but later on an upbeat (measure 68 ff):

"dass die | schöne Mülle- | rin . . ."

The nuance that emerges here is beautiful and, after the middle section, especially meaningful: The miller lad sets the girl who wishes *everyone* a good night against "meinen, meinen treuen Sinn" [*my* true love]. But the listener is affected even more deeply, it seems to me, by the ending of the song, because here—almost in a reminiscing way—the recitative-like passages are set right next to the tone-painting passages, and because the piano part speaks instead of making the wheels "roar" once more in the closing.

"In the delicate four-measure introduction to 'Der Neugierige' [The curious one]," observes Dietrich Fischer-Dieskau, "the miller seems to accompany his question on lute strings. Later the brook joins in as a ground."[59] The miller lad appears to be talking to himself. When he addresses the brooklet:[60] "O Bächlein meiner Liebe . . ." [O beloved brooklet . . .], his speaking turns into singing, but it is a very soft (*pp*), restrained ("sehr langsam" [very slow], heartfelt singing; his song is not the kind one could sing to just anyone, or even sing aloud at all, much less "perform." It is wholly and solely an expression of feeling. The accompaniment, this time in the ordinary sense, continues to suggest lute music, with only a hint of the brook. We would like to agree wholeheartedly with Dietrich Fischer-Dieskau in his sensitive observations, but we no longer can when he goes on to say: "His singing intensifies, becomes increasingly penetrating, finally gaining resolution in recitative, at the point where it seems to refer to life and death." Does the song intensify, does it become increasingly penetrating, so much so that recitative must necessarily result? And to what extent can recitative as such be resolute or give that impression? At best, the speech rendered through recitative can be resolute; the recitative itself cannot. In my view, the recitative comes as a complete surprise here. And it is this element of surprise that makes the text (that one little word "yes") appear to be declaimed completely *differently* all of a sudden, as if actually *spoken*, aloud and audibly, not at all like murmurings to oneself. Is this what gives it that air of resoluteness?

Not this alone, considering that Schubert immediately abandons the recitative diction, at least in the stricter sense of the word, and brings in something new and *unexpected* again with "dem anderen Wörtchen Nein" [the other little word "no"]. This new turn takes us by surprise primarily because of its incredible harmonic effect, which Dietrich Fischer-Dieskau describes as follows: "The change to the G seventh-chord on 'Nein' expresses how unthinkable a refusal would be." I see the harmonics as one of many factors working together here. The element of feeling certainly stands in the forefront, and there is a reason for its placement close to the "musically direct speech"—we observed this in "Am Feierabend" and attempted to describe it. But we should try to understand other aspects of musical effect as well. Other compositional factors are also "at work," and in this passage of "Der Neugierige," the factor we are particularly concerned with, rhythm, seems to be more influential than the rest. It is primarily rhythmic textures that create the special effect and make the text appear in a certain way. This effect is by no means restricted to the musical realms normally associated with feeling and expression.

In the measure with the little word "Nein," a full harmonic-chordal setting begins. No greater contrast to the preceding recitative is conceivable. In contrast to the free text declamation, supported by only two chords, the voice part now corresponds to the upper notes of the piano part and to the piano rhythm. Contrary to the notation, the piano phrase of solid octave chords (measures 35–40) moves in 2/4 time, beginning at the second beat of measure 35, after the "Nein." (In Example 24, the time is shown as it actually sounds, not as it was originally written.) Except

Example 24

for the ornamental notes of the voice part in the repeat, the two sections, placed one below the other here, are alike; one simply follows the other. However, at the point where the repeat begins, a complication turns up. A quarter-note beat is missing! The final syllable of ". . . Welt mir| *ein*" falls on a beat one, and before the corresponding beat two can follow, the repeat comes in with a unison eighth-note pick-up to a new beat one, its own. Example 25 shows what we hear: a disruption of the rhythm. Hereupon we realize something we were hardly aware of before—

Example 25

that the little word "Nein" on a single quarter note was just as isolated as this "ein." It no longer belonged to the preceding recitative section, because of the key change, and did not yet belong to the next section because it stood outside the 2/4 rhythmic order. By citing a relationship between the two rhyming words and comparing their musical positions—we do this automatically in the very sophisticated and discriminating process of hearing—we are at once conscious of the position of the "ein" and, in retrospect, that of the "Nein"—an important piece of the structure in Schubert's musical interpretation of the text. This observation tells us that we subconsciously hear the measure with the little word "Nein" as noted in Example 26, and that our ears tempt us to sneak in an extra quarter at the parallel spot ". . . Welt mir| *ein*" as well (Example 27).

Example 26

Example 27

While we might get away with this the first time, since the beginning of something new at "Nein" is not altogether obvious, it will not work the second time. The two "beat ones" that Schubert has juxtaposed in measure 38 cannot be separated *de facto* as they are in Example 27. The second is just as immovable as the first because of the unison eighth-note pickup. Thereupon we discover that the text line "die beiden Wörtchen . . ." [the two little words] is reproduced in two identical, successive phrases, which do not fit together rhythmically, but are positioned side by side. From the rhythmic structure at the juncture of the repeat, we become musically aware of how Schubert realizes this text that at first speaks only of "ein Wörtchen um und um" [one little word and only one], then also of "another," and finally of "two" little words, "yes" and "no," which embrace the whole world but exclude each other. Now Schubert lets the composition revert to the old key and that restrained song the miller lad sings to himself; no longer will anyone expect an answer to the question, "Sag, Bächlein, liebt sie mich?" [Tell me little brook, does she love me?]. This is romantic irony in musical form.

Oddly enough, up to this point in our cycle the only genuine strophic song was the very first, "Das Wandern." But now we come to four in a row: "Ungeduld" [Impatience], "Morgengruss" [Morning greeting], "Des Müllers Blumen" [The miller's flowers], and "Tränenregen" [Rain of tears]. The miller lad, who in "Der Neugierige" seemed unintentionally to slip from brooding into soft singing to himself ("O Bächlein meiner Liebe"), now really begins to sing—to sing songs, still not loud, but certainly with uplifted voice, and he begins: "Ich schnitt es gern in alle Rinden ein . . ." [I'd like to carve it on all the trees]. So it is no coincidence that, of all the miller songs, "Ungeduld" is the one most often sung individually. Its text is less dependent on the context of the cycle than the others, the only traces occurring in the penultimate lines of the last two stanzas: "Ihr Wogen, könnt ihr nichts als Räder treiben?" [You billows, can't you do anything but turn wheels?] and "Und sie merkt nichts von all dem bangen Treiben" [And she takes no notice of all my anxiety]. None of the other songs stand alone as well.

The four strophic songs are certainly no simpler than their through-composed predecessors; the means by which the texts are given compositional form remain basically the same; the accompaniment is still obbligato, despite the more lyrical melodies and declamation. Five lines in "Ungeduld" begin on an upbeat and are declaimed in short note values, but the sixth line answers our impatient "What is he getting at?" with a downbeat entry and with long note values in crucial positions. The answer comes happily, radiantly, exultingly: "Dein ist mein Herz" [Thine is my heart]. The almost overwhelming power of this part rests on several factors, which we will investigate briefly.

The easiest to recognize is the "colon" effect before "Dein ist mein Herz." It arises from the fact that this crucial line, unlike all the others, begins with falling tones, and that the first four lines of each stanza end in masculine rhyme, the last two in feminine, because they are one syllable longer.

...Rinden ein,
...Kieselstein,
...frische Beet,
...schnell verrät,
...............schreiben:
...............bleiben.

Schubert takes advantage of this by lengthening his line by one quarter as well. It ends on beat three of the measure instead of beat two, so that the next line, if it had an eighth-note upbeat like those preceding, would have to follow immediately, beginning in the same quarter (beat three). But the next line has no upbeat. Where we have come to expect one, there is a rest instead. This device makes the passage function as a colon when the long-awaited "answer" finally comes in: "Dein ist mein Herz!"

Of course, Schubert prepares for this "answer" through rhythm and compositional technique in the narrower sense as well.[61] First of all, in measures 9–16 the stanza strings four two-measure phrases together, and the essential changes in harmony occur from measure to measure; but at measure 17, they suddenly begin to occur from beat to beat. The harmonic sequence is thereby compressed in measures 17 and 18 into a closing phrase with three small parts of two quarters' duration (we might almost say, three 2/4 measures), which fuse into a hemiolic 3/2 measure (Example 28). The ancient device of hemiola is used here in a new way, to set off a section of composition with a "colon effect" before the refrain.

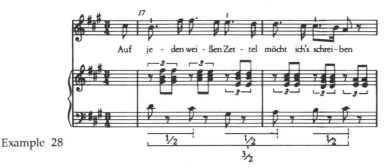

Example 28

The attentive listener will no doubt perceive that the bass d-sharp and its chord on "*Dein* ist mein Herz" refer back to the last measure of the piano introduction, where the same note and chord are stressed—the only forte spot in the song, aside from the final chord. But what seems to me most beautiful and effective is this: The opening melodic interval of the first and second lines, present in the third as well, but concealed, is an ascending sixth. This upswing from the dominant to the third degree of the key, bypassing the tonic, does much to establish all the jubilant, loving, and at the same time yearning impatience of this song. And now "Dein ist mein Herz" comes in directly on the sixth, *without* a pickup, yet fully related to the preceding a' of "schreiben" [write] through the interval. This 'Dein" [thine] no longer needs a leap. It bursts forth from itself, so to speak. And unlike all the foregoing sixth leaps, this is the only one that seems melodically significant. It tolerates only *one* higher interval, the octave of the tonic, so this is what carries the second 'Dein" and the first syllable of the only word that can stand with 'Dein": "ewig" [forever].

The melody of "Morgengruss" [Morning greeting] is also characterized by a rising sixth leap. And here too, Schubert shows the different effect the same interval can create when used in a different way in a crucial spot. In both occurrences, the leap involves an upbeat; but in one place it pushes off from the downbeat toward the middle of the measure, while in the other it goes from an upbeat to the downbeat (Example 29).

Example 29

Gu-ten Mor-gen, schö-ne   Mül-le-rin!

So muß ich wie-der ge - - hen,

What a difference, with almost identical melodics! What intensification of expression—to employ a much-used formula for musical analysis—between the first sixth leap and the second: one is a friendly greeting, the other an expression of heartfelt pain. Thus it seems only logical that the first can be playfully anticipated in the piano introduction, but the second, where it is imitated in the accompaniment, sounds like an echo from the depths of the heart. But now the accompaniment begins to sing. Schubert achieves this effect by the simplest of means—I should say, by the extremely efficient application of his means. He supports the first text lines of each stanza with ordinary chords but the subsequent lines, "Verdriesst dich denn mein Gruss..." [Does my greeting annoy you] only with an eighth-note chordal progression. As a result, the simple accompaniment he brings in on the last line, "So muss ich..." [so I must...] seems almost rich in comparison. Since it also echoes the voice part—and does so with the "new" ascending sixth leap—the effect is perfectly beautiful.

"Des Müllers Blumen" [The miller's flowers] is probably the simplest song of the cycle. While it, too, gives the impression of perfect balance, this balance seems artificial. Like "Halt!" and "Am Feierabend," it is in 6/8 time; but unlike them, it does not have a fast tempo, with whole measures dominating because their six eighth notes belong together (phrases always ending at the beginning of the measure); instead it has a more moderate tempo, "Mässig" [moderato], and each pair of 3/8 measures is loosely connected in one 6/8 measure (phrases always ending in the middle of the measure.[62] Thus the song "sways" a little, helped along by the somewhat meandering melody. This is perfectly appropriate for the speculative mood of the text. However, the final line of each stanza expresses something different from the preceding ones. Gone are the conditional statements; it is no longer "wenn... dann" [if... then], but rather "drum sind es..." [therefore they are...], "Das ist es..." [It is that...], "die will ich..." [those I want...]—resolute statements expressed in a most resolute manner. Schubert matches this precisely in his music. He declaims these lines beginning on a downbeat:

"| drúm sind es..."

In fact he declaims them with a double downbeat, which is significant in that it represents a break from the rhythm thus far established in the song:

"| drúm | sínd es |"

The result is a lengthening of the musical phrase from two measures ending in the middle of a measure to three measures ending at the beginning of a measure. This lengthened, altered phrase now becomes the final phrase. Declaimed thus with conviction on the downbeat and confirmed in the repeat,[63] it constitutes a counterweight to the first part of the song, providing perfect balance to the whole. No song ends like this one, with the period after the last word. A love song of certainty, despite all the "und wenn..." [and ifs]? "Das ist es, was ich meine"! [That's what I mean!] In an ordinary strophic song, through a kind of musical "development," which he disguises in the simple two-part form, Schubert realizes musically the mocking "double image" that lurks in the text.

Of the four strophic songs that conclude the first part of *Die schöne Müllerin*, the first one, "Ungeduld," begins in A major, lovingly jubilant, impatiently yearning. The last one, "Tränenregen" [Rain of tears], ends with a restrained, painfully melancholy mood, with a stanza in A minor. Whereas the former is more suitable than the others for singing by itself, the latter can hardly be imagined out of its context. First of all, though curiously "timeless" in its use of the imperfect tense, the text depicts an incident that reveals the status of plot. The beloved miller maiden is by no means his, as in "Mein!". She turns away when she notices the tears in the miller lad's eyes. But then the text plumbs the depths. The brook calls: "Geselle, Geselle, mir nach!" [Journeyman, journeyman, follow me!]—the brook that lured him into traveling in the first place (remember the text of "Wohin?" [Where?]) and which he will follow one day into "die kühle Ruh, unten, da unten" [the cool stillness below] ("Der Müller und der Bach"). The beckoning call from "hinunter" [downward]—"da unten" [down below]—the thought of his itinerary, "immer dem Bache nach" [always following the brook], and therefore of his final destination, brings tears to his eyes. It is this that evokes the extremely melancholy change to minor, not the lines ending with Heine-like sarcasm: "sie sprach: Es kommt ein Regen, ade, ich geh nach Haus." [She said, "A shower is coming. Good-bye. I'm going home."] So from the standpoint of text, the song holds a key position in the cycle; and in a most careful manner, Schubert acquiesces to this.

Within the group of strophic songs, at the beginning of which we assumed the miller lad was starting to sing songs in the cycle, Schubert holds the music in such restraint that we get the feeling that where text and music reflect jubilation and wanderlust, this is only a starting point. But here the destination comes into view. The last line of "Des Baches Wiegenlied" refers back to the last stanza of "Tränenregen" which concludes the first part of the cycle. Here the sky seems "in den Bach versunken" [submerged in the brook] and seems to pull him "hinunter in seine Tiefe" [down into its depths]. Not until the lad has found death in the brook is it "da oben ... so weit!" [up there ... so far] again. In "Tränenregen," the first six text stanzas are paired into three musical stanzas; then with the seventh, the song flows into the final musical stanza as into a quintessence. It combines minor and major tonalities, summarizes briefly, then links itself to the beginning as it leads into the closing—which begins like the introduction but ends in the dark minor. Contrary to the notation in current editions, the piano introduction should not be repeated between stanzas. A repeat sign should be inserted before the beginning of stanzas 1–3.[64] In this respect, the last stanza is more than a simple musical setting of the text. Indeed there is a flagrant romantic-ironic contradiction between the tone of the music and that of the text. The reason for the painful change to minor tonality lies in the preceding third stanza, which receives no special treatment whatsoever—it is simply one among others in the strophic song.

"Mein!" is so closely related to "Das Wandern" musically, that it seems to begin the cycle anew, to inaugurate a second part. Although the relationship between the two songs may not be recognizable immediately, because of the longer note values, quarter and eighth notes, instead of the eighths and sixteenths, it is nevertheless clear. First of all, the time and tempo are the same. Since "Mein!" is in ¢ (alla breve) or 2/2 time, not 4/4, as many editions erroneously indicate, the half note equals one beat and is the unit by which the tempo is measured. Thus these half notes are to be taken just as 'Mässig geschwind" [allegro moderato] as the quarter notes in 'Das Wandern." Characteristically, the bass vacillates frequently between tonic and dominant harmonies, despite the differentiated harmonic structure—though not from the very first beat and not always in octaves. There is also a striking similarity in the final measures of the two introductions. They have similar internal frameworks. The structural mechanics of "Mein!" in general resemble those of "Das Wandern" and likewise result in a tremendous driving motion that makes it stand out. Finally, the melodic treatment links the two songs, in that both have traces of yodel melodics.

Yet in spite of all this similarity and interrelationship, "Mein!" is characterized by something totally lacking in the opening song because Schubert does not use until later: speech, actual discourse, words articulated musically. This element is critical. It represents something expressly human. This, more than anything else, arouses, justifies, and holds our interest, our attention, our sympathy. Certainly the key word is "mein," and one can hardly imagine a more beautiful rendering of the jubilant 'Die geliebte Müllerin ist mein!" [The beloved miller maid is mine!] than in the four lines that close the first part and the last (a repetition of the first) with a perfect cadence. But we have the feeling that this "mein" would not sound convincing if the speaker had not legitimized himself as human in the middle part of the song, if he had not appeared as someone who refuses to be bound in his speech by the "mechanics" of musical composition or by carefully calculated two- and four-measure phrases, stereotyped verse and song form, uniform declamation units and symmetrical rhythms. He speaks as freely as any man can, ignoring the expectations of those who have a preconceived notion of musical processes and rhythms and who expect something specific: namely, fulfillment of the norm. As listeners, we certainly do not expect the middle section to be in B-flat major, especially after such a short modulation. And once the key change and new sound have captivated us, neither do we expect someone to *speak* prose, using melodic intervals, instead of singing verse. We don't expect him simply to *ask:* 'Frühling, sind das alle deine Blümelein?" [Spring, is that all the flowers you have?] and *immediately* go on to ask: "Sonne, hast du keinen hellern Schein?" [Sun, have you no brighter shine?]. I do not believe our experience with songs in general and with this song so far would lead us to expect this. To put it in musical-technical terms: when all the phrases in almost 40 measures of composition have begun on the downbeat and the word 'Frühling' in the new section also begins on a downbeat, the listener does not expect "sind das| all . . ." to enter on an upbeat, much less an upbeat of two eighth notes, which comes too early and much too abruptly. Since all text-declaiming musical phrases before the transition to the middle section are expressed in "rhythms of 2 or 4 measures," the only exception being "gross und klein" [large and small], but we hear 'Frühling, sind das alle deine Blümelein?" and "Sonne, hast du keinen hellern Schein?" expressed in two "rhythms of 3 measures," then it strikes us either as musically wrong or as meaningful because of what it represents: speech rendered into music.

It cannot be argued that this passage goes by much too quickly for the listener to gain anything that significant from it. Schubert doesn't leave it at that. Instead he draws parallels with earlier passages, and we, the listeners, are able to evaluate the individual factors against our total experience with the complex relationships in his composition. "Ach! so muss ich ganz allein/mit dem seligen Worte mein" is rendered in a "rhythm of 2 × 2 measures," in keeping with the first (and last) part; the next line, "unverstanden in der weiten Schöpfung sein," and its repeat, on the other hand, is in a "rhythm of 2 × 5 measures." [A free translation of these three lines is: Ah, then I must keep this blessed word "mine" to myself and all creation will never know of it.] This is just as unconventional as the preceding 2 × 3 phrase, in which the questions were "spoken"—or at least were supposed to affect us as speech. What we mean by "spoken," in a song whose melody "sings" so far afield, is clarified in the line "unverstanden . . . ," for its cantilena (now with smaller intervals) shines as the epitome of affetuoso singing, making the preceding questions seem as if they were merely spoken. In short, we experience human speech breaking through the music; this experience extends our understanding and prepares us for the rest of the cycle, which in turn surpasses song drama, developing into a story that can truly hold our interest.

After all that has happened musically in the cycle, there can be no variation following "Mein!" in the sense that "Wohin?" was a variation of "Das Wandern." So immediately after the jubilant opening of part two in "Pause," Schubert strikes a note that has not yet been heard. I don't mean a new key tonality, of course, for this song, like "Das Wandern" and the middle section of "Mein!", reminiscent of "Das Wandern," is in B-flat major. I am referring to the basic mood of the song. Can it be called tragic? Perhaps because words fail the love-struck lad: "ich kann nicht mehr singen, . . . weiss nicht, wie ich's in Reime zwingen soll" [I can no longer sing, . . . don't know how to put it into rhyme]? This might be said of the text, but does it apply to the music as well? Do words fail it too? The song seems to be directed inward. The miller lad holds a conversation with his lute, which "answers" in the piano part. But because this part is more independent than that of any other song in the cycle and even seems to oppose the voice part at times, the feeling of disparity, of separation of elements that belong together, grows as the song progresses. The eight-measure introduction is subdivided into antecedent and consequent phrases and forms a nice unit. From this, Schubert extracts the first measure and half of the third and uses them more or less as raw materials in the piano part, without developing them further. He draws nothing from the voice part, nor does he carry anything over to it. All entrances ("Meine Laute . . . ", "Nun, liebe Laute . . . ", "Warum liess ich das Band . . . ", "Oft fliegt's . . . " "fit" perfectly with what we hear from the piano, but it can hardly be said that the piano accompanies them. The melody tries to sing, ascending again and again with the melodic sixth interval; but it is incapable, because the piano part is turned away, instrumentally aloof. It remains fundamentally aloof even where it follows the melody, particularly in the middle section. All the singing comes close to being spoken, while everything instrumental remains stubbornly independent and at the same time fragmentary; indeed, the structure itself seems to crumble toward the end of the song. The characteristic instrumental interlude before the first "Ist es der Nachklang . . . " [Is it the echo . . .] consists of only one measure and is further shortened by the absence of the thirds in the second half; in return, it is burdened with a weighty harmonic progression. Before the second "Ist es der Nachklang . . . ," the interlude has two measures again, shortened and harmonically burdened as above; but whereas before they were identical (nine times!), they are now repeated on a *different* pitch. This repetition on a different pitch relates to the instrumental closing, where major tonality is followed by minor, then immediately by major again. Some have associated this change between major and minor with the miller lad's twofold question. But to me the closing seems more like fleeting reminiscence, where harmony and color are drastically reduced, as in shorthand. In a rare instance, Schubert has distinguished the word "Liebespein" [pain of love] harmonically and stressed its antithesis, "neue Lieder" [new songs], with a perfect cadence. Yet the effect is eerie ("und es durchschauert mich" [and it sends a shiver through me]) precisely because the antithesis is *not* resolved, the question is *not* answered, because the miller lad remains alone and undecided, because his lute can offer nothing in response but a "seufzenden Klang" [sighing sound] that cannot express his "Glückes Last" [the burden of his happiness]; if *he* is unable to sing, how can the lute be expected to "sing" without him?[65]

In "Pause," we encounter the first mention of the color green and the ill-fated ribbon, both of which take on significance as the story develops ("hab sie umschlungen mit einem grünen Band" [(I) have tied a green ribbon around it). The next song is entitled "Mit dem grünen Lautenbande" [With the green lute-ribbon], and one may well ask: why "With . . ."? Does the lad include the poem, when he "sends" her the ribbon? But this is not the first title that raises questions of deeper meaning. Why "Pause" [Interlude]? Why "Der Neugierige" [The curious one]? Why not "Die Laute" [The lute] and "Der Fragende" [The questioner] instead?

"Pause" ends with a B-flat major chord; the same chord, an octave higher, appears under a fermata at the beginning of the next song, "Mit dem grünen Lautenbande." If we follow Alfred Einstein's suggestion[66] and leave out the second chord when performing the songs in context, they move closer together, and the final question: "Soll es das Vorspiel neuer Lieder sein?" [can it be the prelude to new songs?] comes directly before the maiden's words: "Schad um das schöne grüne Band. . ." [it's a shame about the pretty green ribbon], enclosed in quotation marks in both the poem and the song. This seems to be significant, for "Es kommt ein Regen, ade, ich geh nach Haus" [A shower is coming. Goodbye. I'm going home.] was not enclosed in quotation marks by either Wilhelm Müller or Schubert! This sentence now leads into a simple, naive song—the antithesis of the lad's desperate conversation with himself: "ich kann nicht mehr singen" [I can no longer sing]. The miller lad takes over the maiden's song, but he alters its character—perhaps even adding an ironic twist. As he picks up the refrain, he preserves the notes and shape of the first two lines, but transforms the friendly melody into a musical gesture of resolute action (Example 30).

Example 30

The effect is partly due to the shortening of the whole and the change from the simple, folksong-like ascending seventh ("schö*ne* → *grü*ne Band") to an octave leap ("*du* → *Lieb*chen"); but it rests primarily on the continuity established when the miller lad immediately makes the same octave leap again, this time descending to the rhythmic stress point. He sings this as if it were a matter of reporting: "I untied the ribbon at once and sent it!"

Of course, wishes are to accompany the ribbon. They say: "Now enjoy the color green, the green ribbon, I beg you! For we both like green so well." The miller lad takes up the maiden's refrain, and the melodic line, the realization of the action in the text, is toned down, as the stable octave interval dwindles to a pleasantly sentimental descending seventh.

As is often the case in strophic songs, this music was conceived for one text stanza, the first. Consequently, the content of the other stanzas is not expressed in the music—or the musical expression only approximates adequacy. A musical structure on which they were not founded has been assigned to, if not imposed upon them. This is normal for strophic songs, one usually hears it said. Certainly, but where else do musical structures of comparable precision develop so directly from the text as in Schubert's work? Not all his strophic songs, it seems to me, can be compared to those of his contemporaries and successors—and those that can, not without qualification. In "Mit dem grünen Lautenbande," at any rate, the piano introduction, which starts the song rolling, has the added task of announcing the song anew with each stanza, because it is so obviously composed for the first stanza that one does not automatically wish to repeat it with another text.[67]

With "Pause," the cycle threatens to come to a halt. The question is left open, unresolved. The singer is about to fall silent. The lute seems to have only one sighing sound left. In "Mit dem grünen Lautenbande," the maiden rescues the situation, but the cycle has hardly been set back in motion. For this, a new element must be introduced: Enter the hunter. But we should bear in mind that even without the hunter, the cycle has already moved into realms that must be called tragic, through very solemn tones, primarily musical. To the romantic, love is inherently unhappy! It is love that causes the miller lad's sorrow, not his rival and the maiden who grants him her favor. The anger and defiance vented on the hunter have been pent up, and the violence of the eruption is due to long-endured doubt and pain. Not unrequited love, but love itself has set the tone in "Pause," expressing the reverse side of the jubilation in "Mein!" long before the hunter appears and the maiden's fickleness is revealed ("Eifersucht und Stolz" [Jealousy and pride]). The thought of death has already been entertained ("Tränenregen")—the event is yet in the future. But for the moment, jealousy reigns.

So jealous determination and defiance characterize the next two songs, "Der Jäger" [The hunter] and "Eifersucht und Stolz," the only ones in the cycle marked "Geschwind" [allegro]. Just as the eighth-note staccato hammers in the piano part, the text of "Der Jäger" is declaimed relentlessly in a voice part that seems bound to the upper piano notes. The melody moves in the low range in the first part, in the middle range in the middle part, and in the high range in the last part. To simplify it a little: the highest note in each part moves outside the limits of the previous part, as if flung there by centrifugal force. It is also carefully differentiated rhythmically, so that the intensity is doubled. "*Bleib|* trotziger Jäger" [stay, haughty hunter] and "*hier|*wohnt nur ein Rehlein" [here lives only a little doe] are eighth-note pick-ups to second half-phrases. "Hunde zu *Haus*" [dogs at home] and "Saus und *Braus*" [boisterous noise] are quarter notes concluding a phrase in the middle of a measure. However, "Sonst|*scheut* sich" [or else . . . will be frightened] falls in the last half-phrase on the first downbeat, thereby confirming what was established from the beginning: The rhythm is not directed toward the end of the phrase but takes its impetus from each opening measure, making the song sound angry and defiant. The melody itself is defiant; in the motion derived from hunting horn signals, and in the way the text is declaimed, it seems to resist being sung. The piano introduction seems rebellious as well. It only appears to be constructed according to rules. Here the musical effect comes not from the four-measure phrasing of the whole song, but from the three-measure phrase of the right piano hand, which imitates and concludes the primary motif. This phrase does not adhere absolutely to the predominant rhythmic order (6/8 time = 2 × 3/8 time, phrase ending in the middle of the measure, i.e. in the middle of every second 6/8 measure, every fourth 3/8 pulse). If we happen to miss this in the introduction, we know after the first line of the stanza what "right" should sound like, the introduction evidently having been intended only as a "preview" (Example 31). Incidentally, with the canonic imitation of the voices, Schubert draws upon a tradition of musical composition extending back into the 14th century, which stipulates use of canon (in the 14th-century *caccia*) for texts with hunting scenes.

Example 31

In our cycle, "Der Jäger" and "Eifersucht und Stolz" come between the last line of "Mit dem grünen Lautenbande": "dann hab ich's Grün erst gern" [only then will I like green], and the refrain line of "Die liebe Farbe": "mein Schatz hat's Grün so gern" [my sweetheart likes green so much], which are obviously related musically. In this intermediate position, the two songs can be viewed as a sort of intermezzo, especially in light of the downward pull into the water's depths, a kind of death wish that has lain in the background for some time—from the very beginning, in fact. The musical play is not suddenly transformed into a tragedy simply by virtue of the hunter's entrance. If these two songs were omitted, the progress of the theme would be sacrificed, but the underlying trend would hardly be affected. If we reject such an abridgment because it vitiates the unity of the cycle, or because it noticeably weakens an essential feature, we must still concede that in addition to sustaining mood, sensitivity, and the expression of love, jubilation, pain, longing (even for death), the action is and will remain significant. Of course we must qualify this: no action takes place in the narrower sense. What happens or has happened is recorded or finds expression in the miller lad's conversations with himself, for all the songs except the last are "I" songs. These develop musically in various ways; sometimes it is as if the bearing or mood of the subject determines the whole from the ground up, and sometimes as if the subject appears on the scene as a speaking character. Most of the songs contain something of both. But we must bear in mind that in the case of Schubert (in contrast to Robert Schumann, for instance), songs of the second type predominate. Schubert is more inclined to realize human speech in musical form than to make his music serve as a vehicle for emotion, because words can express emotion only imperfectly.

Understood in this way, 'Der Jäger' is governed entirely by a single passion, to which the song gives expression. In the next song, on the other hand, it is not the passions of jealousy and pride themselves that dominate, but rather the person who experiences them. Not only does this person stand at the forefront, he also *speaks*. Like only a few other songs in the cycle, 'Der Jäger' is arranged simply and the text is declaimed simply; no line is interpreted except as the simple musical setting prescribes for the chosen rhythm[68] (Example 32). The emotion is not *articulated* musically; the words "Zorn" [anger], "schelten" [scold], "frech" [impudent]

Example 32    $^6/_8 (= 2 \times ^3/_8)$    » Was sucht denn der Jä - ger am Mühl - bach hier! «

do not appear until the next song, and it is the hunter, not the miller lad, who is accused of being "trotzig" [defiant]. The emotion underlies the whole, a *portrait*—if not a soul painting—of the miller lad, painted at the moment the hunter appears. In the next song, however, the vivid color of this portrait becomes just an undercoating; for Schubert turns again to the other possibility: In his "musical expression of the text," he brings the person to the scene, distinguishing him primarily through speech; he realizes the text as speech, as musically spoken word.

"Eifersucht und Stolz" verifies this formulation, both in general and in every detail. Georgiades has described the extremely complicated composition with loving and accurate thoroughness.[69] We here dwell on only a few of his more obvious points. We know that when Schubert sets out to realize language musically as spoken word in the song, he works primarily with rhythm and meter, subordinating the other musical elements. Through these elements, he is best able to set a norm, direct the listener's expectations toward this norm, then interrupt the norm and thereby—not only thereby!—create the impression of a certain freedom in the declamation, freedom that is peculiar to human speech. The first two lines of 'Eifersucht und Stolz' are expressed in keeping with normal time, in four measures each. The third line forms a five-measure phrase, because the repeat of 'kehr um' [come back] occurs after a whole- rather than half-measure interval. In keeping with the compositional rule that a five-measure phrase should not stand alone but be complemented by a parallel one, forming a "symmetry of 5 × 2," Schubert forms the fourth line, "für ihren leichten, losen . . ." [for her light, careless . . .], into a five-measure phrase as well. Apparently he does not want the first five-measure phrase to draw any more attention than necessary to the exclamatory effect of 'kehr um," which he then repeats three times at the end of the first stanza.[70] With the next line of the poem, "Sahst du sie gestern abend nicht am Tore stehn" [Didn't you see her last night, standing at the gate?], Schubert returns to the normal four-measure phrase, though it is unmelodic and "sings" so suspiciously like recitative that we almost expect direct speech. And indeed the latter comes with the five-measure phrase, now standing alone: "mit langem Halse nach der grossen Strasse sehn" [craning her neck to see down the highway]. "I doubt," says Georgiades, "that humankind ever had the slightest notion, until this passage was set to music, that a neck could be *so* long, stretched so far!"[71] Now the lad is *speaking,* and he does so freely. The running accompaniment has ceased, and there is no four-measure pattern restricting the pick-up to only one eighth-note. Of course the situation is bad enough that at this moment, when through the association with 'hunter', the melody breaks out in imitation of the hunting horn—but is all the worse when the piano takes on this tone. His only hope is to turn directly to the one addressed, the brook, as soon as possible, and address it familiarly, personally, rather than in poetic verse declaimed in sterotypical fashion. We would expect to hear the *line declaimed:*

Example 33    Geh Bäch-lein | *hin* und sag ihr | *das,*

But instead we hear the *words spoken* (Example 34). Through a rearrangement of the stress sequence, a rhythmic trick so to speak, Schubert emphasizes the little word "sag" [tell], freeing it from its unstressed position. When "sag" occurs later in the major section, it carries the emphasis of this spot with it—though now it falls on an upbeat, it retains its emphasis (the "telling"!), it justifies the *fp* in the piano part (the only one in the song!), it intensifies the effect of the gloomy minor—yet because it is consciously heard as an upbeat, it lends emphasis to the "ihr" [her], the pronoun for the recipient of the pathetic love tidings.

Example 34    Geh Bäch-lein | *hin* und *sag* | ihr | das,

The next line is "made to speak" in a different way, again primarily through rhythmic means. Here Schubert completely abandons the poetic lines as the basis for the declamation and obliterates the boundaries between the lines:

"Geh, Bächlein, hin und sag ihr das, doch sag ihr nicht,
Hörst du[72], kein Wort, von meinem traurigen Gesicht;
Sag ihr: Er schnitzt bei mir sich eine Pfeif' aus Rohr,
. . ."
[Go there, brook, and tell her that, but don't tell her—
not a word, do you hear?—of my sad face;
Tell her: He is on my banks, carving a reed whistle,
. . .]

Example 35

And here we do not even notice that Schubert has taken the two last lines of the major section, which are in hexameter, as are all in Müller's poem, and set them to music as if they were in pentameter. In short: the entire song seems like talking, even the parts where it really sings, like the major section. And the dark minor of the sobbing "sag ihr, sag ihr" [tell her, tell her] hurts just as if we, the listeners, were mortally struck by this pain.

It has been said that the title "Die liebe Farbe" [The beloved color] hides the real content of the song (second stanza, fourth and fifth lines): "Das Wild, das ich jage, das ist der Tod,/die Heide, die heiss ich die Liebesnot." [The game that I hunt, it is death,/the field, I call love's affliction.]. Schubert has captured the basic intent of this text in all three stanzas. The interpreter is faced with a difficult task, the 'Durchgestaltung' [through-fashioning] of a simple strophic song. That is, he must "perform each stanza in a different tone. The basic mood is constant; established in the first stanza, it becomes mixed with irony and passion in the second and ends wistfully in the third. The refrain 'Mein Schatz hat's Grün so gern,' because it recurs so many times, demands extremely fine adaptation."[73] The mood is determined to a large degree by the f'-sharp (original key of B minor), which repeats itself uninterruptedly from the first chord to the last, like a death knell.[74] Indeed, the song is deathly solemn and at the same time tranquil and even. However, the balance in the composition is not the result but the source of the fundamental mood. Commensurate with the intended solemnity and dignity, Schubert chooses a highly differentiated structure for his composition, which the listener would hardly suppose lies behind this seemingly simple strophic song "tuned" around a single note.[75]

The first thing we notice about the structure is that the stanza is formed almost symmetrically from eight- and nine-measure phrases $(4 + 4$ and $5 + 4)$; the only deviation from the symmetry is found in the extension of the line "eine Heide von grünen Rosmarein" [a field of green rosemary], with which Schubert probably intended to emphasize the word "Liebesnot" [love's affliction] in the crucial second stanza. This nearly perfect four-measure symmetry and the five-measure introduction/interlude/closing (utterly independent, by the way, and heard nowhere during the stanza) are just as incongruous as the fact that the interlude and closing begin not after the closing of the stanza but directly on its final note. Another striking thing about the structure is that we definitely hear the independent piano passages at the beginning and end as if they were perfectly normal four-measure symmetric units; we even think we perceive in them an element of peace and tranquility. This raises the question: Are we hearing incorrectly? Or do we get a false impression of the compositional result when we separately describe elements that we hear together, stanza vs. introduction/interlude/closing? After all, there is no rest or fermata here to separate the stanza from the introduction, and the immediate onset of the closing reaffirms the lack of separation. The opening and closing piano passage and the stanza are joined in a single musical structure; they are compositionally related and together form a whole. The foundation for the whole is a kind of harmonic framework, the divisions of which are marked off by the recurring tonic B in the bass (Example 36).

We see from this scheme that the song is composed entirely of identically structured symmetrical segments, save for the nine-measure phrase, each of which leaves off on an unresolved dominant tone; thus they are "harmonically linked," and a tonic segment standing alone is needed only at the conclusion. The fermata over this final tonic extends it by one measure, giving it the effect of a two-measure phrase and thus bringing it into alignment with the even-metered symmetry. This harmonic diagram is actualized *as such* only in the piano introduction, interlude, and closing, for this is the only passage without an independent melodic-rhythmic "interpretation" of the harmonic plan—it only seems to fill in the harmony. The voice part, on the other hand, subdivides independently, creating a melodic-rhythmic foreground that is apparently meant to be heard separately.

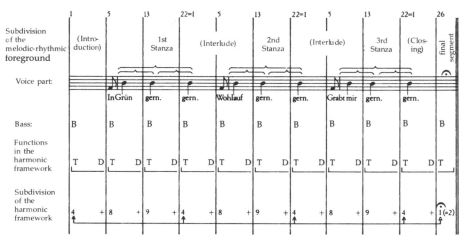

Example 36

So in examining the formation of the phrases and sections, we observe a discrepancy between the melodic foreground in the voice part and the harmonic background. Of course this discrepancy affects the accompaniment, which operates between the harmonic background, represented by the bass, and the foreground of melodic episode, which it is supposed to "accompany." Discrepancy? This may seem an understatement for what we would expect to hear as conflict in the composition. Yet it does not come across as conflict but rather as having a three-dimensional or spatial quality. It has perspective, in that the structural elements of harmony, melody, rhythm, bass, voice part, and middle voice of the piano part are all independent but at the same time inseparably related through the one foundation on which the whole structure is built; together they form what Beethoven called "obbligato accompaniment," which I maintain to be the basis of Schubert's song style as well.

Framed by an introduction and closing that seem to balance each other perfectly and radiate a sense of calm, we hear a simple strophic song, a structure in the Viennese classical tradition, one with the depth and dignity of a major composition. The primary and apparently only thing the listener perceives, that which he feels along with the speaker, what is sounded in such features as the f'-sharp death knell or the exchange between minor and major, seems to be imposed upon the composition. All this is related, because the whole song is organized around a *single* structure that dominates all the elements. The minor-major interplay, which stirs the listener so often and so deeply in this song, may clarify it once again: It is not in the lyrical voice part, with its refrain "mein Schatz hat's Grün so gern" that we recognize the return to minor tonality; it is in the piano part, where the major third changes back to a minor third, gently (*pp, legatissimo*), yet with an emphasis legitimized by the blueprint for the whole. The F-sharp, as the dominant tone, prepares the reentry of the *B* in the low register, which in turn signals a new frame-work subdivision to begin the second part of the stanza.

"Die liebe Farbe" [The beloved color] — "Die böse Farbe" [The evil color] : can anyone imagine a greater contrast in two songs occurring next to each other and related in both text and music? Both are in the key of B. The former, in B minor, conveys the crucial line "mein Schatz hat's Grün so gern" in major the first time; the latter, in B major, vacillates sharply between the modes several times and ends in the minor. The time signatures are the same; the shapes of the melodies are comparable throughout. Is the difference in character perhaps attributable to the tempo, the dynamics, the smaller note values in the piano part (triplets instead of ordinary sixteenth notes), the frequent note subdivisions in the voice part?

No, it is more likely attributable to the totally different compositional style. In 'Die liebe Farbe," the music flows uniformly, evenly, peacefully; in 'Die böse Farbe," it is broken and conveys the sense of inner conflict, of wild despair. In the former, we have a piano part formed around a central tone, a balanced rhythmic arrangement of meticulously connected phrases, and declamation that is consis-tently lyrical throughout the three stanzas; these qualities work together to ensure unity in the development and in the underlying mood. As for the latter song, one cannot help but wonder how such disparate sections of the constantly changing rhythmic structure can possibly result in a unified whole at all, particularly in view of the fact that the declamation varies between "lyrical" and "freely spoken" and the piano part between terse eighth-note chords and driving sixteenth-note triplets reminiscent of the hunt.

Although interrelated, the sections of "Die böse Farbe" are different in style and structure; they affect us like the repeated tone, first announced in measure 22, ". . . totenbleich [deathly pale]", which alludes to the preceding song, though it sounds totally different here; or like the measures "Horch, wenn im Wald ein Jagd-horn schallt . . ." [Hark! when a hunting horn sounds in the wood . . .], which reach even further back to "Der Jäger," so crucial to the plot there, yet sounding only impressionistic here. The listener experiences confusion in all this; but confusion swells to tragic despair when the words "weinen ganz toten*bleich*," [cry all deathly pale]" "das eine Wörtchen *Ade!*" [that one little word, farewell] and "zum Abschied deine *Hand!*" [in parting . . . your hand] all end in the same outburst, the same cry of pain. When the words "O binde von der Stirn dir ab das grüne, grüne Band" [O untie from your brow the green, green ribbon], tainted with madness and hurled out with agitated accompaniment, yield to the melodic and now imploringly simple "Ade! Ade! und reiche mir zum Abschied deine Hand!" [Farewell! Farewell! and offer me your hand in parting!], suddenly in the major again, we then know that the end is near, that the tragedy will in fact occur. This is ultimate despair; it cannot possibly get worse. And therefore the passion is transformed— into resignation. What Müller has laid out, Schubert builds upon in the music.

With the desperate "O binde von der Stirn dir ab das grüne, grüne Band," the maiden is addressed *directly,* as if she were physically present. In the next song, on the other hand, she is only spoken *about:* "Ihr Blümlein alle, die sie mir gab . . . Und wenn sie wandelt am Hügel vorbei" [You flowers all, her gift to me . . . And when she strolls past the mound], as if death had actually already come between the two.

And surely enough, there is a funeral march hidden in "Trockne Blumen" [Withered Flowers].[76] Does the end approach like a funeral march? Or does the miller lad associate the vision of the maiden strolling by his burial mound with that of his funeral procession? (Example 37) Even though the voice part always enters

Example 37    Ihr Blümlein alle, die sie mir gab, euch soll man legen mit mir ins Grab.

on an upbeat, we hear a march in the background, its rhythm beginning on the downbeat rhythm. It persists throughout the piano part, even when it seems to yield here and there to the voice part, as at the pick-up to measure 39. It should be pointed out, however, that a correct rhythmic diagram of a march would have to look like this:

Example 38                                                          or

That is, the first two quarter-note beats of the rhythmic unit of the march should be weighted evenly; the second should not be subordinated to the first by a lesser stress (as in Example 39). Nor do we hear a subordination, as we normally would

Example 39                Ihr Blümlein alle, die sie mir gab,

with 2/4 time (Example 39). If we bring Schubert's notation into line with the corresponding march rhythm (compare Example 38), this is the result:

Example 40    Ihr Blümlein alle, die sie mir gab, euch soll man legen mit mir ins Grab.

Now we discover that Schubert's 2/4 time is, in point of fact, not "genuine." Throughout the song, there is a 2/8 time, a quicker pulsation, which contrasts and conflicts with the restful one. What is barely perceptible in the minor section becomes manifest in the major section. Here the time alternates between 2/4 and 2/8, as Schubert indicates with dynamic symbols such as accents and *fp*[77] (Example 41).

Example 41

What can be the reason for this? Are we supposed to associate the racing 2/8 pulse with the urgent desire for the flowers to bloom expressed in the text,—in other words, are we to regard it largely as an illustrative element? This cannot be ruled out. However, there is something else which is probably more to the point. If we understand the line "der Mai ist kommen, der Winter is aus" [May is come, winter is past] to be the all-important focus, then its jubilant, life-affirming musical expression takes on special meaning and must be grounded in the musical structure. To this end, Schubert deploys the melodic means and the relationship that suddenly emerges between the voice part and the upper line of the piano part; he even grants primacy to the latter, letting it carry the tune a third below. This passage is usually singled out with great admiration, but seldom are the rhythmic devices which play a decisive role in its effect noted. This is the only line in the entire song comprised of two measures that belong together in the stricter sense, that form a unit, two measures of the larger 2/4 order. These two measures do not follow the natural stress pattern, wherein the words "Mai" and "Winter" would receive the emphasis. Rather they are subdivided independently, so that "kommen" [come] is stressed instead of "Mai," and "Winter" follows directly, without an intervening unaccented beat (Example 42). This construction does not necessarily result in a more meaningful emphasis, but it certainly unites the two measures. They appear welded together by the burning desire for that coming. At the same time, the conflict between the 2/4 and 2/8 time is resolved in this atypical two-measure phrase.

Example 42

In this rhythmic-melodic gesture, the world in which a funeral march moves along steadily in a monotone while a restless pulse still beats, a world in which flowers wither, is overcome by a timeless May. The winter of life yields to spring. But this is illusion, not reality. Three times the miller lad shouts jubilantly "der Mai ist kommen, der Winter ist aus!", each time with greater intensity, as if he were possessed. And yet three times the same utterance, as if repetition could prove it true. And when his last note has faded, the vision disintegrates; the musical composition breaks down into individual measures that sink lower and lower, become softer and slower (= *diminuendo*), and end in minor, as melancholy as at the beginning of the song. The first part of the funeral march could follow the "trio" of the major section again; then we would realize that the burning question "wovon so nass?" [what makes them so wet?] and the lovingly recollective phrase "die sie mir gab" [her gift to me] are futile lyrical attempts to break the solemnity of the funeral march.

In "Trockne Blumen" we find the last mention of the maiden, the object of the miller lad's consuming love—or should I call her the agent *through* whom he is consumed with love? After all, the theme of the cycle, as we have seen, is not so much the story of a love for a beautiful miller maiden, but the desire and torment of a loving heart that dies of unfulfilled longing, a romantic yearning for a super-humanly pure, true love—a heart that is bound to die because such love cannot be realized on earth. The flowers will burst into bloom not when a happy pair of lovers goes walking in May but when the maiden comes across the grave of the lad and "denkt im Herzen: der meint' es treu!" [thinks in her heart: his intentions were true!] *Not until then* will they bloom and *not until then* will it be May. The vision of a different, "pure" love is fulfilled in some future May. Müller alludes ironically to this vision when he adds to the title of his song drama the words: "To be read in the winter" and has the poet speak in the prologue ("Dichter, als Prolog"):

Erhoffe, weil es grad ist Winterzeit,
Tut euch ein Stündlein hier im Grün nicht leid.
Denn wisst es nur, dass heut in meinem Lied
Der Lenz mit allen seinen Blumen blüht.

[I hope, since it is now wintertime,
that you won't mind a little time here in the green.
Know that today, in my song,
Spring blooms in all its floral splendor.]

Understood in this light, the cycle could—indeed must—end with "Trockne Blumen." This supposition is confirmed by the tonic E of this song; Schubert has arrived at the key in which he composes "Des Baches Wiegenlied" [The brook's lullaby] as a kind of epilogue: He has come the greatest possible distance, a tritone, from his point of departure, the B-flat major key of the first song "Das Wandern." Therefore "Der Müller und der Bach" seems to be inserted before the last song as an afterthought, perhaps because there has been no recent mention of the brook, which is supposed to give the "funeral oration," according to "Der Dichter, als Epilog" [The poet, as epilogue], or of the alluring "Tiefe da unten" [depths below], to which the miller lad plans to consign himself.

The miller takes his lute and approaches the brook. Fleetingly he strikes chords (measures 1–2, and repeatedly between lines and the stanzas, measures 19, 28, 61, 70; but not while the brook is singing, of course), and, as though improvising, he sings a song in which the melodic lines wander strangely. That significant interval, the ascending sixth—which last occurred at the critical point in "Trockne Blumen"(Example 43)—appears again, but now is split by the phrase

Example 43

break and strikes us as odd, weakened by the subsequent tritone on the word "Liebe" [love] (Example 44). The whole thing wobbles, because the rhythm, despite the stereotype piano part, seems unstable. In the voice part, the rhythm of the similar, successive musical phrases (the intervening measures 19 and 28 have

Example 44

already been discussed) is formed without heed to the text declamation, so that in each first measure of a phrase the longer beat comes first, but in each second measure it comes second (Example 45). Like a companion, the brook comforts the utterly exhausted youth as it picks up the tottering, wobbling music and echos it in its own safe, reliable way.

Example 45

Let us examine the musical devices Schubert uses to achieve this effect. In the foreground, the bright G major and the figuration of the brook in the piano part set the comforting tone. Less noticeable but more effective is the melodic style, no longer wobbling, but stable. For continuity and transition's sake, the first line of the new stanza is still declaimed in the established pattern $|\_\cup|\cup\_|\_\cup|\_$; but then the wobbly formula is replaced by a stabilizing one, wherein the second beat is now the longer one in each first measure of the phrase as well (Example 46).

Example 46

And immediately after the transitional (first major) measure, the melodic sixth swings up so that the word "Liebe" is expressed "naturally" again (measure 30 in contrast to measure 5), and the "Sternlein, ein neues" [starlet, a new one] (measure 34) is pinned into place. What peace streams from this simple, flowing, "folksong-like" G major section! It will cradle the miller lad "da unten" [there below], just as the caressing piano figuration in the third part of the song softly cradles the singing, which wanders and wobbles once again.

Regardless of whether the lad would like to sing along with the brook, he is no longer able to; he sees only one thing: "Ach, unten, da unten die kühle Ruh!" [Ah, below, there below, cool peace!], that which he longs for and which therefore draws him down. But the brook envelops him in that loud rushing sound (in G major) that led him to ask in "Wohin?", the *first* song in one of Müller's early versions: "Was sag ich denn vom Rauschen? das kann kein Rauschen sein: Es singen wohl die Nixen tief unten ihren Reihn." [Why do I speak of rushing? That can't be rushing water. It must be the water sprites singing their dance tunes deep down.]

Schubert often received his inspiration from a single stanza, not necessarily the first, in composing a strophic song so that the others fit the music only roughly. Often he also lifted a single sentence from the text and made it the central point of his song—we have already observed this in several instances. In "Des Baches Wiegenlied", it is the sentence: "Wandrer du müder, du bist zu Haus." [Weary traveler, you are home.] After four measures of introduction (2 + 2 measures, beginning on the upbeat) and four measures for the first two lines of text and the repeat (2 + 2, upbeat), the third line, "Wandrer du müder, du bist zu Haus," comes in on a downbeat, and although the text takes up only two measures, a three-measure phrase results (measures 9–11). Here the two outer voices of the piano part, the soprano and bass, abandon their harmonic fifth sound and descend, in carefully modulated steps, to A major and the subdominant region. The upper voice cuts across the triad of the tonic E major key and at the same time unites the three measures rhythmically by changing the stress pattern that has prevailed up to that point (Example 47). The melodic shape of this line is similar to the previous one (Example 48), but it differs in an essential detail: The important leap to the

Example 47

Example 48

Gu-te   Ruh,  gu-te Ruh,   tu die    Au - - gen zu,

Wan-drer, du mü - der, du    bist   zu— Haus.

highest note, e'', has moved from a metrically inconsequential to a critical position. (Example 49). This lends significance to the point at which the phrase is divided in two: for we hear the second half, "du bist zu Haus," as a statement in the stricter sense of the word, rather than as metaphorical, relating to the brook, as an

Example 49

Ruh, tu die Au - gen zu (mü-)der, du bist zu_ Haus.

announcement of the end: He is dead, he has reached his destination, he is home, safely sheltered, and he will rest there until everyone awakens at the Last Judgment, as confirmed by the fifth and last stanza. This line has a *spoken* effect amid the flow of the singing, and it is therefore the only one left unrepeated. Now all has finally been said; now the brook can sing its lullaby to the miller lad and deliver his "funeral oration in a wet tone."

Aus solchem hohlen Wasserorgelschall
Zieht jeder selbst sich besser die Moral;
Ich geb es auf, und lasse diesen Zwist,
Weil Widerspruch nicht meines Amtes ist.

[From such hollow water-organ sound,
each had best draw his own moral;
I give it up and let this discord be,
because dissent is not my calling.]

Strange, these lines from "Der Dichter, als Epilog," and yet there is a conciliatory note at the end:

So sei des treuen Müllers treu gedacht
Bei jedem Händedruck, bei jedem Kuss,
Bei jedem heissen Herzensüberfluss:
Geb ihm die Liebe für sein kurzes Leid
In eurem Busen lange Seligkeit!

[So may the faithful miller always be recalled
with every hand-squeeze, every kiss,
with every warm o'erflowing of the heart:
May love grant him, for his brief sorrow,
eternal bliss in your bosom!]

The lad who sang "Das Wandern ist des Müllers Lust" as if there were no stopping him, as if stanza after stanza generated new energy from a continually fresh rhythmic impulse, now lies "da unten" [there below] in the "kühlen Ruh" [cool peace] of his brook. The brook sings a lullaby as if to a companion, seemingly to go on forever like the hiking song.

These two songs, the first and the last, are pure strophic songs and the only ones in the cycle with five stanzas; no other is as long, or lasts as long, as the final one. Many and complex are the relationships between these two songs—of which Georgiades has made an impressive study.[78] Though Schubert has set them as far apart as possible in key, he has at the same time drawn them as close together as possible, as if he were spanning the distance from the last back to the first with an arch. The melodies are similar in style, with a hint of yodeling progressions (Example 49a). In both, the critical tritone interval occurs near the very beginning; in "Das Wandern" it is positive, so to speak, directed upward, in "Des Baches Wiegenlied" it descends; indeed, the tones are—be it by chance or intention—the same a' → e"-flat and d"-sharp → a', e"-flat and d"-sharp being enharmonically changed (Example 50).

Example 49a. Alpine yodeling songs typically contain frequent leaps of octaves, sixths and sevenths, within tonic and dominant harmonies, e.g.

*Des Baches Wiegenlied*

*Das Wandern*

Example 50 (based on Georgiades)

In both songs, the piano introduction also serves as closing, though the interlude in "Des Baches Wiegenlied" consists of only the first half; each new beginning provides a new impulse to continue, and the introduction/closing is set apart from the body of the song. In both songs, a second part of the stanza contrasts with the first, particularly in the piano part ("Das Wandern:" measures 13–16; "Des Baches Wiegenlied": measures 16–20).

In other respects "Des Baches Wiegenlied" is of course completely different and indeed unique. The presence of four voices in the piano part strikes us at first glance. The soprano and bass keep repeating a fifth interval in half notes, a sustained e + b′, until measure 8; then after measures 9–11 (the three-measure phrase we discussed), A + e′. The bass descends in the cadence to the low E, here the fifth degree of the subdominant A, to confirm this new and different key range. Encased in this frame, which suggests the sound of drones on bagpipes and the rhythm of a tolling bell (like the f′-sharp in "Die liebe Farbe"), the two inner parts move in shorter note values, melodiously, caressingly. The result is a proper four-part composition, which demands fine tonal and rhythmic differentiation in performance. The voice is added as a fifth part, closely related through the harmonic qualities, yodel-like, yet at the same time separate.[79] Without tampering with it as such, Schubert sheds special light on the line "Die Treu ist hier, sollst liegen bei mir" [I am true, let me cradle you] through his five-part composition. With the modulation to the subdominant and its characteristic color range, he leads the parts away from each other, the piano into a lower, the voice into a higher range. In other words, he brings them into a different tonal relationship.

Another striking thing about the note pattern is that after the line "Die Treu ist hier, sollst liegen bei mir," the piano part is jerked back to the higher range and proceeds in a totally different way, no longer in parts, but with solid chords in both hands. Chords and harmonies now revolve in phrases of 4+1 measures, as if to attract the listener's attention to the rocking by exaggerating its basic rhythm (Example 51) (which, incidentally, is not a "true" lullaby rhythm; for this, it would have to be in 6/8 or 6/4 time), but also as if to transfigure the rocking, to carry it into the realm of the visionary and infinite, through the reference to the sea that "will some day drink up all the brooks." At the same time and in spite of this, Schubert *closes* the song with this musical line, as he brings the melody down, firmly yet

Bsp. 51.

gently. Of course here Schubert's composition is recognizably inspired by the last text line of the poem and cycle, "und der Himmel da droben, wie ist er so weit" [and the heavens above, how vast they are]. Twice he "points above" with a sixth interval, springing from count three of the measure; finally, however, he reduces the sixth to the less expressive, but tonally more stable fifth, this time springing from an upbeat to a downbeat. This last affirmative gesture (like "du bist zu Haus") has the final word: "der Himmel da droben, *wie ist er so weit!*" The magical power of "Ach, unten, da unten, die kühle Ruh!" [Ah, below, there below, cool rest], the death-wish, is countered by "Und der Himmel da droben, wie ist er so weit!" The longing for "the depths below" is stilled through peaceful sleep in the eternally flowing brook, under the infinite heavens. In the epilogue, in "Des Baches Wiegenlied," the cycle finds its end and its fulfillment.

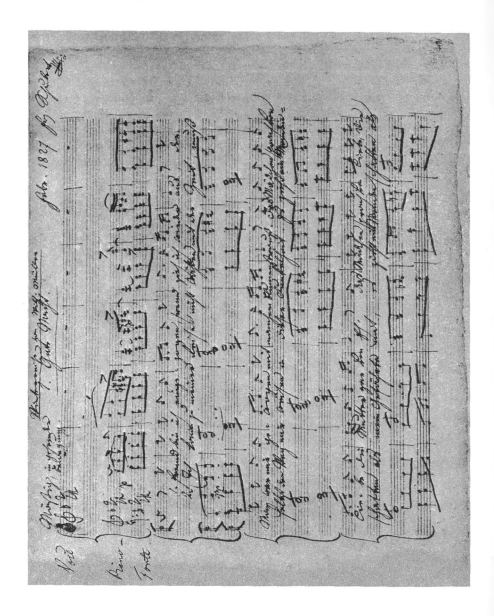

*Winterreise:* First page of the autograph (from the facsimile edition of *Winterreise,* published by Bärenreiter Verlag, Kassel, 1955).

# V. Winterreise

## First Part

*Die schöne Müllerin* has a semblance of plot; and, as we have seen, Schubert has structured each song, both as a single entity and as a link in a chain, in such a way that the plot is showcased in the music. Not that he has set a series of events to music, as in an opera, and linked the songs to one another directly. But he has carried an element of musical composition and sonorous reality, that of motion, so clearly through the whole that the attentive listener experiences it, either consciously or intuitively, accompanying the speaker, the miller lad, on his journey. In the end, he finds himself in another place—we might even say he is another person—than at the beginning.

Not so in *Winterreise*. Here we are also moved and transformed at the end, but in a different way. The text of *Winterreise* lacks the element of plot, and Schubert treats it accordingly. In these songs, he portrays a certain "state of affairs" through music, which he accomplishes primarily by leading the motion not forward but in a circle, appropriate to the text. Despite the "walking tempo" of the first song, nothing is set in motion, and of the songs that relate to the first one stylistically (2/4 time with eighth notes throughout, like the first songs of *Die schöne Müllerin*), not one takes up the motion in order to progress. Correspondingly, the degree of motion also differs from that observed in *Die schöne Müllerin*. "Gute Nacht" [Good Night], "Rast" [Rest] and "Der Wegweiser" [The sign post] are "mässig" [moderate]; "Die Krähe" [The raven] is "etwas langsam" [somewhat slow]; "Einsamkeit" [Solitude] and "Auf dem Flusse" [On the river] are "langsam" [slow] (the latter was originally "mässig"); only "Das Wirtshaus" [The inn] is "sehr langsam" [very slow]. Each song seems in its own way to wander hopelessly in a circle.

Naturally there are many musical elements that contribute to this effect, but one is especially apparent: the closings are either repetitions of the introductions, as if nothing had happened, as if composition and traveler had not moved an inch ("Rast," "Die Krähe," "Das Wirtshaus"), or they come to a stop without really concluding ("Der Wegweiser," "Einsamkeit," "Auf dem Flusse"). This travel has no destination. The second line of the first song, "fremd zieh ich wieder aus" [as a stranger I move out again], conveys no sense of direction; it does not connote the start of a journey; rather, it is exactly the same type of utterance as the opening line, "fremd bin ich eingezogen" [as a stranger I moved in]. "Das Wandern," which opens *Die schöne Müllerin*, awakens an urge to action and a desire to keep singing after the last stanza, to keep traveling onward, so to speak; its closing, which can always serve as a new introduction, allows for no ritardando, no diminuendo.

On the other hand, "Gute Nacht," the first song of *Winterreise*, ends diminuendo, and for Schubert, this typically means becoming slower and softer; it closes as if everything were to come to a standstill. Here no element of musical composition provides impulse for the continuous eighth notes, as the differentiated structure did in the other song.

In contrast to the realistic rushing and clattering characteristics of the "miller songs," the motif of steps from the introductory "Gute Nacht" of *Winterreise* is only hinted at throughout the songs. Here, all associations lie in the inner, psychological realm. (Dietrich Fischer-Dieskau)

"Fremd bin ich eingezogen," the first song starts out; "Wunderlicher Alter, soll ich mit dir gehn?" [Strange old man, shall I go with you?], the penultimate line of the last song asks; and walking and traveling are forever the subject in between. There is no hiking song at the beginning and no reminiscence of a previous song at the end, yet the element of a walking or hiking motion is perceptible in this cycle too. Schubert formulated this sense in his tempo mark for the first song: "Mässig, in gehender Bewegung" [moderate, with a walking motion]. But in *Winterreise* the tempo does not slow down, as from "Das Wandern" to "Wohin?" in *Die schöne Müllerin*, or come to a complete stop, as in "Halt!" Nowhere in *Winterreise* does the "walking motion" appear in concrete form as it does in *Die schöne Müllerin*; here it determines the whole from the ground up, but it functions as an element of a *basic mood*, which Schubert couples with a *basic motion*. This is not only clearly felt, it is recognizable. After seeing the traveler stand and watch the wind play with the weathervane in the second song, "Die Wetterfahne," we get the impression in "Gefrorne Tränen" not that he takes up the walking motion of the first song again and moves on, but that something is getting under way again, albeit somewhat hesitatingly and stumblingly. This effect is demonstrable in the musical structure.

In Schubert's day, the harmonic progression from the fifth to the first degree, leading from the unstressed last beat of one measure to the stressed first beat of the next, served as the simplest and most succinct of all cadences, somewhat like an abbreviation symbol. The song "Gefrorne Tränen" ends with this progression, but it also begins with it. To be sure, the chord sequences at these two spots are not the same. At the end, the leading tone of the upper part leads to the tonic, whereas at the beginning it leads from the fifth of the dominant chord to the third of the tonic. Thus the harmonics and melodics that would have a concluding effect in the opening chord sequence are softened, and the initiatory effect of an upbeat rhythm pattern takes precedence. Such patterns occur in Schubert's work, but in our two cycles less often than is commonly supposed. Only four of the 20 songs in *Die schöne Müllerin* and eight of the 24 songs in *Winterreise* begin on an upbeat, and for this reason alone they merit attention. Here the upbeat is so energetic that it seems to take credit for the high pitch and accent of the half note c'' that follows (c' in the repeat); but the energy is apparently not sufficient to launch a series of quarter notes following this half note. After the upbeat and the wearily stressed half note, the passage stops again and needs another push. And since the new beginning is identical to the first, except the half note is an octave lower, as if it represented the traveler's other foot, everything stops again. The third start would be just as unsuccessful, were it not for the completely unexpected and capricious upbeat entry in the middle of the third measure, one quarter beat too early, leading to the last and weakest quarter rather than to the strong downbeat of the next measure, and nipping in the bud the idea of a measure being the basic unit of motion. If this "false" upbeat in the left piano hand in the third measure did not trigger another upbeat in the right piano hand on the fourth quarter beat, followed by a series of quarter notes, the passage would have come to a halt for the third time. But instead it stumbles on, step by step, as tears drop in the snow. Not until much later does the motion develop any sort of continuity, which comes when the tears no longer drop but flow: "Und dringt doch aus der Quelle der Brust so glühend heiss" [and yet well up so glowing-hot from my heart].

The question of how or whether the basic mood of a song can ever flow from a basic motion may not be at all applicable to the impassioned "Erstarrung" [Numbness]; but at any rate, the 3/4-time songs that follow it, "Der Lindenbaum" [The linden tree] and "Wasserflut" [Flood of tears], seem to stand still, while "Auf dem Flusse" moves again. From this point on, it seems as though all songs in 2/4 time have traces of the initial "walking motion" while those in 3/4 time stand somewhat in contrast to them, "Rückblick," described at length in Chapter III, being an exception. With the 6/8 songs, the situation seems to be different again (the exception "Im Dorfe" is also discussed in Chapter III) —and oddly enough, only three are in 4/4 time: "Erstarrung," "Der stürmische Morgen" [The stormy morning], and "Das Wirtshaus" [The inn]. There is some doubt as to whether the latter two are in true 4/4 time or 2/4 time in disguise.

Meanwhile, we must take another look at "Gute Nacht" and its noted tempo, "moderate, with a walking motion," if we ascribe such importance to the latter. ("Mässig, in gehender Bewegung" appears only on the manuscript; for print, Schubert deleted the more specific second part of the notation, probably because he feared it would be taken too literally.) Apparently the same considerations apply to the tempo of this song as to the first song in *Die schöne Müllerin,* even though it is considerably slower (cf. p. 49f).[80] To really walk to this music is impossible; the eighth notes go too fast, the quarters too slowly. And yet the effect is unmistakable: we don't just form a vague, general impression, which is elaborated on to a certain extent in the text; rather we derive a compelling mental picture of walking from the music itself. In his creation of this kind of reality, in his reliance on such images for the effect of his music, Schubert relates to Haydn, Mozart and Beethoven. We must keep this relationship in mind as we listen and orient ourselves more to them than to Schumann and Brahms. That is, it is not so much a matter of sharpening our sensitivity to the "expression of feeling" or the "tone painting,"[81] but rather of becoming musically active, actually helping to *create* the work rather than passively empathize with it. Such an active posture develops during the listening process if we help *bring it about,* both in the particular and as a whole.

In "Das Wandern," the walking motion is first suggested by the 2/4 time with the steady beat of the eighth notes in the bass, then by the sixteenth-note subdivisions and by a certain "mechanics" in the music, which has its origin in a particular harmonic progression coupled with the "double stops" of the upper piano part. The restless, compelling forward motion in the music of "Das Wandern," which makes the traveling, indeed the traveler himself, seem real, is totally absent in "Gute Nacht." Here something in the composition is separate, which worked as a unit in the other song.

In asking the music lover, or even the musician and singer, how "Gute Nacht" begins—and specify that the piano introduction, not the stanza is meant—he will start with the upper voice of the right piano hand, that is, with the pickup to measure 2. Yet this pickup is preceded by three eighth-notes in the lower and middle voices (measure 1 being a full measure). So *before* either the upper piano voice or the singing voice enters, something is already under way: the steady, seemingly endless eighth-note accompaniment, *over* which the lad then sings,

"Fremd bin ich eingezogen . . ." The piano introduction in "Das Wandern" on the other hand begins with the steady, driving motion as a distinguishing characteristic of the song, thereby establishing itself as independent, despite all accompanying figuration. Nevertheless, the singer begins each new stanza himself—his pickup is unaccompanied and the piano comes in afterwards, even though piano and voice parts constitute a single musical unit.

In "Gute Nacht," by contrast, the accompaniment—one can hardly speak of it as piano composition—leads in, then simply carries on; the upper piano and singing voices come in later, each with the same melody, at a point that does not seem to be determined by the accompaniment—at least it is not dependent on it. We have the impression that this entry is the result of a conscious, voluntary decision, which weariness has made difficult. A test makes us more conscious of this: Because the entry is not tied firmly to the fourth eighth-note of each first measure, of introduction and stanza, the singer can also come in later. Every pianist will automatically repeat the eighths of the first measure until the entry comes; nothing happens, except that the eighth-notes continue. The effect is that of resigned waiting. The listener senses that the piano accompaniment needs the complement or fulfillment of an upper voice, that it longs for it, so to speak, even though it seems to move along independently of all melodic activity. The ending is formed in a corresponding way. A piano closing that does without an upper voice is just as important to the impression the song leaves as the stereotypical melody, which descends deeper and deeper into the steady eighth-note harmonies reminiscent of the voice part and thus of the singer.

So while vocal and instrumental parts in "Gute Nacht" are less independent than in the obbligato style of "Das Wandern," they seem to run along separately side by side, and one might question whether they really form a *single* composition. But they do form one composition, and it is obbligato, even if one considers the accompaniment in many of the *Winterreise* songs to be merely an instrumental realization of the harmony contained in or underlying the voice part. Appearances can be deceiving, so we must hold fast to the idea that vocal and instrumental parts work together in both *Winterreise* and *Die schöne Müllerin,* though in a somewhat different way.

In *Die schöne Müllerin,* the piano part is capricious with its instrumental figures; the accompaniment formulas sometimes support the lyrical voice part and sometimes oppose it. The piano part is treated independently. But on the whole, despite all these departures, the songs strike us as songs in the ordinary sense. In *Winterreise,* on the other hand, the piano part is derived to a large extent from the voice part and blends with it more; the piano part often doubles the voice part and anticipates it in many of the introductions. Accordingly, the voice part has more of an instrumental quality about it, which seems at times to resist not only simple text declamation but melodic-lyric performance as well. A prime example is "Gute Nacht." Though many consider it to be quite singable, possibly even the epitome of song itself, anyone who has actually sung it knows this is not the case.

It is hard not to accent the first syllable and rhythmic pickup, and still to preserve the significance of the initial high note in the wide-ranging melody. For here there are two conflicting elements demanding attention, needing to be balanced. Schubert avoids the unpleasant and rather meaningless text declamation

⏑   ⏒   ⏑   ⏒ ⏑ ⏒ ⏑
Fremd bin ich eingezogen, [literally: strange *have* I *moved in*]

⏑    ⏒   ⏑   ⏒ ⏑  ⏒
Fremd zieh ich wieder aus. [literally: strange *move* I *again out*]

by emphasizing the word "fremd" [strange = as a stranger] melodically, but he leaves it on the unstressed beat, following the meter of the text. The result is a curious floating effect, made possible by the more instrumental character of this melody. In performance there is a strong temptation to scan the syllables, even though the eighth notes are expressed in a line that first falls from the f'' pickup to the e' and then again from the d'' pickup to the final d'. This line itself is also a double pickup because of its instrumental nature, which is also hard to render in performance: not only is its first eighth-note a pickup to the first downbeat, but the two parts of the line are pickups to ". . . zogen" and ". . . aus," and then the whole line through three measures is a pickup to the final syllable ". . . aus."

Once this is understood, our observation that the piano part begins before the voice part gains in significance. We now see that while both voice part and accompaniment form groups or "rhythms" of two or four measures throughout (except the introduction, which is six measures), there, a subtle difference: In the piano part, the divisions fall between full measures, while in the voice part they have a definite upbeat that crosses the bar line.

Example 52

And finally this melody line has the following peculiarity: Schubert does not use all tones of the scale. He is selective and expressly avoids the leading tone, c-sharp[82]; he saves it for the second stanza, ". . . trieb hinaus." Yet he does play with a half-step, f''/e'' and e'/f', at the beginning and at the end of his first melody lines.

This may not strike us as something special, but when the piano comes to the fore for the first time, we soon sit up and take notice; for the same half-step occurs between ". . . Mutter gar von Eh" [her mother even of marriage] and "nun ist die Welt so trübe" [now the world is so dreary] with cutting emphasis.

Not until the last stanza do we appreciate the full significance of the first interval for the basic mood of the song and the nuances that stem from it. For it is not so much the major harmony that creates the moving effect here, as the fact that the starting note is higher, f''-sharp rather than f'', and the incline of the melody line steeper, a whole- rather than half-step:

Fremd bin ich ein-ge - zo - gen,          Will dich im Traum nicht stö - ren,
Example 53

The differing arrangement of whole- and half-steps in the major key—and here, because the series is pentatonic, this means the absence of half-steps in a melody line that otherwise remains the same—has greater impact than such variations would have in the minor. Therefore the stanza has a different sound; the music seems bathed in new light. The reason for this change is the "dich" in the text, the personal form of address, whereupon the subject of the cycle appears for the first time; for by addressing another person, though she is far away, he now becomes a speaking character. This is what prompted Schubert to "strike a different tone" and let it convey the boundless sorrow of the traveler as the basic mood in *Winterreise*.

The second song, "Die Wetterfahne" [The weather-vane], being an example of what is generally called "tone painting," does not belong in the cycle—at any rate, so it must seem, when viewed in isolation. For sung alone the elements of tone painting, which indeed determine its mood to a great extent, become more obvious. But just as this song cannot be sung by itself, neither should it be viewed in isolation, because its very significance lies in the fact that it contributes something essential to a greater whole. Here Schubert elaborates on the two elements we just observed in "Gute Nacht": the arrival of a person on the scene, and this person's state of mind as the basic mood, as if he were being portrayed physically. The person cries out in pain and despair. The song is an eruption, and it must have had an incredible effect in Schubert's day, for nothing even similar had been heard before.

More incredible, in view of how Schubert transformed the very concept of song, is the way the whole is constructed. What other song has ten measures of unison for the introduction and stanza opening, and where else are 26 out of 51 measures written in unison? The harmonies are bold, in the sense of changeable, unpredictable (Example 54); the rhythmics, metrics, and motion are bold in the sense of restless, unsettled; the restless melody, with its large intervals, is bold and completely unconventional, almost ugly! Where else in song does one find recitatives that actually seem to "scoot" up, as they do here; that is, suddenly shift a half- or whole-tone higher without the aid of a sequence of modulation (Example 55)? Where else does a run in the instrumental part, sweeping like a gust of wind (6th measure from the end), set the tempo of a song, so that the voice has to step back, no longer able to execute runs of its own ("des Hauses auf*gestecktes* Schild," "ihr Kind ist *eine* reiche Braut")?

Example 54

Example 55

   Yet, with all its uniqueness, "Die Wetterfahne" still has an inner tie to the
preceding song and to the cycle; and *this* is what gives it meaning beyond the tone
painting. Even though the beginning, with its stormy pickup, contrasts sharply
with that of "Gute Nacht," the descending melody line and above all Schubert's
continued "play" with the half-steps f''/e and e'/f' (the tones are the same, though
the song is in a different key) are direct references to "Fremd bin ich eingezogen."
In order to soften the primary stress of beat one in the second text line ("auf |
*me*ines schönen Liebchens Haus") with a second stress in the same measure ("auf |
meines *schö*nen Liebchens Haus") and to bring out the secondary stress (both are
ironic), Schubert changes the sequence, so that the high point of the melody
moves from the beginning of the measure to the middle. This draws attention to
the interval between the two stresses of the measure, which is the half-step e''/f''.
At the same time, this f'' becomes the highest note—the same note Schubert raised
to f''-sharp in "Gute Nacht" in order to strike that "different tone" in the last stanza.
This f''-sharp would also like to be more prominent here and surpass the f'', but
despite the major tonality of measures 32 ff and 44 ff, it does not quite succeed. It
remains trapped in runs (are they running starts?). Thus no "different tone" is
struck in "Die Wetterfahne."
   Once the listener is aware of the unique features of "Die Wetterfahne" and its
ties to the preceding song, he can recognize what it is that far surpasses the tone
painting in significance: a kind of dramatics that pushes onward despite the lack of
plot.
   With all this inner movement, the traveler remains standing still as he watches
the wind play with the weathervane; not until "Gefrorne Tränen" does he slowly
stumble on. I have already described how Schubert takes up the walking element
from the first song through his choices of ₵ time, and how he sets it in motion. But
now we see that two additional elements underlie the composition and tie the

songs together. One is the modified recitative, used nearly everywhere ("Die Wetterfahne": "Da dacht' ich schon in meinem Wahne . . ." [I thought then, in my delusion] "Was fragen sie nach meinen Schmerzen? . . ." [what do they care about my pain?]; "Gefrorne Tränen": "Ei Tränen, meine Tränen, und seid ihr gar so lau . . ." [Ah teardrops, my teardrops, are you so tepid . . .]). The other is the fervent feeling that comes through again and again, be it in passages that overflow from within, as in "Gefrorne Tränen": "Und dringt doch aus der Quelle der Brust so glühend heiss," or in an entire song, as in "Erstarrung."

Who could ever capture the passion of a song like "Erstarrung" in words? Even if someone were to assemble and present the compositional elements, assuming that all were included and each one fully appreciated, he would still have to concede that, in the study and description of a work of art, the accumulation of the individual elements cannot be considered the whole, that the whole is always more than the sum of its parts. Although this criticism of any esthetics whose interpretations are based on analysis is valid in principle, as noted in the Foreword, the procedure used here still makes practical sense for our purposes, because we are not concerned with an analytical understanding of the whole. Rather, individual insights, gained in the process of structural analysis, should help the musician or music-lover recognize the essence of what he experiences in performing or listening. Such insights sharpen awareness and therefore offer opportunity for further and more profound musical experiences; they are by no means meant as a substitute for an attentive encounter with the work itself. First-hand experience is and must remain the object. This analysis is merely an attempt to pave the way for such experience.

So in discussing the next song, "Erstarrung," I will also single out compositional features that contribute to the essence of the whole. Here voice and instrumental parts are so closely related that for extended sections we can speak of outer voices, and perhaps also of counterpoint. At any rate, we rarely find the lower piano voice articulated as clearly as it is here. In the introduction, we are struck by the following fine distinction: First, a unit is made up of two phrases of two measures each; the broken chord of the right piano hand remains unchanged, despite the various levels in the melody; in the left hand, each quarter beat with a triplet bears an accent; everything is still piano. Then with measure 5, the right-hand harmony begins to travel with the bass melody and is coupled with a crescendo that culminates on the first beat of measure 6. This causes the accent to shift from the triplet in the last quarter of the measure to the downbeat of the following measure, and the result is an extension: the third phrase of the introduction consists of three measures instead of two. It works like a colon before the voice entry, coupling introduction to stanza, accompaniment to song. We note a similar extension in the transition (measures 60–64) to the stanza "Soll denn kein Angedenken . . ." [Shall no remembrance . . .], which is reminiscent of the transition to the recapitulation in sonata form. Here, as in the introduction, the voice part begins with a pickup leading from a dominant measure to a tonic measure. However, before the middle section of the song, "Wo find ich eine Blüte . . .," the interlude (= the introduction shortened to three measures) brings the tonic measure in earlier (measure 47), so that the voice part enters on already existing harmony. The stanza seems to be established in the new key and the sound of a more flattering accompaniment. This suggests remembrance: the unreality of the past, with blossoms and green grass, becomes real, in a sense, through music. The third part, which repeats the music of the first but with dynamics intensified to *ff*, we perceive as all the more passionate, or perhaps at last passionate, because now there is a reason. The ending, which seems to be tacked on and not really to conclude, and the piano closing, in which all trace of the song seems to be obliterated, make the mood all the more hopeless. With unrivaled passion, "Erstarrung" sweeps over us in a single stroke, as if it came in *one* breath. The impetuous eighth-note triplets run uninterruptedly for 108 measures; the one major break in the voice part, between the first and middle sections, only seems to mitigate the painful outcry. Probably no other song in the cycle displays passion of this intensity.

> ... one of those songs—folksong and masterwork at the same time, and through this very dualism earning its special intellectual-philosophical hallmark. ... Why beat around the bush? It was Schubert's "Linden-baum" [The linden tree], none other than that old familiar "Am Brunnen vor dem Tore" [At the well outside the gate] —A tenor performed it with the piano, a fellow with tact and taste, who knew how to handle his simple and superb object with much prudence, musical sensitivity, and careful declamation. We all know that the magnificent song sounds somewhat different in folk or children's vernacular than as art music. In the folk vernacular it is normally simplified and sung straight through in stanzas to the main melody, whereas in its original version this popular theme changes to minor in the second of the eight-line stanzas, only to steer back into major very beautifully on the fifth line; then with the "cold winds" that follow and the hat flying from the head, it breaks down dramatically and does not recover until the last four lines of the third stanza, which are repeated so that the melody can be sung to the end. The really compelling turn in the melody occurs three times, and always in its modulatory second half, the third time at the recapitulation on the last half-stanza "Nun bin ich manche Stunde . . ." This enchanting turn, which we do not wish to approach too closely with words, lies in the sentence fragments "So manches liebe Wort," "Als riefen sie mir zu," and "Entfernt von jenem Ort"; and the light, warm, breath-controlled tenor voice, which was inclined to break a little, sang it each time with such insight for its beauty that it tugged at the listener's heart in a way he had never dreamed of, especially when the artist heightened the effect through especially intimate falsetto tones on the lines "Zu *ihm* mich immer fort" and "Hier *findst* du deine Ruh." On the repeated last line, however, this "Du fändest Ruhe dort!," he sang the "fändest" the first time from a full, yearning heart, and only the second time as the most tender flageolet. —So much for the song and its performance.

Any attempt to improve upon Thomas Mann's[83] complicated description may be "approaching the masterpiece too closely." But perhaps a few observations will not be out of line, especially some dealing with the curious fact that the art song "Der Lindenbaum" has become a folk song—the only one of Schubert's, by the way. First we must bear in mind that with Schubert's song and the folksong, it is really a matter of two different songs, a highly sophisticated, complex one, and a simple one for which a part of the other was extracted. What made this extraction

possible was the loose structure of the composition, as well as the unique character of the part, which was preserved in the folk song. The folk-like quality comes
through much more clearly in "Der Lindenbaum" as folk song than in the context
of *Winterreise*. In the art song, even the first stanza, and especially the last, affect us
like a quotation; they only *sound* like folk song, almost unnaturally. This is
Schubert's intention, this is how he visualized the whole: The introduction
reminds us of a folk singer improvising on his instrument, perhaps a zither, in
order to attune himself and his listeners before the song begins. But the
introduction—its tone-painting features suggested by the rustling of leaves and
branches—only *simulates* improvisation; in reality it is the shaping of an instrumental element that forms a kind of background for the whole song, and from
which the song is set off. The association of the linden tree with the central point of
village life emphasizes the folk tone in the first stanza and again in the last.

But in the middle stanzas, something far removed from folk song and folk
singing, occurs through which Schubert realizes wider concepts and links the
song to the cycle: a recitative-like element. "High range: 'Der Hut flog mir vom
Kopfe'; low range: 'Ich wendete mich nicht.' Only as it reaches beyond music to
represent speech does this passage reveal to us its true content. And conversely:
only by performing it as pure music, not additionally burdened by expression, can
one avoid pathetic declamation."[84] From this stanza on, all the rest falls into the
category of reflection or memory, even though the verbs change to present tense
("Nun bin ich . . ." [Now I am . . .] as opposed to "Ich träumt' . . ." [I dreamed . . .]).
The folk quality in the song no longer creates the illusion of a living folk tune; it
becomes reminiscence—all that is left is an echo.[85] And now Schubert can dare to
round off his art song following the dictates of folk song, to close the stanza with a
repeat (measures 73–76), which the first two stanzas lack.

One last comment: if we consider "Am Brunnen vor dem Tore" a folk song,
then this is against the backdrop of 19th-century tradition, which, to be sure,
Schubert influenced less with his songs than Friedrich Silcher with his choral
compositions—to name not only the most congenial, but probably the best repre-
sentative of the choral movement, which also had political significance.[86] That is,
we do not hear Schubert's melody as a "*Weise*" [traditional tune or way of
rendering a text], which does not really need harmony or accompaniment; rather
we hear it as the upper voice of a four-part composition for male chorus, which as a
whole seems to be a folk song. Admittedly, Schubert suggests this in the first stanza
with his four-part harmonic composition. But in the second and last stanzas, he
avoids reinforcing or even affirming the association. Instead, through a finely differentiated accompaniment and subtle, musically significant variations in the last
stanza, he brings the instrumental element of the composition, which we discussed earlier, to the fore and lets it envelop the voice part of his piano song.

"Der Lindenbaum" ends as it began; the introduction, with very little change,
serves as closing; no progress is made. Does the cycle itself, which for lack of plot is
scarcely coherent in the text, also stay rooted to the spot? Does the song stand
unconnected amid the others? One of the essential differences between *Die Schöne
Müllerin* and *Winterreise* is that in the latter Schubert draws musical-material parallels, thereby establishing coherence beyond the basic style that characterizes and
dominates both the individual song and the cycle, and making it
comprehensible—that is, audible. The means for achieving this, he uses sparingly.
One is the "play with steps and half-steps," which we observed primarily in the

upper regions of the melodic range. The last line of "Gefrorne Tränen," "des
ganzen Winters Eis" [the whole winter's ice] (to be rendered "stark" [strongly] in
the last repeat[87]), again "plays" with that half-step f''/e''(/f'), the highest notes of
the song, the ones with which "Fremd bin ich eingezogen" began. Then the wide-
ranging melody of "Erstarrung" peaks on the a'-flat ("mit mei*nen* heissen Tränen"
[with my hot tears], "schmilzt je *das* Herz mir wieder" [if my heart ever melts
again]) and descends, as in "Gute Nacht," beginning with a half-step and falling in
a long curve, with upbeat phrase attacks. It falls to the half-step a'-flat/g', and only
then is it able to rise again. This melodic curve, "mit meinen heissen Tränen, bis ich
die Erde . . . ," in its length and tension and in its importance for the song, underscores the upper voice of the piano as it retraces it a half-measure behind. Here the
interval g''/a''-flat/g'' (a simple turn) comes to the fore, reinforced by the even
longer curve of the instrumental melody, the imitative entry, the rhythmic-metric
position, and the dynamics: This glow *will* penetrate the ice and snow and relieve
the numbness.

In the next song, "Der Lindenbaum," in the same basic style, the numbness is
indeed relieved, to such an extent that the idea "Du fändest Ruhe dort!" [you
would find peace there] is actually thinkable. Correspondingly, in the instrumental part, which suggests toccata-style improvisation, the high, descending
whole-step (first occurring in measure 2) and the long curve of the descending
bass melody (measure 4 ff), which "plays" with a half-step (Example 56), are
finally expressed as a memory, appropriate to the content and mood of the song.

Example 56

The memory that the music evokes is of course not that of the traveler—
achieved through the text and its concrete associations—but rather its own. Far
from trying to portray something implied by the text with the help of his music,[88]
Schubert realizes *musical* meaning in composing text. In this respect, the elements
that tie the songs together remain purely musical and take on meaning only as they
are heard. In listening, we note that the triplets, which move through the entire
piano part of "Erstarrung," return in the piano part of "Der Lindenbaum" and,
drastically reduced, in the initial figure of the introduction, closing, and stanza
interlude and then in the undulating melodic figures of the voice part in "Wasserflut" [Shower of tears]. We attach no meaning to this recurring usage of the triplets
other than that it provides a musical link through a rhythmic figure, though in each

song it has its own compositional significance.[89] In the first of the three songs that have this usage in common, it does not appear in the voice part at all, and in the second, only in one place, the (repeating) melody. In the third song, on the other hand, it dominates the entire second section of the voice part but turns up in the piano part only as reminiscence. As we perceive all this, we recognize something of the spirit of the whole in the progression, which creates and legitimizes the musical structure, the composition.

Schubert forms two of the four stanzas of "Wasserflut" into a two-part song, whose second part is not totally new but a variation of the first. When the whole is then repeated for stanzas 3 and 4, the result is a strophic song with variations. The music is marked by a strange mixture of extremes, which are mutually exclusive but at the same time seem to depend on each other. On one hand, the motion drags so slowly that it conveys the impression of complete exhaustion, even apathy; on the other hand, the musical outcry on the word "Weh" [grief, woe] is so strong that we are shocked and hurt, for nothing remotely similar has occurred in the cycle heretofore. For this sudden, intense expression, Schubert resorts to a device that he uses sparingly, unlike the Romantics, and rarely in this manner: that of dissonance and related harmony. The powerful effect of the passage "durstig ein das heisse *Weh,* durstig ein das heisse Weh" [thirstily (absorb) my burning grief] (measures 11–14, especially measure 12—note the half-step e''/f'' at this spot) depends largely on the fact that Schubert leads his composition in a direction other than that which the listener expects. We expect the dominant seventh chord and the ascending melody above it (beat three of measure 11: "heisse") to be followed by a tonic chord on beat one of measure 12. But instead we hear an altered chord, containing the expected root tone e, not as the lowest, but as the highest tone (in the voice part; 5/6 position of the chord); this functions primarily as another dominant seventh chord and therefore tends toward the fourth degree of the scale. But the e moves immediately to f, resulting in the sharply dissonant diminished seventh chord g-sharp/b/d/f. Since this chord has no particular resolution tendency, it waits dissonantly, as it were, leaving open various possibilities for resolution. But Schubert uses none of the "attractive" possibilities. Instead he turns to the conventional cadence IV—I$^6_4$V$^7$—I, as if the diminished seventh chord were nothing but a substitute for the preceding dominant seventh chord of the fourth degree, as if the dissonance, in spite of its sharpness, were nothing but a harmonic alteration. (Harmonic theory, in such cases, actually speaks of "secondary dominants" and "passing modulations.") The effect is that of someone's sinking back in total exhaustion after writhing in pain. After this, the second stanza can pick up the thread of the story, but it can hardly lead to this point again. Now we understand why the second stanza differs from the first, why the line "und der weiche Schnee zerrint" [and the soft snow melts away], despite the high range and the forte, is strangely pale and disappointing in comparison to "Weh:" The energy that would crack ice and melt snow is gone. The instrumental interlude, and thus the introduction and closing, can also be better understood now. Notable here is the articulation, which does *not* bridge from the last tone of the first measure to the first of the second measure, from the leading tone to the tonic of the scale, even though a connecting articulation in the third measure (from first to second beat) is indicated (Example 57). This articulation seems somewhat unnatural. As a result, each of the two first measures seems bogged down, as if a new decision to continue were needed; there is no coherence at all, in the strict sense of the word. This

Example 57

result of structure and articulation determines the effect of the song appreciably from the very first measure. Finally, we also understand now why we are no longer offended by the senselessness of the renewed outcry on the text line "nimmt dich bald das Bächlein *auf*' [soon the brook will take you *in*]. After the "Weh" of the first stanza and the conscious reversion to a kind of narrative tone in the second, the parallel spot in the third comes across only as reminiscence. Even though new text is presented, we hear little else than that terrible outburst of "Weh!"

By now the cycle has reached the point where a listener following along is bound to wonder whether a continuation of this "winter journey" is at all possible. All will to go on seems paralyzed, every utterance beyond the simple narrative tone exudes pain. Schubert seems to have given up the "walking motion" and its corresponding images, as well as the element of simulated speech (which I call "recitative" for simplicity's sake), for the structure of his cycle. Instead, he allows feelings to dominate as he rarely does: the basic mood is oppressive. But at the same time, in this description of the situation in the sixth song, the way in which Schubert seeks to proceed is suggested, the only conceivable way.

In "Auf dem Flusse," Schubert takes up the style of "Gute Nacht" and once again lets the traveler "speak." As listeners, we immediately feel that we are "on track" again, on the course that was laid out in the first song, the course which we know from experience ties the songs together. We are again caught up in an event, even though the cycle has no clear plot line—we believe the event is happening to us, even though we are only listeners. Rarely do we encounter so earnest a song. And now, in this earnest tone, as if a first act (6 of 24 songs) were over, Schubert begins anew with a song in 2/4 time, styled after the walking songs. The tempo was originally marked "mässig" [moderato], as in "Gute Nacht," but later Schubert changed this to "langsam" [slow], because a different mood requires a different tempo. Of course, to begin the same way as before is impossible. The listener not only perceives the darkening mood but also understands how it came to be, and Schubert uses this opportunity to combine structure-forming elements that were introduced to the listener earlier in separate songs. He compresses his structures henceforth, but the listener is in a position to grasp them, because he has been drawn into the development of the composition step by step.

An illustration of compressed or intensified structure in "Auf dem Flusse" that immediately comes to mind is the stirring line "wie still bist du geworden" [how still you have become]. Here, in keeping with the text, Schubert reduces the dynamic level from *pp* to *ppp*; "sehr leise" [very softly] in the voice part, brings the melody line down a half-step from the highest tone so far used, and follows with a harmonic change in the accompaniment. With this dynamic-melodic-harmonic shift, the word "still" suddenly reaches into the realm of feelings, where it has a strangely dissonant effect, though we are not yet aware that the real dissonance occurs much later, at the forte spot: "Ob's unter seiner Rinde wohl auch so reissend schwillt" [Are there ripping torrents under its crust too?]. But I am thinking more in terms of how, in the third part, Schubert modifies the "walking" 2/4 time and symmetrical phrasing that dominated the first part. The four-measure phrasing is emphasized rather than disturbed by the insertion of the single modulatory measures 13 and 22 between text stanzas one and two, then between three and four (D-sharp minor → E minor).

Schubert approaches the third part ("Mein Herz..." [My heart...]) from another direction. Here he introduces recitative-style text declamation, which results not only in stanza variations but in an interruption of the characteristic pattern of constant eighth-note subdivisions. For example, in measure 52, despite the figure in the right hand, we no longer hear the two quarter beats in the bass (the second is merely ornamented by a written-out trill) as subdivided into eighths; and in measure 53, we hear the eighths as independent beats of a 4/8 time (Example 58). With the return to minor (measure 41) after the "recollection

Example 58

stanza" (in E major, like 'Der Lindenbaum'), the melody from the voice part of the two first stanzas appears in the piano bass. After four measures it shifts to D-sharp minor, as in measure 9. But now Schubert does something different. Instead of a four-measure phrase plus a single modulatory measure, he forms a unified three-measure phrase (measures 45–47). Then he interprets the D-sharp minor of this phrase as the dominant for the G-sharp minor of the first four measures of the six-measure phrase that follows (48–53); the last two measures of this phrase modulate back to the main key, which begins in measure 54 ("schwillt? Mein..."). In this six-measure phrase, the voice part is now coupled to the piano bass, as if it had lost its independence and relinquished its function to the instrumental part. We have this impression not only because the melody lies in the piano bass, but because the voice part stops singing, as it were; it turns the singing over to the instrument and only seems to speak now. The vocal part actually ceases to be an independent part, a coherent melody, with the reentry of the minor, that is, with the poem's fifth stanza and its text repetitions (34 measures, compared to the 40 of stanzas 1–4). "Mein Herz—in diesem Bache—erkennst du nun dein Bild?" [My heart—in this brook—do you now recognize your image?] in measures 41–47 comes across as *spoken* to music, on musical pitch levels. The entrances are willful, as if the person, recognizing his situation, were speaking with increasing agitation and deepening emotion.[90] His speech becomes louder and the pitch rises, picking up melodic strains from the instrumental part, and thus indirectly from the first stanzas. Something rarer in Schubert's work than is generally believed moves the listener deeply here: intensification. Clearly, harmony and dynamics contribute much to this effect. However, they only serve to emphasize what is going on and moving the listener more deeply *at the foundation level:* We experience how the song develops from the first two stanzas to the major section; how it blossoms there as song, both in the melody and in the progressive variation of the accompaniment; how, with the return to minor, something breaks in and threatens the unity of the composition, especially since the voice part and instrumental bass are curiously related; but how it is then restored again, indeed formed anew; and how this newness carries the whole far beyond the lyric quality from which the composition originated. The text no longer seems "set to music" in the usual sense; it is "spoken musically." Even if the listener approaches this work naively or sentimentally at first, at this point he will not be able to escape Schubert, who claims him fully, draws him into his *Winterreise,* and transforms him.

The way Schubert combines elements of simple song composition in "Auf dem Flusse" (in melody, periodic organization and three-part form) with others that do not really fit with them (recitative with free declamatory rhythm and phrasing, striking modulations, and harmonic shifts) raises the question of whether the listener can perceive such a musical creation as a unified whole. The open-minded and experienced listener will immediately answer the question affirmatively, because he is familiar with the song; but he can also affirm it on the basis of insight, since structural analysis shows how the parts and the whole are fashioned and fitted together, how the elements are applied with respect to the desired musical effect, which, as I have said, is more than just setting a text to music. A structural analysis of the next song, "Rückblick" [Glance back], was presented in Chapter III; it is quite detailed because the question of unity is especially pressing, in the absence of a unifying rhythm for this song. There we saw how Schubert's concept was sparked by the text but then developed in purely musical form; and how the active involvement of the listener is necessary in order for the work to come into being, because only then do the various elements in the text and composition, as well as the interrelationship of the musical structures, function together and therefore reveal the meaning of the work.

Schubert picks up the "walking motion" in "Auf dem Flusse," but does not allow it to function as such, tying it instead with an element somewhat comparable to recitative. This motion is also a premise for "Rückblick," though he does not continue it; he alludes to it in the distancing of a hastily stumbling, panicky flight.

I will leave open the question of whether a little of the "walking" tempo from the beginning of our cycle, which comes through again and again in varied form, is also present in the "slow" tempo[91] of "Irrlicht" [Will-o'-the-wisp]. At least the 3/8 time seems to me not to rule this out, for the melodic-harmonic and rhythmic elements have a distancing effect as well. Indeed, the two descending intervals at the beginning represent not only the descent "in die tiefsten Felsengründe" [into the deepest rock caverns] but also "das irre Gehen" [confused wandering]. Just as the normal progression of the basic harmonic steps of a scale I-IV-V-I is reversed to I-V-IV-I, the sequence of long and short rhythmic values, usually perceived as natural in 3/8 time, is also changed (Example 59). Thus the first two measures express a certain instability. But the following two measures are immediately con-

Example 59

tradicted melodically, harmonically, and rhythmically by a fully-developed, confident cadence, in which the step to the tonic marks the first beat of measure 4 as a stress point reached via an upbeat. The four-measure phrase concludes with the first chord of its last measure (Example 60). What follows this concluding chord is an addition, an abbreviated repetition of the melodic, harmonic, and rhythmic occurrence of measures 3–4 (Example 61). But more than a repetition, this addition is a melodic and rhythmic reversal of the interval that opened the composition (Example 62). Thus the beginning and ending of the phrase are related structurally like a weight and its counterweight: they create uncertainty, then resolve it. One could think of them as the determinants of a musical structure.

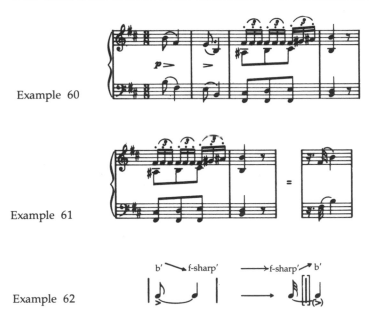

Example  60

Example  61

Example  62

Turning back to the text now, we recognize it as the force that triggered Schubert's concept and led to its expression, and we see that both extend far beyond simply setting a text to music: The beginning is as uncertain as the will-o'-the-wisp; the ending, as certain the grave.

Thus we observe that the whole of ''Irrlicht'' is contained in the piano introduction. Actually, the unfolding of what is encapsulated in the first four measures has the character of a theme development, less so in the first two stanzas, more so in the third. The line ''Bin gewohnt das irre Gehen'' [I'm used to confused wandering], with its suddenly rising melody, as well as the return of the earlier rhythmic figure that began on the downbeat, this time with an upbeat pickup (Example 63)remind us of the treatment of musical material from the exposition in a sonata development, as does the varying of the interval that first occurred in measures 3–4 and is so often repeated, typically enough (Example 64). The fact that the basic compositional problem presented in the piano introduction is touched upon at each of these occurrences becomes clear at the end of the last stanza and the transition to the closing.

Example 63

Example 64

According to Schubert's plan, one expects the last line "jedes Leiden auch sein Grab" [every sorrow (finds) its grave] to be declaimed like the last lines of the other stanzas:

Measures 13–14: "│liegt nicht schwer mir in dem│ Sinn."
                        [does not lie heavily on my mind]
Measures 25–26: "│alles eines Irrlichts│ Spiel."
                        [all the play of a will-o'-the-wisp]
Measures 39–40: "jedes│ Leiden auch sein│ Grab."
                        [every sorrow (finds) its grave]

As can be seen, the correlation is not perfect, for the last text is declaimed with an upbeat, like the rest of the third stanza. Another observation goes along with this. In the first two stanzas, the one-syllable nouns at the ends of the lines appear in separate final measures:

| Sinn ⅞ | and: | Spiel. ⅞ |

Each is followed by two instrumental measures, which are basically only a variation of the cadence in measures 3–4. The final syllable "Grab" [grave] stands alone in a concluding measure, but it is not followed by the corresponding measures from the second half of the piano introduction. Rather, this introduction begins at the same time as the final syllable, but with the first, not the third measure, so that the entire introduction forms the closing of the song. Therefore, in the fourth measure from the end, the final chord (thus the final measure) of the last stanza and the beginning (and thus the first measure) of the closing coincide. Technically speaking, we have an example of what music theorists of Schubert's day called a *Takterstickung* [measure suffocation] or *Taktunterdrückung* [measure suppression], because when two measures fall simultaneously, one must be eliminated or "suppressed" (Example 65). And now if, as we have seen, the last measures of all stanzas basically correspond to the last measure of the piano introduction, then the first and the last measure, beginning and ending of the four-measure musical phrase in which we found the whole encapsulated (measures 1–4), fall together here on the key word "Grab."

Example 65

After seeing, hearing, and experiencing this coming together, we can recognize in retrospect the significance of the alternation between downbeat and upbeat entrances and the change to continual upbeat entrances in the third stanza. The caesura that clearly divides the first and second stanzas is bridged between the second and the third by the pickup "Durch des..." [Through the...]; and now here, where the piano closing begins, it is completely closed—though at the price of an abrupt curtailment of the last phrase of the last stanza from four to three measures. As beautifully as Schubert has finished out each line of the last stanza and tied it to the following with a gentle upbeat bridge, he does not allow the final word "Grab" to resound; there is no bridge leading beyond the grave. Since the introduction begins with chords, it now assumes the character of a funeral march.

"In eines Köhlers engem Haus hab Obdach ich gefunden" [In a charcoal burner's small house, I have found shelter]. For the first time, the traveler rests. And yet "Rast" is a "walking song": strange paradox, which of course is just as familiar in the realm of folk song as in art song. In "Der Lindenbaum," for example, which is close to a folk song, Schubert creates the impression of actual folk-singing, at least in the first stanza, though the text speaks of the past and the singer is only reminiscing: "Ich träumt' in seinem Schatten. . . . Ich musst' auch heute wandern . . ." [I dreamed in its shadow. . . . I had to travel today too . . .]. Just as tenses sometimes become muddled in folk song, quite naturally,[92] Schubert can mix the points of reference in his art song. Paradox, in this case the walking motion of "Rast," is the only way reality can adequately be portrayed:[93] a reality in which the traveler does not notice how tired he is until he lays himself to rest and finds that his limbs cannot relax even while resting, that his heart can find neither new energy nor peace; a reality in which his feet walk on alone, so to speak. "Things" keep going on involuntarily in the person who is singing: the instrumental part moves ahead without stopping, and the voice part is powerless to influence it, to subdivide it, no matter how great the melodic and dynamic range, no matter how eloquent the declamation, as in the line: "der Rücken fühlte keine Last" [my back did not feel its burden], or, equally expressive: "der Sturm half fort mich wehen" [the storm helped blow me onward].

The musical structure, and within this—again more clearly—the rhythmic structure of the phrasing, can help us recognize what we experience when listening. At first the piano introduction seems strangely long, almost too long, and one must ask whether this six-measure phrase is necessary per se. But the closing verifies it unmistakably; the tonic needed for the conclusion is tacked on in an extra seventh measure. With this six-measure phrase, Schubert indicates that the instrumental part neither follows the periodization of the voice part nor establishes its own symmetrical grouping of measures. Between the simple four-measure phrases of the first two half-stanzas (measures 7–10, 12–15) and again before the beginning of the second stanza (measure 17: "Die Füsse . . .), there is a measure in the piano, not tacked on, not anticipated, not inserted: it is without relationship to the phrasing that is going on "above it." Between lines 2 and 3 of the second stanza (". . . zum Stehen; der Rücken . . .") there is no corresponding measure; between lines 3 and 4 (". . . Last, der Sturm . . .") it is suddenly there again—likewise before the repeat of the last line; but between the end of the stanza and the beginning of the piano closing, it is missing again. If we relate this irregularity in the construction to the fatigue expressed in the text, or the reverse: if we trace the impression of crippling fatigue in this song back to the irregularity just described, then we have identified the motive but hardly explained it sufficiently. For these rhythmic switches in Schubert's composition are related to other devices and have "consequences"—and these are what create the impression for the listener. The line "der Rücken fühlte keine Last" (measure 21) begins one measure too early, in terms of the listener's expectations based on his experience with the song so far, and is suddenly withdrawn (*pp* in the piano, "leise" [softly] in the voice part], melodically venturesome, of course, but creating an unpleasant dissonance with a diminished seventh chord. Then this dissonance hangs on for three measures (the listener expects only two!), so uncannily eerie that it seems as though nothing less than a simple perfect cadence to the principal key, on a higher dynamic level, can break the spell and bring the composition to a standstill. But this cadence fails because of the deceptive cadence, the recurring pianissimo and the limbo of the "empty" measure (26), in which the eighths fall like separate "droplets" again. Not until the second attempt (measure 27 ff) will the cadence succeed, so it seems. But again Schubert "suffocates" or "suppresses" the tonic measure that should close the cadence and immediately (measure 31) brings in the first measure of the piano introduction.[94] And the composition continues relentlessly—inevitable as fate. The musical reality opposes the will of the traveler.

With the memory of "Gute Nacht" called forth by the accented second appoggiaturas in the right piano hand (measures 17–20), it becomes at the same time glaringly apparent that the original concept of motion, not cheerful but at least somewhat relaxed, has been transformed into an obsession, a compulsion to travel. Schubert embroils the listener in this transformation, even though there is no plot.

> We could still enjoy the songs of *Die Schöne Müllerin,* even if we accepted them only as trivial 'pretty songs.' But most of the songs of *Winterreise* defy classification as trivial 'pretty songs' (the melody of 'Der Lindenbaum,' perhaps; but then again, not the middle section); they go straight to the heart. Most of the time the piano part does not provide accompaniment but tends to fuse with the song; it cooperates in presenting the content and is caught up in its seriousness.[95]

We might ask ourselves whether this is also true of 'Frühlingstraum" [Spring dream], or whether this song should be regarded as "merely pretty." If each of its three parts appeared as a separate song, each displaying a mood, then we would have to answer the question affirmatively. But in this context—musically non-cohesive in both the narrow and the broad sense (the three parts in the one song and the song in the cycle)—"Frühlingstraum" takes on an oppressive realism. With the illusion of the dream, then with the immediacy of reality, reflected here through simple musical devices, and finally with the initial cheerful outlook becoming darkly clouded at the end by the knowledge that the question "When will the leaves at the window turn green, when will I hold my sweetheart in my arms?" has no answer, this realism is all too evident. Beginning and ending, that is, the piano measures of the introduction and closing, must therefore be "heard together." Then of course the song no longer appears as "a ray of hope," as it has been called. If "Frühlingstraum" seems not to belong in the cycle, it is because here—and only here—there is nothing to suggest motion; the compulsion to keep moving on is suspended here, in the dream.

To conclude the first part of *Winterreise,* Schubert once again takes up the elements I have identified as most important to him in the composition of his cycle: the "walking motion" and the quasi-recitative style. In 'Einsamkeit" [Solitude], these are related and at the same time counterposed. "Sluggish of foot" but still "walking," the song moves on, and the motion changes character in the course of the song. In the first two lines, the eighth notes fall in droplets; despite their division between the two hands of the piano part from quarter to quarter, they have no closer relation to one another metrically. From the third line on, Schubert accents each first and third eighth note, thus giving priority to the quarters, which were designated as the counting units but seem to have lost the beat amid the dragging eighth notes, especially at a slow tempo. It is this, and not just the melodic upswing, that gives the text lines in which the traveler speaks of himself, "so zieh ich meine Strasse . . ." [so I make my way . . .], a firmer, less tired declamation, more as if they were spoken. After the end of the first song stanza (". . . ohne Gruss" [. . . without greeting]), at measure 22, when half notes replace the quarters as the basic structural unit, the stage is set, rhythmically and metrically, for Schubert's recitative. Here it is of a type known as *recitativo accompagnato*. In the instrumental part, Schubert recalls earlier stages of this story-without-a-plot through characteristic passages that, if not quoted literally from the first songs, are at least reminiscent of them. With the sharply accented appoggiatura of measures 25, 27, 37, and 39, he alludes to "Gute Nacht" and the only place where the piano emerges independently; with the chordal section "war ich so elend . . ." [I was (not) so miserable] in E-flat major (first printing: C major; Schubert originally composed 'Einsamkeit' in D minor, the key of "Gute Nacht"), he recalls the line "Und dringt doch aus der Quelle der Brust so glühend heiss" in "Gefrorne Tränen." With these allusions, Schubert also brings to consciousness the fact that the voice was still singing in the two "quoted" songs, but that the person who sang then is only speaking now. In this new awareness, the traveler of our songs achieves simultaneously an unparalleled musical reality and the reality of his mortality. We know what lies behind the statement that back then "war ich so elend, so elend nicht" [I was not so miserable, so miserable]; we are witnesses to this tale of woe; we experience it musically as tragedy.[96]

## Second Part

A reality of a completely different sort greets us at the beginning of the second part of *Winterreise*. With the old musical device of naive imitation, Schubert paints 'Die Post' [The mail coach], so we already know what the subject is by the time the text begins: "Von der Strasse her ein Posthorn klingt" [From the street, the postilion's horn sounds]. But Schubert does not leave it at that. In each of the two identically structured parts of his song (the text has four stanzas), he sets the first half of the text, which merely reports "Von der Strasse her ein Posthorn klingt" and "Nun ja, die Post kommt aus der Stadt . . ." [Well yes, the mail comes from the city . . .], in sharp contrast to the following half, which contains the directed question:

Die Post bringt keinen Brief für dich.
Was drängst du denn so wunderlich,
Mein Herz?

[The mail coach brings no letter for you.
Why do you leap so strangely,
my heart?]

and:

> Willst wohl einmal hinübersehn
> Und fragen wie es dort mag gehn,
> Mein Herz?

> [Do you want to have a look over there
> and ask how things are going,
> my heart?]

E. Schwarmath[97] has described the effect:

> Schubert creates the abrupt effect when he allows the dotted note values, the *outward* manifestation of motion, to ignore the tonic conclusion of the phrase (measures 24 f and 69 f) and commence again with fresh activity even on the final notes (compare the double occurrence of *fp*). The darkening of the tonality into minor (compare "Auf dem Flusse," "Der Wegweiser") signals the entry into an *inner realm*. The new smoothed rhythm in the piano part contrasts with the dotted rhythm of the first, and third, text stanza, which sounds like a real horn signal. The new rhythm becomes neutral (*pp*) and allows the voice part to come to the fore, whereas in the first stanza the voice part functioned increasingly as mere commentary on what was happening in the piano part.

The change from an "outward" to an "inner" realm occurs *de facto* in the two rest measures (26 and 71). It is the change from naive word painting and a lyrical narrative tone to the stark reality of a musical utterance, a speaking person.

One can also view the song as a scene, so to speak. From a distance one hears the mail coach approaching, announced by the coachman's horn. With horses trotting, it rolls into view, turns the corner, and suddenly is no longer visible—yet the heart of the beholder continues to beat in the rhythm of the coach. Suddenly the coach is there again, it drives on by, then disappears—what remains is the heart that beats in its rhythm. Like an apparition The mail coach (and the song) flashes by. When sung alone, "Die Post" is an idyll, nothing more. In the context of the cycle, however, the song carries weight—especially in that its function in the second part is similar to that of "Gute Nacht" in the first part. "Die Post" picks up the story again—that is, it sets something in motion, initiating a continuous motion. It is not a coincidence that "Die Post" has no real conclusion.

Of course the element of motion is not the same here as at the beginning of the cycle. The important difference is not that it was walking motion there and the motion of a coach and horses here, but that the power that initiated the motion before is now crippled or broken, as I tried to show in our discussion of "Einsamkeit." When the traveler moves on despite his exhaustion, it is only because "things" keep going on inside him, inexorably, until the end. We sense that his search for death in the wintery elements will not be in vain, that he will find it—even if no text exists to report it. All potential for action seems to be spent; therefore the "walking songs" relate differently to the "walking motion" established at the beginning, which moves through the whole but changes markedly as the basic mood darkens; they also relate differently to the non-"walking songs." In the second song, "Die Wetterfahne," for example, we can almost see the traveler stop and look up at the weathervane; we sense the great effort with which he turns to go, and we also hear him move on. But the stopping in "Der greise Kopf" [The gray head] is of another sort, as is the motion that picks up again in "Die Krähe" [The raven] (significantly, both bear the same tempo mark "etwas langsam" [somewhat slowly]). The fact that Schubert seems to capture reality more in the first part and tends toward abstraction in the second is not a sufficient explanation for the difference, for these two qualities are actually combined in the second part. Nowhere do we find reality more clearly portrayed in music than in "Der Leiermann" [The organ-grinder] with his hurdy-gurdy; and yet nowhere does Schubert wander so far from traditional song into the abstract as in "Leiermann," so that he seems to redefine the nature of the Lied in his cycle. Musical reality, effective musical reality, cannot be pinpointed or identified in either part.[98] However, we know through the process of active interpretation, of listening and understanding, that the turning from an outer to an inner realm, which was discussed in connection with "Die Post" and could be clearly grasped there as musical fact, occurs again and again, be it within a song or from song to song. Sometimes it is more perceptible, sometimes less; it takes place throughout the whole, as the cycle turns increasingly inward. And naturally the relationship of word and tone— to us a familiar phrase—also changes within the cycle, though on the whole in Schubert's late work, this relationship is different from that found elsewhere in song, and from what is generally associated with Schubert, for that matter.

> The word is not directly enhanced by the melody here, and the melody does not originate directly from the text, as in folk song and the tunes of *Die Zauberflöte*. Rather, the word inspires the musical idea, which is first expressed in purely instrumental form in the accompaniment, with the unmistakable ring of a poetic world apart, if only in introductory measures or in a single chord. From this basic musical idea, from this sheer poetic utterance, and with the addition of the melody, poetic song emerges, which accompanies its own words in the tone language discovered by the tone poet, who actually sets them to music. It appears almost as a matter of pure chance, as something inconsequential, that words should accompany this song and express a verbal sense together with a tonal sense when, as an instrumental phenomenon, it already includes both text and composition.[99]

"Der greise Kopf" illustrates this tone language in a special way in the first and third stanzas, where the song text seems merely to chime in, as if to accompany the "instrumental phenomenon," which already contains the essentials. The other stanzas are in conflict with this interpretation, however. Through a kind of recitative, they produce speech that seems, in this highly compressed musical form, to have absorbed the instrumental element. Here, at the beginning of the second part and midpoint of the composition, Schubert sets in unison the line that points to the pathway and the destination: "wie weit noch bis zur Bahre! wie weit noch bis zur Bahre!" He has used unison several times before—the first time at length in "Die Wetterfahne," the last time briefly on a key text phrase in "Einsamkeit": "dahin mit trägem Fuss."[100] The greatest possible reduction in means has the most powerful effect. The song seems to be composed for this line alone, and with this line it serves as a road sign.

"Die Krähe" is another in the group of "walking songs," as I have labeled them for the sake of simplicity, and thus it belongs to that set whose composition and structure can be understood more easily and described more clearly. Of the three stanzas, the middle one constrasts sharply with the first and the beginning of the third; the third stanza starts like the first but then takes on certain aspects of the middle one. Schubert imposes on this simple structure a kind of accelerando, which, on the surface, seems aimed at supporting the melodic and dynamic heightening in the third stanza. The piano introduction is clearly set off from the beginning of the stanza; there are two measures of piano interlude between the first and second stanzas but only one between the second and third; the closing begins immediately, without a transitional measure. If this accelerando extends into the closing, as it obviously does, then it cannot be aimed at the high point in the middle of the third stanza. Now that our attention has been called to it, we also perceive how firmly this accelerando undergirds another feature of the song, one that goes beyond mere intensification and must be regarded as fundamental in the strictest sense. This feature has its origins in the compositional structure, which we shall now examine.

The melodic line of the piano introduction is immediately audible, its tendency easily perceptible. Several factors contribute to its powerful effect:

1. In two runs of two and three measures respectively, the melody falls an octave, that is the interval at the lower end extending to the leading tone below the tonic.

2. The same melodic figure occurs at the beginning and end of this passage, but

3. the figure begins once on a downbeat and once ends on an upbeat (Example 66).

Example 66

4. "The weighted whole step in measure 4, e''-flat/d''-flat, together with a sinking of the harmonic progression into the deceptive cadence level and the Neapolitan sixth chord, creates the impression that the melody is being compelled downward, unlike the corresponding cadence in measure 9: e'-flat/d'/c', where the descent seems like a natural fall.

5. The three-measure unit (measures 3–5) has its own pitch-space, where the subdominant is represented exclusively by the Neapolitan sixth (measure 3, first eighth-note; measure 4, second eighth-note; compare the six-five chord [first inversion of the seventh] of the second degree in measure 8).

6. The C minor space of the introduction is partitioned off from that of the song."[101]

7. The independence and ultimate power of the introduction is underscored by the five-measure phrasing as such and as compared with the "normal" four-

measure phrasing of the corresponding sections that follow in the stanza.

On the one hand, the lyrical style of the first stanza mitigates what seemed so emphatic in the introduction; on the other, the five-measure phrase (1–5) makes its mark as such once again, when we recognize the four-measure phrase (6–9) as its original form. Thus the listener draws a connection between introduction and stanza, in which relationship and difference register equally in our consciousness. Incidentally, the perceptive listener will also notice a relationship to the preceding song: namely, between the unison there and the unison coupling of the voice part to one piano hand here. This bridge of association also spans the texts, in that both poems follow the same meter and their last lines correspond in content and in their rhyme words: "wie weit noch bis zur Bahre!" [how far yet to the bier!] and "Treue bis zum Grabe!" [faithfulness unto the grave].

Schubert does away with the unison coupling of a piano voice with the singing voice in the second stanza. With repeating minor second steps, he leads the piano in a strangely unsteady—perhaps we might call it wobbling—sequence. But more importantly, he declaims the text so that it seems to have drifted into a different meter, if one can think of this recitative-like declamation in terms of verse and poetic meter at all. Here, for the first time in the cycle, an "other" is addressed, a living creature, even though it is only the bird, the crow, that is accompanying the traveler. Here Schubert formulates the question "willst mich nicht verlassen?" [so you don't want to leave me?] as if it said: "wirst du mich verlassen?" [are you going to leave me?]. Correspondingly, in the third part of the song, he reformulates the last line *musically, compositionally*, from the command: "Krähe, lass mich endlich sehn!" [Crow, let me finally see!] to the *answer:* "Treue bis zum Grabe!" [The whole line translates: "Crow, let me at long last behold a faithfulness that endures to the grave!]

The third part of the song begins like the first: lyrically, in two two-measure phrases (= in a four-measure phrase), voice part and left piano hand in unison. The situation changes abruptly with the third line. The voice part imitates the recitative second stanza in its rhythmic declamation, but it goes far afield in its emotion-charged melody. In contrast, the minor second steps in the piano part come to the fore again, though here, with their harmonic chords, they press toward a cadence. Powerful dynamic devices are suddenly brought in for intensification;[102] the phrase (measures 29–33) consists of five (2+3) measures, like the introduction; in a kind of deceptive cadence the five-measure phrase leads to the sharply dissonant diminished seventh-chord. In other words, on the lines "Krähe, lass mich endlich sehn Treue bis zum Grabe!" (first occurrence, measures 29–33), the question and the command in the text are expressed as the outcry of a tormented man, so that any further intensification is ruled out, and a repetition is tolerable only if the cutting dissonance is cancelled in a conciliatory resolution, a compelling cadence, a reassuring answer. To accomplish this, Schubert fuses the last five-measure phrase of the stanza (measure 34 ff) to that of the piano closing, for which we expect five measures, not six, so that the two become inseparable (measure 38). Because one measure is "suppressed" in the process, the last group of stanza measures is reduced in the piano part to a four-measure phrase (measures 34–37), which requires, as metric-rhythmic equivalent, another "symmetrical" group of measures for completion—that is, an extension of the closing from five to six measures (38–43). Thus the composition ends in a manner and in metric rhythms that release all tension. The five-measure phrase which as introduction is separated from the stanza and contains a compelling downward motion, is tied to the stanza in the closing, comes to a peaceful conclusion, and has lost its compulsive tendency. The vision of the crow—a strange metaphor for faithfulness—rises above the grave, so to speak (measures 37–38).

In the well known dialogue "What Is Atonality?" broadcast over the Wiener Rundfunk in 1923, and which I quoted earlier, Alban Berg tried to correct the most widespread of his "opponent's" misconceptions: that all melodies from significant and popular works of the classical composers were easy to sing. Indeed, he showed that many remain incomprehensible if the underlying or accompanying harmonies are not immediately heard, recognized, and understood.

> ... A melody combined with diverse, frequently changing harmonies, which is almost the same thing, can easily appear "crimped" if one does not understand this harmonic interpretation, which is no less true of a highly chromatic style—there are hundreds of examples of this in Wagner. But instead, listen to a melody by Schubert from the famous song "Letzte Hoffnung" [Last hope]:

Example 67

Is that crimped enough for you? ... And to continue with Schubert, this melodist par excellence, what would you say about his treatment of the voice part in the song "Der stürmische Morgen" [The stormy morning]:

Example 68

Are these not typical examples of a richly serrated voice part? And here is one with especially long leaps:

Example 69

You will find similar passages with an almost instrumental quality in Mozart's voice lines.

Alban Berg's argument is convincing in context. Yet it seems improper for him to insinuate that he has identified Schubert particularly as melodist, "albeit" an unusually progressive one for his time. "Letzte Hoffnung" in particular clearly demonstrates that the accompaniment in Schubert's composition is obbligato, which means that vocal and instrumental parts are conceived as a unit and that only in this way does the composition achieve its musical effect.[103] When the voice part is separated from the rest of the composition, not only does it yield no melody, it yields no musical sense at all. When the first stanza begins: "Hie und da . . .", something of consequence has already occurred instrumentally. The listener already knows that he can depend on nothing, that the compositon is unstable, that neither the time nor the key are assured, for the prescribed 3/4 time cannot be verified by simply listening; so it comes as no surprise that the voice part comes in on the same notes as the piano but one eighth note (!) behind, and that the entry note (c''-flat) must lead at once to the sharpest of all melodic dissonances, the tritone (c''-flat/f'). What then follows virtually knocks us flat: instead of the tritone, we hear the fifth b'-flat (middle of measure 6) to e'-flat (middle of measure 7), which is traversed diatonically; instead of eighth notes falling arbitrarily, with no relation to scale and meter, we hear a resolute 3/4 time in a harmonic cadence that leads to the tonic. That is, on these two lines of text, which form a unit and agree in linguistic "tone," Schubert forms a musical structure with extreme contrasts, and the listener experiences far more than the "musical picture" of dry leaves dangling loosely from branches. After an uninterrupted sequence of complementary eighth notes (the two piano hands complement each other), what a chasm opens up, when a rest—a hole, in effect—turns up in measure 6 (last eighth note)! Of course this is "only" the seam between the "unmetered" eighth notes and those tied into 3/4 time. But at this moment, the listener is gripped by fear; with this structure, the music produces what we might almost call live fear, because suddenly the eighth notes *are* the dry leaves dangling there on the branches, and because one of them suddenly . . . The rest occurs again (measures 10, 20), and other rests are added (measure 21, first eighth note; measure 24). The fear does not abate, but it changes as we listen and comprehend more fully. We grasp the truth of the metaphor of dry leaves for hope, we understand it musically, we recognize the opening chasm, the sense of tragedy that comes over us—and then, with the traveler, we can pour out our fear, pain, and sadness in music; we can cry our hearts out with the traveler in his song: "auf unsrer Hoffnung Grab" [on the grave of our hope].

It seems to me that such a heightening of expression precludes any further intensification, and that the cycle can continue only if a new direction is opened. If the situation reached in "Letzte Hoffnung" is not to lead to a standstill, if the element of inner happening is to be preserved in the cycle, then action must be revived. If the claim is to be taken seriously that this person, the traveler, his words and actions, are a kind of musical reality, then this action must result from a voluntary decision by the person, which must be the "subject of the music" as such. And in fact, this decision is the subject of the next song, "Im Dorfe," as the detailed analysis in Chapter III has shown. Its special position and function in the cycle help to explain the structure and the particular technique with which the relationship between the vocal and instrumental parts is handled. First of all, the piano part is more independent here than anywhere else in *Winterreise*—it "cannot be regarded as mere instrumental accompaniment, nor does it fuse with the song."[104] But though voice and piano parts are initially completely separated, nowhere do we find the two so completely fused as in the last stanza. (We are not concerned here with the middle stanza, which is totally different in form.) Our traveler asserts his resolution and will against himself, when he *says* to himself: "was will ich unter den Schläfern säumen?" [Why should I tarry among the sleepers?]. Schubert realizes this "episode" through a musical structure in which the vocal part asserts itself against the instrumental part; the listener understands this compositional 'tone mechanism" as an "Analogon der Empfindung" [equivalent of feeling] derived from the text.[105]

The decision, the turning point represented in 'Im Dorfe," is liberating, so to speak. In 'Der stürmische Morgen," our traveler once again has strength—tempo mark: "ziemlich geschwind, doch *kräftig*' [quite fast, but forcefully]—he has mustered a second wind for his journey. For the first time in the cycle, we have a song that can move at a hiking pace—or the reverse: a song by which a hiker can set his pace. The effect is astounding. Although the text does not say a word about hiking, we have the impression that it is a hiking song. We can picture the traveler striding forth in the stormy morning, grimly prepared to brace himself against the storm. The forthright introduction—opening on a full-measure downbeat, striving upward from quarter to quarter (d-e-f-sharp-g) and from eighth to eighth (g-sharp-a-b-flat), leading to the harsh, but not goal-oriented dissonance of a diminished seventh chord, then concluding with a terse phrase that has an upbeat[106]—the persistent unison of voice and piano, the relentless forte (the only one in *Winterreise*—in the second part, it is actually fortissimo), the resolute declamation, the sharp accentuation in the instrumental part, the repetition of the introduction as interlude and closing, all contribute to the effect described. But what seems to me of greater significance, particularly because of its effect, is the position of the song in the cycle. The listener knows that the traveler has gathered strength and courage again because he has torn himself loose in the preceding song, 'Im Dorfe," because he has broken the spell and freed himself. Of course anyone who allows himself to be carried along with the "story" also knows that the upswing will soon become a downswing, that the traveler's feet cannot carry him much farther, because the energy picked up here cannot be great; it is weak, like the musical structure, which never crystallizes into a differentiated composition as in the other songs. The listener senses that the motion is of a lesser intensity than that of the earlier walking songs, which move along persistently, if not as loudly.

Friendly A major, a dancing 6/8 time—why doesn't 'Täuschung" [Deception] leave us in good spirits? Are not 'Licht" [light] and "tanzt freundlich vor mir her" [dances friendly before me] the key words? Not only those! The third and most important is "deception." While Schubert develops the first two key words in the foreground with naive tone painting, he lays the basic structure of his composition in such a way that we are actually deceived, and we perceive this deception, especially in the context of the cycle, as tragic.

As in 'Letzte Hoffnung' and contrary to the sense of the text and the structure of the line, Schubert separates the first word from the rest of the text, isolates it, and gives it musical emphasis—there it was 'hie und da," here 'Ein Licht." We see the light, as it were; it is really there—so it seems. This effect stems first from stretching the one-syllable word 'Licht" over a whole measure, so that the whole line takes up a total of three measures; then from the melodic distinction, the extreme contrast between short pickup and held-out tone; and finally from the rhythmic structure of the three-measure phrase, which sets the first measure apart but then ties it back in by forming the last measure correspondingly (Example 70). The piano measure, which amplifies the three measures of the voice line into a four-measure phrase, has an inherent tone painting quality, for it calls forth the image of some-one running along in pursuit, although there is a trace of parody.

Example 70

More important, however, is the significance of this amplifying piano measure to the structure and its perceptibility—that is, its effectiveness. In the voice part, all phrases are three measures long. In the first section of the song, with the form A-B-A', they are always amplified in the piano part into four-measure groups, into "rhythms of four measures," but never in the middle section. So the first and second sections contrast in their overall structure and internal rhythms, and only secondarily in key and in the declamation, which sheds special light on the transitions and structural characteristics. Whereas the downbeat opening of the middle section and the following upbeat with two eighth-notes, "Ach! wer wie ich . . ." [Ah! Someone like me . . .] stand in stark contrast to the line openings in the first section (Example 71), a true Schubertian "manipulation" of the rhythmic values (Example 72[107])—which corresponds to the crossing of singing voice and upper piano voice in the preceding section—creates a compelling transition to the third section (Example 73). This transition takes on special significance in connection with the interpretation of the text. The recapitulation (Section A' of the overall structure, measure 31 ff) begins not with a new text couplet but with the second line of the fourth couplet, out of a total of five. The last word of the middle section,

Example 71

Example 72

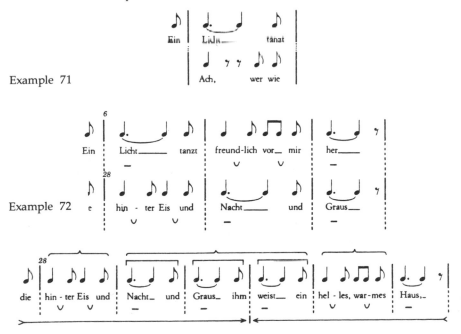

Example 73

"Graus," doesn't find its rhyme, "Haus," until the recapitulation. This results in a musical coupling of the first line of the last couplet ("und eine liebe Seele drin") to the preceding line ("ihm weist ein . . .) as a postscript, though it has no relation to it as far as rhyme is concerned (Example 74). Thus the last text line "nur Täuschung

Example 74

ist für mich Gewinn!" is left to stand alone. What of it? one might say the last section of the stanza can always be completed with a text repeat! But here Schubert expressly avoids this device, which he has used in all the other songs in *Winterreise.* Rather than form a two-part unit corresponding to measures 14–21 of the first section ("ich folg ihm gern . . ."), he forms a unique one-part unit from various elements. "Nur Täu(schung)" corresponds to the other opening measures: "Ein Licht," "ich folg," and "ihm weist;" "(Täu)schung ist für mich Gewinn" corresponds to the conclusion of the first stanza, measures 19–20, "verlockt den Wandersmann" (Example 75). However this unique unit (measures 38–41) does

Example 75

not correspond to the parallel passages with the inserted piano measure, amplifying the three measures of the voice phrase into a four-measure phrase; rather, it follows the preceding unit immediately, suddenly, too early (in measure 38 instead of 39), and contrary to our listening experience and expectations. At the same time, the cadence corresponding to measure 12–13 or 20–21, which would have created detachment, is eliminated. The extra unit is attached to the preceding one through a deceptive harmonic cadence on the word "Täuschung" (Example 76). The last line, in keeping with the word "Täuschung" and the tightening of its

Example 76

melody and metric-rhythmics, seems to summarize the song. At the same time, it destroys the structure, which up to now has been carefully divided into distin guishable phrases (Section A: 3 + 1 measures; B:3;A':3 + 1), by unexpectedly establishing a firm bond with the line to which it was supposed to be loosely tied as before. The two lines seem welded together; in the musical setting, their textual content seems brought to an ironic equivalency: "eine liebe Seele" [a friendly soul] = "Täuschung" [deception].

> The conclusion of the song, as a metric and harmonic entity, withholds everything expected and familiar: the symmetry of periodic half-phrases, the ending of the final phrase in the tonic, a leading function for the piano part, corresponding to section A. The periodic structure seems predestined to realize a "deception" through musical composition: the form established as dependable during the song turns out, at an essential place, to be undependable.[108]

Toward the end of the cycle, Schubert's sequence for the songs deviates not inconsiderably from Wilhelm Müller's (cf. page 24ff). In Müller, it is as follows:

Täuschung
Der Wegweiser
Das Wirtshaus
Das Irrlicht
Rast

Die Nebensonnen
Frühlingstraum
Einsamkeit
Mut!
Der Leiermann

In Wilhelm Müller's sequence, therefore, the following lines from "Irrlicht" are:

Bin gewohnt das irre Gehen,
's führt ja jeder Weg zum Ziel:
Unsre Freuden, unsre Wehen,
Alles eines Irrlichts Spiel.

Durch des Bergstroms trockne Rinnen
Wind ich ruhig mich hinab.
Jeder Strom wird's Meer gewinnen
Jedes Leiden auch ein Grab."

[I am accustomed to confused wandering, and every path leads to the goal anyway. Our joys, our woes, all the play of a will-o'-the-wisp. Through the mountain streams's dry bed I calmly wind my way down. Every stream will reach the sea and every sorrow find a grave.]

These lines, which point beyond the aimless wandering to the end of the road, to the grave, come *after* those of "Täuschung." If, in "Irrlicht," Schubert has taken the only possible route in his musical interpretation of the text, as I have tried to show, then after "Täuschung" he must point all the more emphatically to the inevitability of the end.

Thus "Der Wegweiser" [The sign post] must really come as a surprise, for it relates more closely than any of the other "walking songs" to the first song, "Gute Nacht." However, in addition to the similarities we also hear differences, and these are of greater significance, as we shall see. The most important differences have to do with the eighth-note motion: here it only seems to be endless and uninterrupted; it is by no means a matter of course, as if it were the foundation for the composition, as in "Gute Nacht."

If we disregard the ending of "Der Wegweiser" for the time being and examine the places at which the eighth notes are interrupted, the first thing that strikes one is the rest at the end of the major section. It marks a change[109] similar to that in "Die Post," this time from the traveler's reflection on his own behavior: "welch ein törichtes Verlangen treibt mich in die Wüstenein?" [what foolish craving drives me into the wastelands?] to a reference to the outer world, the theme "Wegweiser:" "Weiser stehen auf den Wegen . . ." [Signposts stand along the paths]. But once we are aware of this change in orientation, we also notice that the eighth-note motion stagnates almost immediately in the second measure, then in the fourth, in the fifth, and again and again in the first two stanzas; each time it must be, and is, taken up anew—which is especially clear, for example, at the caesura between the introduction and the beginning of the stanza—and always with the help of a rising pickup of two sixteenth notes. So we must immediately ask where that illusion of eighth-note continuity originates, which we remember from this song. It stems from the chain of eighth notes in the last stanza, but certainly also from its relation to the eighth-note motion of the first song, which also moves at the same moderate tempo. But this song differs fundamentally from "Gute Nacht." What is it that is so different? Does a different mood, a different feeling prevail? Hardly, for mood and feeling recede equally in favor of an unmistakable motion that is totally different despite all similarity. In "Gute Nacht" it is disappointed, resigned, weary, yet still walking with a purpose; in "Der Wegweiser" it is irrevocable, irresistible, walking as if driven.

Schubert achieves this starkly contrasting effect in "Der Wegweiser," as contrasted with "Gute Nacht," by making the eighth notes and their motion the compositional theme, as it were. So while uninterrupted motion is the *foundation* for the first song, here it is the *result*. As we become aware of the structure and its changes, we discover how far it is from the four eighth notes of the first measure (which stagnate in the second measure) to the eighth notes that no longer wander (beginning with measure 67) but only hammer out the tonic of the scale, pointing to it as a signpost points the way and not leaving it except to secure this tonic in the cadence. We can see from the composition what a long journey it is from the timidly hesitant eighth notes of the first stanza to the relentlessly compelling ones of the last. We realize how much room Schubert's compositional structure still has to play with at the beginning, if we line up and compare various related positions and combinations in which the four eighth-notes with pickups appear (Example 77).

The example shows that the figure is treated as a musical motif in the earlier stanzas, that a kind of motivic work characterizes the composition and comes through in the effect. But it also shows that the motif is "processed" and how, in the "processing," its very substance is altered. The pickup loses or changes its melodic component ("welch ein"; "treibt mich"; piano part, measure 29); on the other hand, a melodic component comes through on the eighth-notes that originally sounded only a single tone (measure 32: "in die Wüstenein?"); eighth-note values are transformed rhythmically into dotted notes ("törichtes"; measure 31: "treibt mich"); the motif diminishes to three eighth-notes (measure 29), then finally to one with a pickup (measure 31).

The consequence of all this becomes evident at the end of the major middle section. Once clearly defined and distinguished by definite features, the motif is now dismantled to such an extent that it seems merely to be raw material for a chain of eighth notes accompanying the development of heavily chromatic harmonic sequences, which now crowd to the forefront. After the first section is repeated with variations ( = A' of the overall structure: A-B-A'-C), the text steers from "den Weisern, die auf Strassen stehen" [the signs that stand on streets] to the one sign "der dem Wanderer vor dem Blick steht" [that stands before the traveler's eyes]. Consequently Schubert immediately guides his composition in the direction suggested at the end of the B section. At the same time, he narrows the way, both literally and figuratively, when he gradually removes the melodic element from the voice part, then affixes the eighth-note chain to a single tone, then forces the piano voice into chromatic lines, and finally suppresses the voice's attempt to assert itself in a melodic cadence one last time (measure 65 ff, 75 ff), so that it merely reaffirms the tonic keynote. Nowhere in the cycle do we find the logic of the concluding sequence as convincing as here. In the final measures, the eighth notes are not so much slowed as ossified into quarter notes. We no longer hear that the piano phrase begins on an upbeat (measure 77, second quarter), or that on the

Example 77

last line the voice part comes in one quarter beat later than the piano, rises above the upper piano voice again in measure 79 ("keiner"), but seems tied to the instrumental part in its last two measures, leading inevitably downward—into the depths that we perceive as metaphor for the grave.

In the next song, "Das Wirtshaus" [The inn], the music, following the text, leads to the churchyard. This becomes clear when we picture the following scene: The road leads the traveler past the cemetery, where a burial is in progress. As the traveler stops and watches from a distance, his thoughts mingle with the music of the wind band playing in the funeral procession. (Felix Mendelssohn-Bartholdy has transcribed the song, typically enough, for wind instruments; especially characteristic of wind composition are measures 12–15, for example, where the upper voice of the accompaniment is higher than the melody.) *Here* a person speaks, and, murmuring into space, finds a reflection of self in this event; *over there* musicians play, which, transcending the personal, reflects the realm of a liturgical event. The liturgical act, the funeral, is linked with music that as processional music is part of the event. With this as background, Thrasybulos Georgiades has shown how Schubert's melody is rooted in the "Kyrie" from the Gregorian *Requiem,* in the processional chant of the requiem mass. Indeed, the entire song is fashioned after this chant, with which Schubert must have been familiar as a youth in Lichtental and in the Vienna *Konvikt:* "The overall form and the individual parts of the 'Kyrie,' the musical gestures, are paraphrased and reinterpreted in 'Das Wirtshaus.'"[110]

Here, I suggest, is the key to a question that has occupied musicians and listeners for ages: How can a song based on this human situation be so calm? It is the only one in the cycle with the tempo mark "Sehr langsam" [very slowly]. What is it that lends such solemnity to this composition? It is a liturgical style, the composition's tie to old liturgical forms, which have not lost their power to this day. A detailed substantiation of this claim would become too involved here, but we will at least cite the reference to the key:

> The F tonality here is not the major we are familiar with. It reflects that which is composed, dispassionate, serene, at ease, peaceable, even consecrated. It is the embodiment of something that did not become possible only with the development of the harmonic major in about the 17th century. We find works in F with a similar style even earlier: For example Palestrina's *Improperia* for Good Friday. We also encounter this type of F tonality in monophonic music. For instance, the air of composure and solemnity that we note in the instrumental introduction of 'Das Wirtshaus" is also a characteristic of the stately and solemn "Alleluia" of Holy Week in the Greek Orthodox Church [Example 78]. The same style

Example 78

is found in a Gregorian chant in F, the "Kyrie" from the Mass for the Dead. (Another musical setting by Schubert with a similar touch is the opening song "Wohin soll ich mich wenden" [Whither shall I turn] in F major from the Songs for the *German Mass,* D 872, 1.) Is the conception of a song like "Das Wirtshaus" based on concrete knowledge and experience? Or is it the result of a latent tradition, an underground stream, so to speak? The association of the unusual F scale in "Das Wirtshaus" with the motion of a funeral procession now directs our attention to this "Kyrie" from the Gregorian *Requiem.* For the style of the funeral procession litany has left its imprint on this song."[111]

It has been said that "Mut" [Courage] is unique and hence isolated in the chain of songs whose boundless grief exposes this defiant challenge as false, and therefore no connection, not even a transition, is attempted.[112] Well, if the cycle lacks unity, as has also been claimed,[113] a unity that can be demonstrated in musical connections and transitions, then we might accept such an assertion. On the other hand, if we believe that Schubert's *Winterreise* has recognizable musical coherence, even though it does not manifest itself in motifs or the like, then the position of "Mut" must also be accounted for.

Of central importance in the cemetery episode, "Das Wirtshaus," is the tension between the traveler's standing off to the side and his longing to be included in the scene being enacted before his eyes, the duality of his feeling drawn to the scene and being turned away by the "unbarmherz'ge Schenke" [unmerciful inn]. Tension and duality are brought to bear in Schubert's composition through an agreement of vocal and instrumental parts in the simple song setting and by the independence of the "accompaniment" in the "wind music," which not only serves as introduction and closing but also separates and links the stanzas and lines of the voice part with "interludes." Unity is established only in the overall "tone," by which all the musical elements work together: key, melodics, harmonics, simple rhythmics, lyrical structure, etc. This tone results from the tie with old familiar musical forms, and vice versa: it seems to unite the "I" of the song, who speaks in text and music, and the listener on the common ground of a tradition. Here at the churchyard, the traveler, who wants to bear his fate alone and therefore seeks solitude, becomes conscious of this tie to community and to doing what is traditional. It is this consciousness that makes him storm onward and sing rebelliously out of a sense of defiance: "will kein Gott auf Erden sein, sind wir selber Götter!" [if there is no God on earth, then we ourselves are gods!]

With "Mut"—as once before, in "Im Dorfe"—the traveler tears himself away from what his heart depends on, whereof it speaks, what his ears want to hear. He strides forth in order to escape: "Mut," like "Der stürmische Morgen," is a walking song with which one can match step.[114] He sings in order to drown out[115] "what his heart bemoans in his bosom".

"Mut" is clearly a song which belongs in the cycle. But the traveler also sings in order to detach himself from what lies behind him: "Mut" is no simple, "ordinary" song. The first melody line of three measures is not constructed in the way it is solely to achieve a particular text declamation. The way the melody line makes a bounding start, only to be pulled down by a kind of rhythmic counterweight at the end, is anything but lyrical (Example 79). Behind this musical form is the compositional technique of Viennese classic instrumental music—and with it the com-

Example 79

poser's intention to create musical realities that go beyond what is generally designated as "musical expression" and held to be the only purpose of composition. "Mut" does not *give expression to* the rebellion by setting it to music, to intensify and clarify what is expressed in the text. *As music*, "Mut" actually *is* the rebellion of the person in Schubert's song cycle, in whose destiny we participate, so that we surrender our detachment from the work of art and feel ourselves to be one with him, though only listeners.[116]

Musically real in the same sense as the rebellion in "Mut" is the end, the final doom, in "Die Nebensonnen" [Rival suns]. The devices Schubert uses here derive from another realm of musical possibility, yet the actual effect is due again to the blending of a primarily instrumental element into the song. The basic two-measure rhythmic structure (Example 80) seems like that of a carefully measured

Example 80

walking dance, serious and slow. One can envision the last act of a tragedy concluding with a grand exit to the instrumental accompaniment of such a dance, with the motion stylized to the utmost. First of all, our rhythm is in many respects so complicated that it produces a stylized motion rather than a natural, even flow. This is determined above all by the following characteristics. First we note that the two-measure phrase ends on the second beat of the measure, as in a sarabande. Then too, the phrase of this slow dance rhythm begins with an upbeat, but lacks it internally. That is, the eighth note before the first measure has a different function and meaning from the one before the second measure—the latter only *seems* to correspond exactly. The first main beat is prepared for by an eighth-note pickup, but not the second, because the "middle" eighth note is expressly bound to the preceding dotted quarter by a slur. So this rhythm is to be understood as a complex unit of two measures, not as a coupling of two identical parts—that is, not as noted in the first but as in the second half of Example 81. This interpretation is con-

Example 81

firmed not only in the introduction, but also in the interlude (measures 14–15) and the closing (minus the last measure). Here, in addition to the slur, Schubert shifts the accentuation, so that the dotted quarter seems welded to the eighth note in a rhythmic gesture (Example 82). He thereby prevents the reinterpretation of the "middle" eighth note as a pickup to the second measure—otherwise the complex

Example 82

"rhythmic unit of two measures" would degenerate into a compound "rhythm of two measures" with a banal effect. Meanwhile, in spite of, or because of, its complexity, the rhythmic structure we have described is unstable and in danger of collapsing at any cadence. The fascinating impression of mid-air suspension that we get in the introduction and at the beginning of each new four-measure group in this rhythm can also be attributed to the subdivision of the downbeat and the lingering of the unstressed beat two of the measure, to the harmonic progression tonic → dominant *within* the first beat, and not least of all to the fact that in each case the upper voice falls only one step and then levels off (Example 83). The

Example 83

moment something of this is given up, when the harmony progresses from the first to the second quarter beat of the measure (instead of within the first), this time from the dominant to the tonic, and the melody descends a third to the tonic keynote (Example 84), at that moment, what seemed to hover before seems to fall

Example 84

now; the cadence manages to pull the "middle" eighth note of the first two-measure phrase to itself, thereby setting off as a repeat cadence a part that was previously a component of a closed unit (Example 85).

Example 85

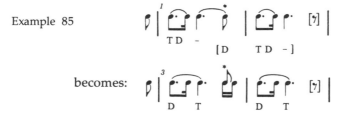

becomes:

All this is laid out in the piano introduction and occurs repeatedly in the course of the song; but only in the closing is it conclusive, played once and for all (Example 86). (The instrumental measure [9] inserted after the first text couplet does not correspond to the last measure of the song, in that the upper voice falls from the fifth to the third degree, while at the end it falls from the third to the tonic.

Example 86

The still-imminent danger of stagnation after this short repetition figure of measure 9 [compare the interlude, measures 10–11, in "Das Wirtshaus"] leads to an immediate continuation with the next couplet and an almost violent forte, which otherwise does not seem completely justified.) In three measures, in the tightest possible musical formulation, we hear the rise and fall of a musical structure; we witness how a stylized striding motion, no longer walking, begins, threatens from the outset to stagnate, and finally comes to a standstill.

Remember that so far we have dealt not with the song but only the compositional unit, which occurs in four measures in the introduction, in three in the closing, and in several repeated variations in the course of the song, and which, with its special structure, strongly influences both the parts and the whole. Consequently the repeat of this particular unit or variation of it is especially significant. While not always noticeable in the first part, we become quite conscious of it in the second, when right after the lines: "Ach, meine Sonnen seid ihr nicht, schaut andern doch ins Angesicht!" [Ah, you are not my suns; go look others in the face!], which are rendered in quasi-recitative (that is, "unformed" relative to the established form), we hear the following: "Ach, neulich hatt'ich auch wohl drei; nun sind hinab die besten zwei," [Ah, recently I had three, but now the best two are gone], in a suddenly lighter major (C major!) and in a high range. Both of these changes surprise us and remind us of the melody in "Gute Nacht," which falls from this same height and changes to major in the last stanza. But the way from that first song to this one was long, and too much has happened for a key change to be able to alter the "tone" as it did there. Instead, a "solemn drama" begins here:

> With majestic simplicity, taking their final leave, the melody and the accompaniment, like the one whom fate has struck, climb down the broad steps of the edifice. First step (measure 20 f) on e'' (third degree), accompaniment in C major. Second step (measure 22), the melody still in C major, descending to the tonic c'', the accompaniment moving to A minor, which is the key reached in a deceptive cadence, that is, picking up the version of the second couplet: measure 22 = measure 12 transposed a minor third higher. Third step (measure 23), the melody does not repeat the tones of the preceding measure, as with the other couplets (thus the connective, rising triplet is also missing), so it does not return to C major as expected (parallel to the A major in measure 13), but again climbs down a third, to a', so that we hear a change to A minor (compare also the text in measure 22 f: "Nun sind hinab die besten zwei" [now the best two are gone]). But at the same time, the accompaniment continues with the a' of the melody through the deceptive cadence in F to the fourth step, which is still lower, and the a' becomes the third of the F scale, which moves on toward the bottom. Fifth step, the piano part makes the descent

from a to g-sharp after picking up the cadence of the melody once again (c''-b'-a'': c'-b-a, and then the g-sharp), and on beat one the bass has already reached E. Last step, the upper piano voice, reminiscent of the somber, hollow sound of a bass clarinet, takes the significant last step to e (by way of a and d) where the song reaches the ground, the bottom that cannot be penetrated further. The controlled progression in these six measures (20–25) forms one motion, one descent. It does not end on beat two of the measure like the other phrases, but rather on beat one (measure 25), creating a deep rift.

After this musical "naming" of the grief, regarded as a physical-spatial occurrence, the last text couplet begins. A verbal expression that proceeds relentlessly without looking back. ...[117] "Die Nebensonnen" is set to music as the closing song of *Winterreise.*[118]

In light of this view, a connection one can't help but notice, the connection to 'Das Wirtshaus," sets us to thinking. Wasn't that song, in terms of the composition, also to be understood as a "final word?" Aside from the text "nun weiter denn, nur weiter" [well onward then, onward . . .], could the cycle not end with that closing, which for the first and only time has the cadence beginning on the downbeat of the measure, thus concluding the song?

"Das Wirtshaus" and 'Die Nebensonnen" are closely related in their simplicity, despite the differentiated structures; in their bearing, far from melancholy, yet deeply sorrowful; and in the fact that they both seem to bring something to a close. But why the double ending, and why the rebellion of "Mut" in between? As has already been indicated, Schubert, like Wilhelm Müller, obviously wanted to avoid ending with an allusion to tradition and community. Alone, in the solitude that he has sought and found, the traveler, the person, should sink like the setting sun: 'Im Dunkeln wird mir wohler sein" [I will be better off in the dark].

Now that we have interpreted and understood Schubert's song in this way, we have made the very discovery of which Arnold Schönberg speaks in the essay quoted earlier (cf. p. 44). "Without knowing the poem," we have "grasped the content . . . , the real content" of Schubert's song, "perhaps even more fully than if [we] had clung to the surface of the actual semantic concepts." The text, with which we have not been concerned up to now, is indeed obscure in its meaning. It speaks of three suns twice, and the first ones cannot be the same as the last ones. As certainly as the last ones refer to the eyes of the girl and the sun in the sky:

> "Ach neulich hatt' ich auch wohl drei:
> nun sind hinab die besten zwei.
> Ging' nur die dritt' erst hinterdrein!
> Im Dunkeln wird mir wohler sein."

> [Ah, recently I had three,
> but now the best two are gone.
> If only the third would follow!
> I will be better off in the dark.]

just as certainly do text lines three and five refer to other suns: "und sie auch standen da so stier . .." [and they stood there so blankly] and: "Ach *meine* Sonnen seid ihr nicht . . ." [Ah, you are not *my* suns . . .]. But then, what were the first three suns which the traveler saw in the sky?

The only sensible explanation, it seems to me, is this: When a person with tears in his eyes turns his head at a certain angle to the sun with an unfocused glance, then in addition to the sun itself, he can see its reflections on and under the tears, and there is something strangely unreal and glassy about this phenomenon. It was obviously familiar to the readers of lyric poetry in Schubert's and Müller's day, in which much was written about tears and people seemed to be moved to tears more easily than in our time.

To use E. T. A. Hoffmann's expression quoted on p. 37 and elaborated upon as it applied to Schubert's composition: It seems indeed that Schubert's "melody [= composition] shines forth" from a "focal point," and that "these sounds in turn . . . symbolize all the various elements of inner feeling contained in the poet's song." But for Schubert it is not primarily the ideas of the poet, which are associated here with the vision of the rival suns, with sorrow and tears, that are to be understood as in a focal point; rather it is his own *musical* ideas, which proceed from the sinking sun to the sinking of the traveler of *Winterrreise* to the motion reminiscent of a grand exit in a final scene. Actually, "the real content" of Schubert's song is "inspired by the song's [the poet's] deep meaning" in the ground of creative consciousness; but because it is musically autonomous, it is also understandable to the listener who is less familiar with the content of the poem— musically autonomous within the song genre, of course, which still has the task of conveying the text.

The cycle is at its end, the play is over, the curtain has fallen. Like the fool in Shakespeare's *Twelfth Night,* who at the end, or more correctly *after* the end, steps onto the ramp or leans on the stage railing and sings:

"For the rain it raineth every day,"

Müller's and Schubert's traveler, at the end of his winter journey (here too, *after* the end is more accurate), sings "Der Leiermann" [The organ-grinder], the embodiment of timeless events, removed from human beings and the human condition. Accordingly, the elements of musical composition here remain unformed in time. The song rolls on, sadly monotonous, like a piece of instrumental folk music on a hurdy-gurdy.[119] The basis for the harmony and tonality is the fifth of the drones, which is sustained from the first to the last measure, that is, a sound instead of a key; there is a complete lack of any key-defining cadence. Only at the end do we sense a trace of the "I," when on the last question, "Willst zu meinen Liedern deine Leier drehn?" [Do you want to accompany my songs on your organ?], the span of an octave is overstepped in the melody for the first and only time, and the instrumental part ventures two accompanying chords, with the result that the four instrumental closing measures (new in this arrangement) seem to tremble as they recede. The basis for the rhythm and meter is a grinding triple meter, which is rendered mechanically—that is, independent of the person and without a structured rhythm.

However, the end of the song is worked out in finest rhythmic detail, and in such a way that once again we encounter direct human speech. For the last text lines, "Wunderlicher Alter . . ." [Strange old man . . .], Schubert falls back on the device of "recitative" declamation, but interweaves it with the inhumanly monotonous triple meter of the instrumental part. Above the triple meter, he forms declamation units that seem so free, as if actually spoken, because on one hand they are bound in a duple meter and thus stand out from the triple meter of the piano, but on the other hand they clash with this duple meter. (The two eighth notes of "Liedern" are shortened quarter notes of a whole measure corresponding to that of the text "Alter," and it is from these that the rhythmic order of the 2/4 measures: 4 + 4, detectable beneath the surface, seem to be established.)

Example 87

After Schubert has demonstrated the blending of accompaniment and melody in the majestic song 'Die Nebensonnen," we come to 'Der Leiermann," which establishes melody and accompaniment epigrammatically as two different, equally tangible realities: the instrumental playing here on the street corner, where the organ-grinder stands and cranks his hurdy-gurdy; the singer there watching him and speaking about it in his song.[120]

Some have tried to see in 'Der Leiermann," this final song of *Winterreise*, something of an ironic Schubert self-portrait. There could be no objection to this concept, it seems to me, if at the same time it led to the realization that in a way Schubert marks the end of western music here, as the thousand-year history of polyphonic composition, from the 9th to the 19th century, has defined it. In 'Die Nebensonnen," but also in other songs, such as "Halt!", the musical structure has become fragile and brittle; in 'Der Leiermann", but also in other songs, such as 'Die Stadt," D 957, No. 11, 1828, tonality as foundation of music is ignored—a new age of music has dawned.

That is why there is no pathway from Schubert to the perfection of a genre or to art that glorifies the soil (*Schollenkunst*), but only one to deepest depravity and another to the rarely discussed reality of a free music of the transformed man and a transformed culture. In irregular strokes, like a seismograph, Schubert's music has recorded the message of the qualitative transformation of man. The proper response is weeping: weeping over the utter sentimentality of "Dreimäderlhaus" [a once popular musical about Schubert—ed.] being no different from weeping because of an emotional upheaval that shakes one to the core. With Schubert's music, tears gush from our eyes without consulting our soul—so directly and immediately does it penetrate us. We cry without knowing why, because we have not yet reached the state that the music intimates. Though we cannot read it like a book, the music holds before our failing, overflowing eyes the symbols of eventual reconciliation.[121]

# VI. The Texts of Wilhelm Müller's Two Cycles

Sieben und siebzig
Gedichte
aus den hinterlassenen Papieren
eines
reisenden Waldhornisten.
Herausgegeben
von
W i l h e l m   M ü l l e r
Deßau 1821
Bei Christian Georg Ackermann[122]

———

D i e   s c h ö n e   M ü l l e r i n
(Im Winter zu lesen.)

---

Der Dichter, als Prolog (not composed)

Ich lad euch, schöne Damen, kluge Herrn,
Und die ihr hört und schaut was Gutes gern,
Zu einem funkelnagelneuen Spiel
Im allerfunkelnagelneusten Stil;
Schlicht ausgedrechselt, kunstlos zugestutzt,
Mit edler deutscher Roheit aufgeputzt,
Keck wie ein Bursch im Stadtsoldatenstrauß,
Dazu wohl auch ein wenig fromm für's Haus.
Das mag genug mir zur Empfehlung sein,
Wem die behagt, der trete nur herein.
Erhoffe, weil es grad ist Winterzeit,
Tut euch ein Stündlein hier im Grün nicht leid;
Denn wißt es nur, daß heut in meinem Lied
Der Lenz mit allen seinen Blumen blüht.
Im Freien geht die freie Handlung vor,
In reiner Luft, weit aus der Städte Tor,
Durch Wald und Feld, in Gründen, auf den Höhn;
Und was nur in vier Wänden darf geschehn,
Das schaut ihr halb durch's offne Fenster an,
So ist der Kunst und euch genug getan.

Doch wenn ihr nach des Spiels Personen fragt,
So kann ich euch, den Musen sei's geklagt,
Nur e i n e präsentieren recht und echt,
Das ist ein junger blonder Müllersknecht.
Denn, ob der Bach zuletzt ein Wort auch spricht,
So wird ein Bach deshalb Person noch nicht.
Drum nehmt nur heut das Monodram vorlieb:
Wer mehr gibt, als er hat, der heißt ein Dieb.

Auch ist dafür die Szene reich geziert,
Mit grünem Sammet unten tapeziert,
Der ist mit tausend Blumen bunt gestickt,
Und Weg und Steg darüber ausgedrückt.
Die Sonne strahlt von oben hell herein
Und bricht in Tau und Tränen ihren Schein,
Und auch der Mond blickt aus der Wolken Flor
Schwermütig, wie's die Mode will, hervor.
Den Hintergrund umkränzt ein hoher Wald,
Der Hund schlägt an, das muntre Jagdhorn schallt;
Hier stürzt vom schroffen Fels der junge Quell
Und fließt im Tal als Bächlein silberhell;
Das Mühlrad braust, die Werke klappern drein,
Man hört die Vöglein kaum im nahen Hain.
Drum denkt, wenn euch zu rauh manch Liedchen klingt,
Daß das Lokal es also mit sich bringt.
Doch, was das Schönste in der Mühle ist,
Das wird euch sagen mein Monodramist;
Verriet' ich's euch, verdürb' ich ihm das Spiel:
Gehabt euch wohl und amüsiert euch viel!


## 1. Wanderschaft

### [Das Wandern]

Das Wandern ist des Müllers Lust,
    Das Wandern!
Das muß ein schlechter Müller sein,
Dem niemals fiel das Wandern ein,
    Das Wandern.

Vom Wasser haben wir's gelernt,
    Vom Wasser!
Das hat nicht Rast bei Tag und Nacht,
Ist stets auf Wanderschaft bedacht,
    Das Wasser.

Das sehn wir auch den Rädern ab,
    Den Rädern!
Die gar nicht gerne stille stehn,
Die sich mein Tag nicht müde drehn [gehn],
    Die Räder.

Die Steine selbst, so schwer sie sind,
    Die Steine!
Sie tanzen mit den muntern Reihn
Und wollen gar noch schneller sein,
    Die Steine.

O Wandern, Wandern, meine Lust,
    O Wandern!
Herr Meister und Frau Meisterin,
Laßt mich in Frieden weiter ziehn
    Und wandern.

## 2. Wohin?

Ich hört' ein Bächlein rauschen
Wohl aus dem Felsenquell,
Hinab zum Tale rauschen
So frisch und wunderhell.

Ich weiß nicht, wie mir wurde,
Nicht, wer den Rat mir gab,
Ich mußte auch hinunter
Mit meinem Wanderstab.

Hinunter und immer weiter,
Und immer dem Bache nach,
Und immer heller rauschte[123]
Und immer heller der Bach.

Ist das denn meine Straße?
O Bächlein, sprich, wohin?
Du hast mit deinem Rauschen
Mir ganz berauscht den Sinn.

Was sag ich denn von [vom] Rauschen?
Das kann kein Rauschen sein:
Es singen wohl die Nixen
Tief unten ihren Reihn.

Laß singen, Gesell, laß rauschen,
Und wandre fröhlich nach!
Es gehn ja Mühlenräder
In jedem klaren Bach.

## 3. Halt!

Eine Mühle seh ich blicken [blinken]
Aus den Erlen heraus,
Durch Rauschen und Singen
Bricht Rädergebraus.

Ei willkommen, ei willkommen,
Süßer Mühlengesang!
Und das Haus, wie so traulich!
Und die Fenster, wie blank!

Und die Sonne, wie helle
Vom Himmel sie scheint!
Ei, Bächlein, liebes Bächlein,
War es also gemeint?

## 4. Danksagung an den Bach

War es also gemeint,
Mein rauschender Freund,
Dein Singen, dein Klingen,
War es also gemeint?

Zur Müllerin hin!
So lautet der Sinn,
Gelt, hab ich's verstanden?
Zur Müllerin hin!

Hat s i e dich geschickt?
Oder hast mich berückt?
Das möcht ich noch wissen,
Ob s i e dich geschickt.

Nun wie's auch mag sein,
Ich gebe mich drein:
Was ich such, hab ich funden,
Wie's immer mag sein.

Nach Arbeit ich frug,
Nun hab ich genug,
Für die Hände, für's Herze
Vollauf genug!

## 5. Am Feierabend

Hätt' ich tausend
Arme zu rühren!
Könnt' ich brausend
Die Räder führen!
Könnt' ich wehen
Durch alle Haine,
Könnt' ich drehen
Alle Steine!
Daß die schöne Müllerin
Merkte meinen treuen Sinn!

Ach, wie ist mein Arm so schwach!
Was ich hebe, was ich trage,
Was ich schneide, was ich schlage,
Jeder Knappe tut es [mir's] nach.
Und da sitz ich in der großen Runde,
In der stillen kühlen Feierstunde,
Und der Meister spricht [sagt] zu allen:
Euer Werk hat mir gefallen;
Und das liebe Mädchen sagt
Allen eine gute Nacht.

## 6. Der Neugierige

Ich frage keine Blume,
Ich frage keinen Stern,
Sie können mir alle nicht sagen,
Was ich erführ' so gern.

Ich bin ja auch kein Gärtner,
Die Sterne stehn zu hoch;
Mein Bächlein will ich fragen,
Ob mich mein Herz belog.

O Bächlein meiner Liebe,
Wie bist du heut so stumm!
Will ja nur eines wissen,
E i n Wörtchen um und um.

Ja, heißt das eine Wörtchen,
Das andre heißet Nein,
Die beiden Wörtchen schließen
Die ganze Welt mir ein.

O Bächlein meiner Liebe,
Was bist du wunderlich!
Will's ja nicht weitersagen,
Sag, Bächlein, liebt sie mich?

## Das Mühlenleben (not composed)

Seh ich sie am Bache sitzen,
Wenn sie Fliegennetze strickt,
Oder sonntags für die Fenster
Frische Wiesenblumen pflückt;

Seh ich sie zum Garten wandeln,
Mit dem Körbchen in der Hand,
Nach den ersten Beeren spähen
An der grünen Dornenwand:

Dann wird mir die Mühle enge,
Alle Mauern ziehn sich ein,
Und ich möchte flugs ein Fischer,
Jäger oder Gärtner sein.

Und der Steine lustig Pfeifen,
Und des Wasserrads Gebraus,
Und der Werke emsig Klappern,
's jagt mich schier zum Tor hinaus.

Aber wenn in guter Stunde
Plaudernd sie zum Burschen tritt,
Und als kluges Kind des Hauses
Seitwärts nach dem Rechten sieht;

Und verständig lobt den Einen,
Daß der Andre merken mag,
Wie er's besser treiben solle,
Geht er ihrem Danke nach –

Keiner fühlt sich recht getroffen,
Und doch schießt sie nimmer fehl,
Jeder muß von Schonung sagen,
Und doch hat sie keinen Hehl.

Keiner wünscht, sie möchte gehen
Steht sie auch als Herrin da,
Und fast wie das Auge Gottes
Ist ihr Bild uns immer nah.

Und wo wer zum Fallen strauchelt,
Hält es ihn im Sinken schier,
Und wo ich die Hände falte,
Kniet es still zur Seite mir –

Ei, da mag das Mühlenleben
Wohl des Liedes würdig sein,
Und die Räder, Stein' und Stampfen
Stimmen als Begleitung ein.

Alles geht in schönem Tanze
Auf und ab, und ein und aus:
Gott gesegne mir das Handwerk
Und des guten Meisters Haus!

## 7. Ungeduld

Ich schnitt' es gern in alle Rinden ein,
Ich grüb' es gern in jeden Kieselstein,
Ich möcht es sä'n auf jedes frische Beet
Mit Kressensamen, der es schnell verrät,
Auf jeden weißen Zettel möcht ich's
         schreiben:
Dein ist mein Herz, und soll es ewig bleiben.

Ich möcht mir ziehen einen jungen Star,
Bis daß er spräch' die Worte rein und
         klar,
Bis er sie spräch' mit meines Mundes Klang,
Mit meines Herzens vollem, heißen Drang;
Dann säng' er hell durch ihre
         Fensterscheiben:
Dein ist mein Herz, und soll es ewig bleiben.

Den Morgenwinden möcht ich's hauchen ein,
Ich möcht es säuseln durch den regen Hain;
O, leuchtet' es aus jedem Blumenstern!
Trüg' es der Duft zu ihr von nah und fern!
Ihr Wogen, könnt ihr nichts als Räder
         treiben?
Dein ist mein Herz, und soll es ewig bleiben.

Ich meint', es müßt' in meinen Augen stehn,
Auf meinen Wangen müßt' man's brennen
         sehn,
Zu lesen wär's auf meinem stummen Mund,
Ein jeder Atemzug gäb's laut ihr kund;
Und sie merkt nichts von all dem bangen
         Treiben:
Dein ist mein Herz, und soll es ewig bleiben!

## 8. Morgengruß

Guten Morgen, schöne Müllerin!
Wo steckst du gleich das Köpfchen hin,
Als wär' dir was geschehen?
Verdrießt dich denn mein Gruß so schwer?
Verstört dich denn mein Blick so sehr?
So muß ich wieder gehen.

O laß mich nur von ferne stehn,
Nach deinem lieben Fenster sehn,
Von ferne, ganz von ferne!
Du blondes Köpfchen, komm hervor!
Hervor aus eurem runden Tor,
Ihr blauen Morgensterne!

Ihr schlummertrunknen Äugelein,
Ihr taubetrübten Blümelein,
Was scheuet ihr die Sonne?
Hat es die Nacht so gut gemeint,
Daß ihr euch schließt und bückt und weint,
Nach ihrer stillen Wonne?

Nun schüttelt ab der Träume Flor,
Und hebt euch frisch und frei empor
In Gottes hellen Morgen!
Die Lerche wirbelt in der Luft,
Und aus dem tiefen Herzen ruft
Die Liebe Leid und Sorgen.

## 9. Des Müllers Blumen

Am Bach viel kleine Blumen stehn,
Aus hellen blauen Augen sehn;
Der Bach der ist des Müllers Freund,
Und hellblau Liebchens Auge scheint,
Drum sind es meine Blumen.

Dicht unter ihrem Fensterlein
Da will ich pflanzen die Blumen ein,
Da ruft ihr zu, wenn alles schweigt,
Wenn sich ihr Haupt zum Schlummer neigt,
Ihr wißt ja, was ich meine.

Und wenn sie tät die Äuglein zu,
Und schläft in süßer, süßer Ruh,
Dann lispelt als ein Traumgesicht
Ihr zu: Vergiß, vergiß mein nicht!
Das ist es, was ich meine.

Und schließt sie früh die Laden auf,
Dann schaut mit Liebesblick hinauf:
Der Tau in euren Äugelein,
Das sollen meine Tränen sein,
Die will ich auf euch weinen.

## 10. Tränenregen

Wir saßen so traulich beisammen
Im kühlen Erlendach,
Wir schauten so traulich zusammen
Hinab in den rieselnden Bach.

Der Mond war auch gekommen,
Die Sternlein hinterdrein,
Und schauten so traulich zusammen
In den silbernen Spiegel hinein.

Ich sah nach keinem Monde,
Nach keinem Sternenschein,
Ich schaute nach ihrem Bilde,
Nach ihren Augen [ihrem Auge] allein.

Und sahe sie nicken und blicken
Herauf aus dem seligen Bach,
Die Blümlein am Ufer, die blauen,
Sie nickten und blickten ihr nach.

Und in den Bach versunken
Der ganze Himmel schien,
Und wollte mich mit hinunter
In seine Tiefe ziehn.

Und über den Wolken und Sternen
Da rieselte munter der Bach,
Und rief mit Singen und Klingen:
Geselle, Geselle, mir nach.

Da gingen die Augen mir über,
Da ward es im Spiegel so kraus;
Sie sprach: Es kommt ein Regen,
Ade, ich geh nach Haus.

## 11. Mein!

Bächlein, laß dein Rauschen sein!
Räder, stellt eu'r Brausen ein!
All ihr muntern Waldvögelein,
Groß und klein,
Endet eure Melodein!
Durch den Hain
Aus und ein
Schalle heut e i n Reim allein:

Die geliebte Müllerin ist  m e i n !
M e i n !
Frühling, sind das alle deine Blümelein?
Sonne, hast du keinen hellern Schein?
Ach, so muß ich ganz allein,
Mit dem seligen Worte  m e i n ,
Unverstanden in der weiten Schöpfung sein!

## 12. Pause

Meine Laute hab ich gehängt an die Wand,
Hab sie umschlungen mit einem grünen Band –
Ich kann nicht mehr singen, mein Herz ist zu voll,
Weiß nicht, wie ich's in Reime zwingen soll.
Meiner Sehnsucht allerheißesten Schmerz
Durft' ich aushauchen in Liederscherz [*Liederschmerz*],
Und wie ich klagte so süß und fein,
Meint' [*glaubt'*] ich doch, mein Leiden wär' nicht klein:
Ei, wie groß ist wohl meines Glückes Last,
Daß kein Klang auf Erden es in sich faßt?

Nun, liebe Laute, ruh an dem Nagel hier!
Und weht ein Lüftchen über die Saiten dir,
Und streift eine Biene mit ihren Flügeln dich,
Da wird mir [*mir so*] bange und es durchschauert mich.
Warum ließ ich das Band auch hängen so lang?
Oft fliegt's um die Saiten mit seufzendem Klang.
Ist es der Nachklang meiner Liebespein?
Soll es das Vorspiel neuer Lieder sein?

## 13. Mit dem grünen Lautenbande

»Schad um das schöne grüne Band,
Daß es verbleicht hier an der Wand,
Ich hab das Grün so gern!«
So sprachst du, Liebchen, heut zu mir;
Gleich knüpf ich's ab und send es dir:
Nun hab das Grüne gern!

Ist auch dein ganzer Liebster weiß,
Soll Grün doch haben seinen Preis,
Und ich auch hob es gern.
Weil unsre Lieb ist immer grün,
Weil grün der Hoffnung Fernen blühn,
Drum haben wir es gern.

Nun schlinge in die Locken dein
Das grüne Band gefällig ein,
Du hast ja's Grün so gern.
Dann weiß ich, wo die Hoffnung wohnt
[*grünt*],
Dann weiß ich, wo die Liebe thront,
Dann hab ich's Grün erst gern.

## 14. Der Jäger

Was sucht denn der Jäger am Mühlbach hier? [*!*]
Bleib, trotziger Jäger, in deinem Revier!
Hier gibt es kein Wild zu jagen für dich,
Hier wohnt nur ein Rehlein, ein zahmes, für mich.
Und willst du das zärtliche Rehlein sehn,
So laß deine Büchsen im Walde stehn,
Und laß deine klaffenden Hunde zu Haus,
Und laß auf dem Horne den Saus und Braus,
Und schere vom Kinne das struppige Haar,
Sonst scheut sich im Garten das Rehlein, fürwahr.

Doch besser, du bliebest im Walde dazu,
Und ließest die Mühlen und Müller in Ruh.
Was taugen die Fischlein im grünen Gezweig?
Was will denn das Eichhorn im bläulichen Teich?
Drum bleibe, du trotziger Jäger, im Hain,
Und laß mich mit meinen drei Rädern allein;
Und willst meinem Schätzchen dich machen beliebt,
So wisse, mein Freund, was ihr Herzchen betrübt:
Die Eber, die kommen zu Nacht aus dem Hain
Und brechen in ihren Kohlgarten ein,
Und treten und wühlen herum in dem Feld:
Die Eber, die schieße [*schieß*], du Jägerheld!


## 15. Eifersucht und Stolz

Wohin so schnell, so kraus, so wild [*so kraus und wild*], mein lieber Bach?
Eilst du voll Zorn dem frechen Bruder Jäger nach?
Kehr um, kehr um, und schilt erst deine Müllerin,
Für ihren leichten, losen, kleinen Flattersinn.
Sahst du sie gestern abend nicht am Tore stehn,
Mit langem Halse nach der großen Straße sehn?
Wenn von dem Fang der Jäger lustig zieht nach Haus,
Da steckt kein sittsam Kind den Kopf zum Fenster 'naus.
Geh, Bächlein, hin und sag ihr das, doch sag ihr nicht,
Hörst du, kein Wort, von meinem traurigen Gesicht;
Sag ihr: Er schnitzt bei mir sich eine Pfeif aus Rohr,
Und bläst den Kindern schöne Tänz und Lieder vor.
[*Sag ihr's, sag ihr's!*]


### Erster Schmerz, letzter Scherz (not composed)

Nun sitz am Bache nieder
Mit deinem hellen Rohr,
Und blas den lieben Kindern
Die schönen Lieder vor.

Die Lust ist ja verrauschet,
Das Leid hat immer Zeit:
Nun singe neue Lieder
Von alter Seligkeit.

Noch blühn die alten Blumen,
Noch rauscht der alte Bach,
Es scheint die liebe Sonne
Noch wie am ersten Tag.

Die Fensterscheiben glänzen
Im klaren Morgenschein,
Und hinter den Fensterscheiben
Da sitzt die Liebste mein.

Ein Jäger, ein grüner Jäger,
Der liegt in ihrem Arm –
Ei, Bach, wie lustig du rauschest,
Ei, Sonne, wie scheinst du so warm!

Ich will einen Strauß dir pflücken,
Herzliebste, von buntem Klee,
Den sollst du mir stellen an's Fenster,
Damit ich den Jäger nicht seh.

Ich will mit Rosenblättern
Den Mühlensteg bestreun:
Der Steg hat mich getragen
Zu dir, Herzliebste mein!

Und wenn der stolze Jäger
Ein Blättchen mir zertritt,
Dann stürz, o Steg, zusammen
Und nimm den Grünen mit!

Und trag ihn auf dem Rücken
In's Meer, mit gutem Wind,
Nach einer fernen Insel,
Wo keine Mädchen sind.

Herzliebste, das Vergessen,
Es kommt dir ja nicht schwer –
Willst du den Müller wieder?
Vergißt dich nimmermehr.

### 16. Die liebe Farbe

In Grün will ich mich kleiden,
In grüne Tränenweiden,
Mein Schatz hat's Grün so gern.
Will suchen einen Zypressenhain,
Eine Heide von grünem [*grünen*] Rosmarein,
Mein Schatz hat's Grün so gern.

Wohlauf zum fröhlichen Jagen!
Wohlauf durch Heid und Hagen!
Mein Schatz hat's Jagen so gern.
Das Wild, das ich jage, das ist der Tod,
Die Heide, die heiß ich die Liebesnot,
Mein Schatz hat's Jagen so gern.

Grabt mir ein Grab im Wasen,
Deckt mich mit grünem Rasen,
Mein Schatz hat's Grün so gern.
Kein Kreuzlein schwarz, kein Blümlein bunt,
Grün, alles grün so rings und rund
                    [*so ringsumher*]!
Mein Schatz hat's Grün so gern.

### 17. Die böse Farbe

Ich möchte ziehn in die Welt hinaus,
Hinaus in die weite Welt,
Wenn's nur so grün, so grün nicht wär'
Da draußen in Wald und Feld!

Ich möchte die grünen Blätter all
Pflücken von jedem Zweig,
Ich möchte die grünen Gräser all
Weinen ganz totenbleich.

Ach Grün, du böse Farbe du,
Was siehst mich immer an,
So stolz, so keck, so schadenfroh,
Mich armen weißen Mann?

Ich möchte liegen vor ihrer Tür,
In Sturm und Regen und Schnee,
Und singen ganz leise bei Tag und Nacht
Das eine Wörtchen Ade!

Horch, wenn im Wald ein Jagdhorn ruft
                    [*schallt*],
Da klingt ihr Fensterlein,
Und schaut sie auch nach mir nicht aus,
Darf ich doch schauen hinein.

O binde von der Stirn dir ab
Das grüne, grüne Band,
Ade, ade! und reiche mir
Zum Abschied deine Hand!

### Blümlein Vergissmein (not composed)

Was treibt mich jeden Morgen
So tief in's Holz hinein?
Was frommt mir, mich zu bergen
Im unbelauschten Hain?

Es blüht auf allen Fluren
Blümlein V e r g i ß m e i n n i c h t,
Es schaut vom heitern Himmel
Herab in blauem Licht.

Und soll ich's niedertreten,
Bebt mir der Fuß zurück,
Es fleht aus jedem Kelche
Ein wohlbekannter Blick.

Weißt du, in welchem Garten
Blümlein V e r g i ß   m e i n   steht?
Das Blümlein muß ich suchen,
Wie auch die Straße geht.

's ist nicht für Mädchenbusen,
So schön sieht es nicht aus:
Schwarz, schwarz ist seine Farbe,
Es paßt in keinen Strauß.

Hat keine grüne Blätter,
Hat keinen Blütenduft,
Es windet sich am Boden
In nächtig dumpfer Luft.

Wächst auch an einem Ufer,
Doch unten fließt kein Bach,
Und willst das Blümlein pflücken,
Dich zieht der Abgrund nach.

Das ist der rechte Garten,
Ein schwarzer, schwarzer Flor:
Darauf magst du dich betten –
Schleuß zu das Gartentor!

## 18. Trockne Blumen

Ihr Blümlein alle,
Die sie mir gab,
Euch soll man legen
Mit mir in's Grab.

Wie seht ihr alle
Mich an so weh,
Als ob ihr wüßtet,
Wie mir gescheh'?

Ihr Blümlein alle,
Wie welk, wie blaß?
Ihr Blümlein alle,
Wovon so naß?

Ach, Tränen machen
Nicht maiengrün,
Machen tote Liebe
Nicht wieder blühn.

Und Lenz wird kommen,
Und Winter wird gehn,
Und Blümlein werden
Im Grase stehn,

Und Blümlein liegen
In meinem Grab,
Die Blümlein alle,
Die sie mir gab. [!]

Und wenn sie wandelt
Am Hügel vorbei,
Und denkt im Herzen:
D e r   meint' es   t r e u !

Dann Blümlein alle,
Heraus, heraus!
Der Mai ist kommen,
Der Winter ist aus.

## 19. Der Müller und der Bach

D e r   M ü l l e r.

Wo ein treues Herze
In Liebe vergeht,
Da welken die Lilien
Auf jedem Beet.

Da muß in die Wolken
Der Vollmond gehn,
Damit seine Tränen
Die Menschen nicht sehn.

Da halten die Englein
Die Augen sich zu,
Und schluchzen und singen
Die Seele zu Ruh.

D e r   B a c h.

Und wenn sich die Liebe
Dem Schmerz entringt,
Ein Sternlein, ein neues,
Am Himmel erblinkt.

Da springen drei Rosen,
Halb rot, [*und*] halb weiß,
Die welken nicht wieder,
Aus Dornenreis.

Und die Engelein schneiden
Die Flügel sich ab,
Und gehn alle Morgen
Zur Erde herab.

D e r   M ü l l e r.

Ach, Bächlein, liebes Bächlein,
Du meinst es so gut:
Ach, Bächlein, aber weißt du
Wie Liebe tut?

Ach, unten, da unten,
Die kühle Ruh!
Ach, Bächlein, liebes Bächlein,
So singe nur zu.

*20. Des Baches Wiegenlied*

Gute Ruh, gute Ruh!
Tu die Augen zu!
Wandrer, du müder, du bist zu Haus.
Die Treu ist hier,
Sollst liegen bei mir,
Bis das Meer will trinken die Bächlein aus.

Will betten dich kühl,
Auf weichem [*weichen*] Pfühl,
In dem blauen kristallenen Kämmerlein.
Heran, heran,
Was wiegen kann,
Woget und wieget den Knaben mir ein!

Wenn ein Jagdhorn schallt
Aus dem grünen Wald,
Will ich sausen und brausen wohl um dich her.
Blickt nicht herein [*hinein*],
Blaue Blümelein!
Ihr macht meinem Schläfer die Träume so schwer.

Hinweg, hinweg,
Von dem Mühlensteg,
Böses Mägdlein [*Mägdelein*], daß ihn dein Schatten nicht weckt!
Wirf mir herein
Dein Tüchlein fein,
Daß ich die Augen ihm halte bedeckt!

Gute Nacht, gute Nacht!
Bis alles wacht,
Schlaf aus deine Freude, schlaf aus dein Leid!
Der Vollmond steigt,
Der Nebel weicht,
Und der Himmel da oben [*droben*], wie ist er so weit!

### Der Dichter, als Epilog (not composed)

Weil gern man schließt mit einer runden Zahl,
Tret ich noch einmal in den vollen Saal,
Als letztes, fünf und zwanzigstes Gedicht,
Als Epilog, der gern das Klügste spricht.
Doch pfuschte mir der Bach in's Handwerk schon
Mit seiner Leichenred' im nassen Ton.
Aus solchem hohlen Wasserorgelschall
Zieht jeder selbst sich besser die Moral;
Ich geb es auf, und lasse diesen Zwist,
Weil Widerspruch nicht meines Amtes ist.

So hab ich denn nichts lieber hier zu tun,
Als euch zum Schluß zu wünschen, wohl zu ruhn.
Wir blasen unsre Sonn und Sternlein aus –
Nun findet euch im Dunkel gut nach Haus,
Und wollt ihr träumen einen leichten Traum,
So denkt an Mühlenrad und Wasserschaum,
Wenn ihr die Augen schließt zu langer Nacht,
Bis es den Kopf zum Drehen euch gebracht.
Und wer ein Mädchen führt an seiner Hand,
Der bitte scheidend um ein Liebespfand,
Und gibt sie heute, was sie oft versagt,
So sei des treuen Müllers treu gedacht
Bei jedem Händedruck, bei jedem Kuß,
Bei jedem heißen Herzensüberfluß:
Geb' ihm die Liebe für sein kurzes Leid
In eurem Busen lange Seligkeit!

U r a n i a

Taschenbuch
auf
das Jahr 1823

Neue Folge, fünfter Jahrgang.

Leipzig, bei F. A. Brockhaus
und
Berlin, bei F. A. Herbig

1823

V.
Wanderlieder
von
W i l h e l m  M ü l l e r

Die Winterreise. In 12 Liedern.[124]

## 1. Gute Nacht!
[*Gute Nacht*]

Fremd bin ich eingezogen,
Fremd zieh ich wieder aus.
Der Mai war mir gewogen
Mit manchem Blumenstrauß:
Das Mädchen sprach von Liebe,
Die Mutter gar von Eh' –
Nun ist die Welt so trübe,
Der Weg gehüllt in Schnee.

Ich kann zu meiner Reisen
Nicht wählen mit der Zeit,
Muß selbst den Weg mir weisen
In dieser Dunkelheit.
Es zieht ein Mondenschatten
Als mein Gefährte mit,
Und auf den weißen Matten
Such ich des Wildes Tritt.

Was soll ich länger weilen,
Daß man mich trieb' hinaus?
Laß irre Hunde heulen
Vor ihres Herren Haus.
Die Liebe liebt das Wandern –
Gott hat sie so gemacht –
Von Einem zu dem Andern –
Fein Liebchen, gute Nacht!

Will dich im Traum nicht stören,
Wär' schad um deine Ruh;
Sollst meinen Tritt nicht hören –
Sacht, sacht, die Türe zu!
Schreib im Vorübergehen
An's Tor dir [:] G u t e  N a c h t,
Damit du mögest sehen,
Ich hab an dich [*An dich hab ich*] gedacht.

## 2. Die Wetterfahne

Der Wind spielt mit der Wetterfahne
Auf meines schönen Liebchens Haus:
Da dacht' ich schon in meinem Wahne,
Sie pfiff' den armen Flüchtling aus.

Er hätt' es ehr [eher] bemerken sollen,
Des Hauses aufgestecktes Schild,
So hätt' er nimmer suchen wollen
Im Haus ein treues Frauenbild.

Der Wind spielt drinnen mit den Herzen,
Wie auf dem Dach, nur nicht so laut.
Was fragen sie nach meinen Schmerzen? –
Ihr Kind ist eine reiche Braut.

## 3. Gefrorene Tränen
### [Gefrorne Tränen]

Gefrorne Tropfen fallen
Von meinen Wangen ab:
Ob es mir denn entgangen,
Daß ich geweinet hab?

Ei Tränen, meine Tränen,
Und seid ihr gar so lau,
Daß ihr erstarrt zu Eise,
Wie kühler Morgentau?

Und dringt doch aus der Quelle
Der Brust so glühend heiß,
Als wolltet ihr zerschmelzen
Des ganzen Winters Eis? [.]

## 4. Erstarrung

Ich such im Schnee vergebens
Nach ihrer Tritte Spur,
Wo sie an meinem Arme
Durchstrich die grüne Flur.

Ich will den Boden küssen,
Durchdringen Eis und Schnee
Mit meinen heißen Tränen,
Bis ich die Erde seh.

Wo find ich eine Blüte,
Wo find ich grünes Gras?
Die Blumen sind erstorben,
Der Rasen sieht so blaß.

Soll denn kein Angedenken
Ich nehmen mit von hier?
Wenn meine Schmerzen schweigen,
Wer sagt mir dann von ihr?

Mein Herz ist wie erfroren [erstorben],
Kalt starrt ihr Bild darin:
Schmilzt je das Herz mir wieder,
Fließt auch das [ihr] Bild dahin.

## 5. Der Lindenbaum

Am Brunnen vor dem Tore,
Da steht ein Lindenbaum:
Ich träumt' in seinem Schatten
So manchen süßen Traum.

Ich schnitt in seine Rinde
So manches liebe Wort;
Es zog in Freud und Leide
Zu ihm mich immer fort.

Ich mußt' auch heute wandern
Vorbei in tiefer Nacht,
Da hab ich noch im Dunkel
        [First edition: *Dunkeln*]
Die Augen zugemacht.

Und seine Zweige rauschten,
Als riefen sie mir zu:
Komm her zu mir, Geselle,
Hier findst du deine Ruh!

Die kalten Winde bliesen
Mir grad in's Angesicht;
Der Hut flog mir vom Kopfe,
Ich wendete mich nicht.

Nun bin ich manche Stunde
Entfernt von jenem
        [Autograph: *diesem*] Ort,
Und immer hör ich's rauschen:
Du fändest Ruhe dort!

## 6. Wasserflut

Manche Trän aus meinen Augen
Ist gefallen in den Schnee;
Seine kalten Flocken saugen
Durstig ein das heiße Weh. [!]

Wann [*Wenn*] die Gräser sprossen wollen,
Weht daher ein lauer Wind,
Und das Eis zerspringt in Schollen,
Und der weiche Schnee zerrinnt.

Schnee, du weißt von meinem Sehnen:
Sag mir, wohin [*Sag wohin doch*]
        geht dein Lauf?
Folge nach nur meinen Tränen,
Nimmt dich bald das Bächlein auf.

Wirst mit ihm die Stadt durchziehen,
Muntre Straßen ein und aus –
Fühlst du meine Tränen glühen,
D a ist meiner Liebsten Haus! [.]

## 7. Auf dem Flusse

Der du so lustig rauschtest,
Du heller, wilder Fluß,
Wie still bist du geworden,
Gibst keinen Scheidegruß!

Mit harter, starrer Rinde
Hast du dich überdeckt,
Liegst kalt und unbeweglich
Im Sande ausgestreckt.

In deine Decke grab ich
Mit einem spitzen Stein
Den Namen meiner Liebsten
Und Stund und Tag hinein:

Den Tag des ersten Grußes,
Den Tag, an dem ich ging;
Um Nam und Zahlen windet
Sich ein zerbrochner Ring.

Mein Herz, in diesem Bache
Erkennst du nun dein Bild? –
Ob's unter seiner Rinde
Wohl auch so reißend schwillt?

    } repeated

## 8. Rückblick

Es brennt mir unter beiden Sohlen,
Tret ich auch schon auf Eis und Schnee;
Ich möcht nicht wieder Atem holen,
Bis ich nicht mehr die Türme seh. [,]

Hab mich an jedem [*jeden*] Stein gestoßen,
So eilt' ich zu der Stadt hinaus;
Die Krähen warfen Bäll und Schloßen
Auf meinen Hut von jedem Haus.

Wie anders hast du mich empfangen,
Du Stadt der Unbeständigkeit!
An deinen blanken Fenstern sangen
Die Lerch und Nachtigall im Streit.

Die runden Lindenbäume blühten,
Die klaren Rinnen rauschten hell,
Und ach, zwei Mädchenaugen glühten! –
Da war's geschehn um dich, Gesell!

Kömmt mir der Tag in die Gedanken,
Möcht ich noch einmal rückwärts sehn,
Möcht ich zurücke wieder wanken,
Vor i h r e m Hause stille stehn.

## 9. Das Irrlicht

[*Irrlicht*]

In die tiefsten Felsengründe
Lockte mich ein Irrlicht hin:
Wie ich einen Ausgang finde,
            [Autograph: ? mit Fermate]
Liegt nicht schwer mir in dem Sinn.

Bin gewohnt das irre Gehen,
's führt ja jeder Weg zum Ziel:
Unsre Freuden, unsre Wehen [*Leiden*],
Alles eines Irrlichts Spiel.

Durch des Bergstroms trockne Rinnen
Wind ich ruhig mich hinab –
Jeder Strom wird's Meer gewinnen,
Jedes Leiden auch ein [*sein*] Grab.

## 10. Rast

Nun merk ich erst, wie müd ich bin,
Da ich zur Ruh mich lege;
Das Wandern hielt mich munter hin
Auf unwirtbarem Wege.

Die Füße frugen nicht nach Rast,
Es war zu kalt zum Stehen,
Der Rücken fühlte keine Last.
Der Sturm half fort mich wehen.

In eines Köhlers engem Haus
Hab Obdach ich gefunden;
Doch meine Glieder ruhn nicht aus:
So brennen ihre Wunden.

Auch du, mein Herz, in Kampf und Sturm
So wild und so verwegen,
Fühlst in der Still erst deinen Wurm
Mit heißem Stich sich regen.

## 11. Frühlingstraum

Ich träumte [Autograph: *träumt'*]
            von bunten Blumen,
So wie sie wohl blühen im Mai,
Ich träumte von grünen Wiesen,
Von lustigem Vogelgeschrei.

Und als die Hähne krähten,
Da ward mein Auge wach;
Da war es kalt und finster,
Es schrieen die Raben vom Dach.

Doch an den Fensterscheiben,
Wer malte die Blätter da?
Ihr lacht wohl über den Träumer,
Der Blumen im Winter sah?

Ich träumte von Lieb um Liebe,
Von einer schönen Maid,
Von Herzen und von Küssen,
Von Wonn [First edition: *Wonne*]
      und Seligkeit.

Und als die Hähne krähten,
Da ward mein Herze wach;
Nun sitz ich hier alleine
Und denke dem Traume nach.

Die Augen schließ ich wieder,
Noch schlägt das Herz so warm.
Wann grünt ihr Blätter am Fenster?
Wann halt ich dich, Liebchen,
      [*ich mein Liebchen*] im Arm?

## 12. Einsamkeit

Wie eine trübe Wolke
Durch heitre Lüfte geht,
Wenn in der Tanne [First edition: *Tannen*]
      Wipfel
Ein mattes Lüftchen weht:

So zieh ich meine Straße
Dahin mit trägem Fuß,
Durch helles, frohes Leben,
Einsam und ohne Gruß.

Ach, daß die Luft so ruhig!
Ach, daß die Welt so licht!
Als noch die Stürme tobten,
War ich so elend nicht.

Gedichte
aus den hinterlassenen Papieren
eines
reisenden Waldhornisten.
Herausgegeben
von
W i l h e l m   M ü l l e r.
2. Bändchen.
Deßau 1824
bei Christian Georg Ackermann

---

Lieder des Lebens und der Liebe.
D i e   W i n t e r r e i s e[125]

---

### 13. (1.) Die Post

Von der Straße her ein Posthorn klingt.
Was hat es, daß es so hoch aufspringt,
    Mein Herz?

Die Post bringt keinen Brief für dich:
Was drängst du denn so wunderlich,
    Mein Herz?

Nun ja, die Post kömmt aus der Stadt,
Wo ich ein liebes Liebchen hatt',
    Mein Herz!

Willst wohl einmal hinübersehn,
Und fragen, wie es dort mag gehn,
    Mein Herz?

### 14. (2.) Der greise Kopf

Der Reif hatt' [hat] einen weißen Schein
Mir über's Haar gestreuet.
Da meint' [glaubt'] ich schon ein
    Greis zu sein,
Und hab mich sehr gefreuet.

Doch bald ist er hinweggetaut,
Hab wieder schwarze Haare,
Daß mir's vor meiner Jugend graut —
Wie weit noch bis zur Bahre!

Vom Abendrot zum Morgenlicht
Ward mancher Kopf zum Greise.
Wer glaubt's? Und meiner ward es nicht
Auf dieser ganzen Reise!

## 15. (3.) Die Krähe

Eine Krähe war mit mir
Aus der Stadt gezogen,
Ist bis heute für und für
Um mein Haupt geflogen.

Krähe, wunderliches Tier,
Willst mich nicht verlassen?
Meinst wohl bald als Beute hier
Meinen Leib zu fassen?

Nun, es wird nicht weit mehr gehn
An dem Wanderstabe.
Krähe, laß mich endlich sehn
Treue bis zum Grabe!

## 16. (4.) Letzte Hoffnung

Hier [*Hie*] und da ist an den Bäumen
Noch ein buntes [*Manches bunte*]
          Blatt zu sehn,
Und ich bleibe vor den Bäumen
Oftmals in Gedanken stehn.

Schaue nach dem einen Blatte,
Hänge meine Hoffnung dran;
Spielt der Wind mit meinem Blatte,
Zittr' ich, was ich zittern kann.

Ach, und fällt das Blatt zu Boden,
Fällt mit ihm die Hoffnung ab,
Fall ich selber mit zu Boden,
Wein auf meiner Hoffnung Grab.

## 17. (5.) Im Dorfe

Es bellen die Hunde, es rasseln die Ketten.
Die Menschen schnarchen
   [*Es schlafen die Menschen*] in ihren Betten,
Träumen sich manches, was sie nicht haben,
Tun sich im Guten und Argen erlaben:
Und morgen früh ist alles zerflossen. –
Je nun, sie haben ihr Teil genossen,

Und hoffen, was sie noch übrig ließen,
Doch wieder zu finden auf ihren Kissen.

Bellt mich nur fort, ihr wachen Hunde,
Laßt mich nicht ruhn in der
          Schlummerstunde!
Ich bin zu Ende mit allen Träumen –
Was will ich unter den Schläfern säumen?

## 18. (6.) Der stürmische Morgen

Wie hat der Sturm zerrissen
Des Himmels graues Kleid!
Die Wolkenfetzen flattern
Umher in mattem Streit.

Und rote Feuerflammen
Ziehn zwischen ihnen hin.
Das nenn ich einen Morgen
So recht nach meinem Sinn!

Mein Herz sieht an dem Himmel
Gemalt sein eignes Bild –
Es ist nichts als der Winter,
Der Winter kalt und wild!

## 19. (7.) Täuschung

Ein Licht tanzt freundlich vor mir her;
Ich folg ihm nach die Kreuz und Quer;
Ich folg ihm gern und seh's ihm an,
Daß es verlockt den Wandersmann.
Ach, wer wie ich so elend ist,

Gibt gern sich hin der bunten List,
Die hinter Eis und Nacht und Graus
Ihm weist ein helles, warmes Haus,
Und eine liebe Seele drin –
Nur Täuschung ist für mich Gewinn!

## 20. (8.) Der Wegweiser

Was vermeid ich denn die Wege,
Wo die andren [andern] Wandrer gehn,
Suche mir versteckte Stege
Durch verschneite Felsenhöhn?

Habe ja doch nichts begangen,
Daß ich Menschen sollte scheun –
Welch ein törichtes Verlangen
Treibt mich in die Wüstenein?

Weiser stehen auf den Straßen [Wegen],
Weisen auf die Städte zu,
Und ich wandre sonder Maßen,
Ohne Ruh, und suche Ruh.

Einen Weiser seh ich stehen
Unverrückt vor meinem Blick;
Eine Straße muß ich gehen,
Die noch keiner ging zurück.

## 21. (9.) Das Wirtshaus

Auf einen Totenacker
Hat mich mein Weg gebracht.
Allhier will ich einkehren:
Hab ich bei mir gedacht.

Ihr grünen Totenkränze
Könnt wohl die Zeichen sein,
Die müde Wandrer laden
In's kühle Wirtshaus ein.

Sind denn in diesem Hause
Die Kammern all besetzt?
Bin matt zum Niedersinken [,]
Und [Bin] tödlich schwer verletzt.

O unbarmherz'ge Schenke,
Doch weisest du mich ab?
Nun weiter denn, nur weiter,
Mein treuer Wanderstab!

## 22. (10.) Mut!
[Mut]

Fliegt der Schnee mir in's Gesicht,
Schüttl' ich ihn herunter.
Wenn mein Herz im Busen spricht,
Sing ich hell und munter.

Höre nicht, was es mir sagt,
Habe keine Ohren,
Fühle nicht, was es mir klagt,
Klagen ist für Toren.

Lustig in die Welt hinein
Gegen Wind und Wetter!
Will kein Gott auf Erden sein,
Sind wir selber Götter.

### 23. *(11.)* Die Nebensonnen

Drei Sonnen sah ich am Himmel stehn,
Hab lang und fest sie angesehn
         [*angeschaut*];
Und sie auch standen da so stier,
Als könnten [*Als wollten*] sie nicht weg
         von mir.
Ach, m e i n e Sonnen seid ihr nicht!

Schaut andren [*andern*] doch in's Angesicht!
Ja [*Ach*], neulich hatt' ich auch wohl drei:
Nun sind hinab die besten zwei.
Ging' nur die dritt' erst hinterdrein!
Im Dunkel [*Dunkeln*] wird mir wohler sein.

### 24. *(12.)* Der Leiermann

Drüben hinter'm Dorfe
Steht ein Leiermann,
Und mit starren Fingern
Dreht er was er kann.

Barfuß auf dem Eise
Schwankt [*Wankt*] er hin und her;
Und sein kleiner Teller
Bleibt ihm immer leer.

Keiner mag ihn hören,
Keiner sieht ihn an;
Und die Hunde brummen [*knurren*]
Um den alten Mann.

Und er läßt es gehen
Alles, wie es will,
Dreht, und seine Leier
Steht ihm nimmer still.

Wunderlicher Alter,
Soll ich mit dir gehn?
Willst zu meinen Liedern
Deine Leier drehn?

# VII. Wilhelm Müller and Romanticism

by Rolf Vollmann

In the last year of his all too short but certainly not joyless life—despite the deep hypochondria which had taken possession of him when he was a mere 33 years old—Wilhelm Müller made his way to Württemberg. He visited Uhland, Schwab, and Kerner, and then one last beautiful moment was bestowed upon him: the singers of Stuttgart gathered in his honor, took him into their midst, and celebrated the man and his achievements. Uhland, Schwab and Kerner, and then these singers! Müller had traveled far from his native place, but all this must have seemed like a homecoming to him. At any rate, the Württembergers fully accepted him as one of their own.

A few years later, Heinrich Heine, in his *Romantische Schule* [Romantic School] —a still very worthwhile, stimulating writing—reflected on this period for his German and French readers:

> And this is the place where I can still praise several poets of the Romantic School, who, as I said, show an eloquence comparable to Mr. Uhland's with respect to the subject matter and tone of their poetry, but who needn't stand in his shadow in the matter of poetic worth, and who are perhaps distinguishable from him only in being less assured in matters of form. Indeed, what a superb poet Baron von Eichendorff is; the songs that he has woven into his novel *Ahnung und Gegenwart* [Intimation and the Present] are totally indistinguishable from those of Uhland, even from the best of them. The only discernible difference consists in the greener forest freshness and the more crystalline truth of the Eichendorff poems. Mr. Justinus Kerner, who is virtually unknown, also merits honorable mention here; he too composes valiant songs in the same style and tone; he is a compatriot of Mr. Uhland. The same is true of Mr. Gustav Schwab, a more famous poet, who likewise blossomed in Swabian regions and continues to refresh us yearly with lovely, fragrant songs. He has a special talent for ballads and frames local sagas most delightfully in this form. Here we must also mention Wilhelm Müller, whom death snatched from us in the happiest fullness of his youth. In his emulation of German folk song, he is in the same class as Mr. Uhland; it seems to me that in this regard he was sometimes even more successful, surpassing Uhland in his natural style. Because he recognized the spirit of the old song forms more fully, he was not compelled to imitate them in their externalities; therefore we find a freer handling of transitions in his work and a sensible avoidance of antiquated words and expressions.

So then, if we set Eichendorff aside for the moment (we will come back to him), Heine, in his reflections, shares the same sense of the man that our look at Müller's last year revealed: The Swabians celebrated the man from Dessau as one of their own; indeed, they celebrated the younger one perhaps as the greater—strangely enough, for today, Müller, as a poet in his own right, is doubtless the least familiar of all those whom Heine names.

A good dozen years before, Heine had written to Wilhelm Müller, who had just published his *77 Gedichte aus den hinterlassenen Papieren eines reisenden Waldhornisten* [Seventy-seven poems from the papers left behind by a traveling French horn player], among them the poems about the lovely miller maid. Here Heine uses words of highest praise for Müller—he even goes so far as to call him the most significant song poet after Goethe. This may seem an exaggeration; on the one hand, Heine undoubtedly wished to ingratiate himself with Müller, who was known as a harsh critic, before his own debut; but on the other, he must have discovered some quality in the older poet which set him apart from the ranks of contemporary second-rate song poets and which aroused in Heine a sense of kinship. When he read in Müller's "Tränenregen":

> Wir sassen so traulich beisammen
> Im kühlen Erlendach,
> Wir schauten so traulich zusammen
> Hinab in den rieselnden Bach.
>
> Der Mond war auch gekommen,
> Die Sternlein hinterdrein . . .

> [We sat together so cozily,
> in the cool shade of the alder,
> we looked down so cozily
> into the trickling brook.
> The moon had also come,
> the stars, close behind . . .]

and then when the song ended:

> Da gingen die Augen mir über,
> Da ward es im Spiegel so kraus;
> Sie sprach: Es kommt ein Regen,
> Ade, ich geh nach Haus."

> [Then my eyes filled with tears,
> and the mirror became clouded;
> She said: A shower is coming,
> Good-bye, I'm going home.]

Heine must have recognized in this unaffected simplicity, in this utterly unembellished, relaxed tone ("Der Mond war auch gekommen") and in the charmingly prosaic style of the closing lines an absolutely stunning anticipation of what he himself had in mind. Müller was almost a modern poet for him.

Of course, after Heine had found, at about the same time as Müller's *Winterreise*, the tone for the middle sections of his *Buch der Lieder* [Book of songs], had gone through it, and to some extent rejected it again, Müller gradually fell in his estimation back into the ranks of the Romantic song poets. The more Heine distances himself from all of them, the more they become as one to him. Shortly before the passage cited from *Die Romantische Schule,* Heine writes:

> Mr. Uhland represents an entire era, and he now represents it almost alone, since the other representatives of the same are sinking into oblivion or are really all summed up in this author. The predominant tone of Uhland's songs, ballads and romances was the tone of all his Romantic contemporaries.

Heine is even more blunt a few pages earlier, where he quotes Uhland's "Der schöne Schäfer zog so nah" [The handsome shepherd drew so near] and then writes:

> I have the same book in hand again, but 20 years have since gone by; I have heard and seen much in the meantime, much indeed; I no longer believe in headless beings and the old spook no longer affects me. The house in which I now sit and read lies on the Boulevard Mont-Martre; and there the wildest billows of the day surge, there the loudest voices of modern times shriek; there is laughing, rumbling, hammering; in double-quick step, the National Guard marches by; and everyone speaks French.

As I said, this is only a few years after Müller's visit in Württemberg! And then Heine continues, as if he were aiming directly at Müller:

> Perhaps, too, I have grown cool toward such poems since I discovered that there is a far more painful love than poetic love in which one never gains possession of the beloved object or loses her through death. It is actually more painful when the beloved object lies in our arms day and night but through incessant conflict and ridiculous caprices ruins our days and nights, so that we thrust from our heart that which our heart loves the most, and we ourselves are forced to bring the cursed, beloved woman to the mail coach and send her away: Good-bye, little princess!

Heine's inconsistent assessment of Müller reflects something deeper and more unsettling: that beneath the surface of the Romantic current that seemed to flow on peacefully for decades, as personified in the Swabian Romantics, this period was basically one of the fastest moving in Europe's cultural and intellectual history. Within the rapidly changing world of trends and fashions, Müller occupies that unusual position wherein he can be at once a model for Heine and yet be cast into the still waters of Uhland, Schwab, and Kerner.

The Romantic school or movement can be considered a unit only when viewed from afar, for on closer scrutiny it is composed of several groups or periods. The fact that these periods can be identified by dates is neither coincidental nor arbitrary. The reason is simply that each new impulse came from a circle of like-minded friends of about the same age. One must keep in mind that this circle was almost always composed of very young people, and generally of city-dwellers. Whatever else we may link with the name Romanticism, youth, city, and modernity are always associated with it.

The first Romantic wave was triggered by the age-group born in 1772 and 1773: Friedrich Schlegel was born in 1772; Novalis, also 1772; Tieck, 1773;

Wackenroder, also 1773. Schlegel was an agile and brilliant philosopher and literary scholar; originally from Dresden, he later lived in Berlin and Jena. Tieck, who came from Berlin where he and Wackenroder were friends, then went to Jena, was a shrewd operator who once hoped to become an actor. Tieck was of that bent of mind we would call "sophisticated" today. Novalis, a precocious lad, came from more rural, though certainly elevated, circumstances, then studied in Leipzig and finally also landed in Jena. And whatever the "Blue Flower" of Romanticism may mean to us, Novalis, who invented it, was an extremely sensitive and bold thinker. Certainly Jena was no great metropolis; but it was here that Fichte and Schelling taught, and they were the philosophers who, from 1794–1806 (further evidence of the tremendously fast pace of this period), set the tone for Germany; they represented the very latest in modern thinking.

Friedrich Schlegel, later derided by Heine for his Catholic-reactionary obduracy, was the principal theoretician and formulator of the early Romantic period. So-called "Romantic irony" owes its being to him. Early Romanticism, certainly related in this aspect to the work of the "idealistic" philosophers Fichte and Schelling, is characterized by a striving for "the absolute" that we can neither readily nor fully understand. Or to express it in terms of emotion: it is characterized by a longing for the perfect, for something that lies beyond all limits of earthly and human finitude and inadequacy, in a realm of pure creative freedom, of liberated fantasy. In this ethereal sphere, life and poetry, mind and nature, were thought to merge. Of course Schlegel was aware that the greatest freedom of poetic genius cannot successfully leap the gap between the finite and the infinite, which is the decisive difference. This freedom can do one thing: it can immediately turn upon and destroy or abandon as imperfect any creation it has made, be it in a work of art, a way of life, or perhaps a love. The object will of course reestablish itself, but only to live on in a state of intellectual suspension. All that endures is this eternal uncertainty, this remaining-in-limbo itself. As for any permanence which might be attributed to a life or art form, this endless limbo results in a refusal to take it seriously; an almost ironic disregard for everything. It is not as if everything counted as nothing; it is just that in the final analysis the mind is only free when it has progressed beyond this contradiction, because it has intended something more all along.

Therefore, Romantic irony, on the wings of a great yearning, is a highly artificial mind game. Indeed, Heine was the one who found it perfectly natural that anyone who tired of this strenuous and insubstantial game but who retained a Romantic yearning would be forced to turn to Catholicism.

However, in artistic undertakings by this group, we find scarcely a trace of this comprehensive irony which they repeatedly proclaimed. Schlegel's creative powers were less well developed than his intellectual powers; only in his rather frivolous novel *Lucinde* did he make some artistic use of his ideas. Tieck's *Mondbeglänzte Zaubernacht* [Magic moonlit night] contains no trace of irony. And even in the case of Novalis, little irony is to be found, neither in his *Hymnen an die Nacht* [Hymns to the night] or in the underlying romantic feeling of yearning in these thoroughly beautiful verses:

"Wenn nicht mehr Zahlen und Figuren
sind Schlüssel aller Kreaturen,
wenn die, so singen oder küssen,

mehr als die Tiefgelehrten wissen,
wenn sich die Welt ins freie Leben
und in die Welt wird zurückbegeben,
wenn dann sich wieder Licht und Schatten
zu echter Klarheit werden gatten
und man in Märchen und Gedichten
erkennt die wahren Weltgeschichten,
dann fliegt vor einem geheimen Wort
das ganze verkehrte Wesen fort."

[When numbers and figures are no longer keys to all creatures, when those who sing or kiss know more than learned men, when the world betakes itself into free life and the world again, when light and shadow then unite as true clarity and the world's true histories are recognized in fairy tales and poems, then the whole topsy-turvy essence flees at the mention of a secret word.]

How far removed this emotional yearning and the intellectuality of a Schlegel are from Müller's "Sie sprach: Es kommt ein Regen, /Ade, ich geh nach Haus," hardly bears discussion. Equally far removed from this emotional yearning is Müller's convivial, droll bracketing of the miller romance in a prologue and epilogue with a condescending smile; but we will come to that presently. The dissimilarities between the Romantics are also evident in that the vision of Wackenroder, Schlegel, Tieck, and Novalis hiking with Fichte and Schelling along a brook while singing has something decidedly incongruous about it.

The next generation of Romantics comes on the stage a few years later, with Achim von Arnim and Clemens Brentano. Brentano was born in 1778, Arnim in 1781. Fouqué (1777) and Chamisso (1781) also belong to this generation. The distinguishing characteristic here is the encounter with folk poetry and the Middle Ages. Certainly this direction had already been heralded in Wackenroder's *Herzensergiessungen* [Effusions from the heart] and in Novalis' *Die Christenheit oder Europa* [Christianity or Europe], but it was only fully evident in the lyric poetry of Arnim's and Brentano's *Des Knaben Wunderhorn* [The youth's magic horn]. Even before the publication of this collection, Romantic poetry was surely extraordinarily melodious and lyrical, and for this very reason it was in a position to take up the impulse of the folk song at once. In contrast to the musical subtlety and rhythmic sensitivity of art poetry, the fresh, unspent quality of the folk song came across as the essence of pure nature. It is as if a new spring had been discovered at which the pampered poetry of the day would be able to quench its secret thirst, to find the innocence, the magical mixture of folk and nature, of which it had completely lost sight. True, Brentano himself, certainly the greatest of the Romantic lyricists, allowed this new discovery to influence him only very indirectly; his poems appear to be simple but are really highly complex and polyphonic; but then, Brentano too became increasingly pious. But the discovery of folk poetry had its fullest effect in the following generation.

Lest one misunderstand: This division into generations is somewhat artificial, as are all such generalizations. Clearly there were always close connections between the generations. Eichendorff, for instance, who must be included with the next generation to emerge, belongs to the Heidelberg Romantic circle of Arnim and Brentano. Nevertheless, each of these Romantic currents remains a matter of youth, and at that level five or six years make a great difference. Speaking of Heidelberg, this too is a university town.

Now then, Eichendorff was born in 1788. Rückert was born in the same year, Uhland one year earlier; Kerner, in 1786. Eichendorff and Uhland emerge as the two lyricists who had the greatest influence on the concept of Romantic poetry in the folk tradition. Both adopt the simple tone of the folk song, though each in his own way. Both maintain their characteristic tone for many years. Both infuse their poetry with an almost timeless quality, as if it were the epitome of lyric poetry, or at least a substantial part of it, aside from Goethe perhaps. The journeymen now appear en masse, and traveling becomes a lyric folk sport.

At the same time, what was more or less a mere metaphysical idea of folk and folk community in the early Romantic period now becomes both a national and especially a Catholic issue. The 1813 War of Liberation contributed more than a little to this national sentiment. Again, Heine summarizes this sense rather well when he writes:

And it is easily understandable that the ballads and romances of our excellent Uhland earned the greatest applause not only from patriots of 1813 and pious youths and charming maidens, but also from many of the more vigorous modern thinkers. I have added the date 1813 to the word 'patriots' in order to distinguish them from today's friends of the Fatherland, who no longer feed on memories of the so-called War of Liberation. Those older patriots must take the sweetest pleasure in Uhland's muse, since most of his poems are impregnated with the spirit of their time, a time when they themselves could still indulge youthful emotions and proud hopes. They passed this preference for Uhland's poems on to their blind followers, and for the boys on the athletic fields, collecting Uhland's poems once counted as patriotism.[121a]

Heine's words are not without some malice, but they do offer an explanation of how the powerful "feeling for nature" was gradually reduced to mere wanderlust and how the powerful idea of a strong western Europe gradually dwindled to one of class-conscious restoration and to "athletic-field" patriotism. Of course these are negative effects; they did not emerge until later. The Romantics themselves were still highly educated men, scholars, literary figures with manifold interests, as always.

Romanticism now became a major cultural stream; it is no longer possible to define the boundaries of the movement, as it was during the first generation. The Berlin salons of Varnhagen and Rahel Levin were also Romantic, if you will. Romanticism became modern, almost mundane. It was a way of life; one could practice it or not, yet this freedom itself was a part of it. Into this world, almost 15 years later, came Heine, the derisive city-dweller who sensed the great pressure in the fast-moving era and who fully surrendered to it. Wilhelm Müller, born in 1794, falls between the generation of Eichendorff, Uhland, Kerner, and Rückert, and that of Heine.

Müller studied in Berlin and was a popular guest in learned circles. He is portrayed as having a zest for life, even as happy-go-lucky, but as his diary reveals, he was an upright, God-fearing and innocent youth. He threw himself into old German literature with enthusiasm, tried his hand at the *Nibelungenlied* [Song of the Nibelungs], and praised the War of Liberation, in which he himself had been involved. But at about this time he came to realize that with all his liveliness of wit—or with all his social talents, at any rate—his soul still longed for simpler things and a simpler life. He destroyed his early writings, and in 1821 the collection *77 Gedichte aus den hinterlassenen Papieren eines reisenden Waldhornisten* appeared. The title, in its deliberate, elaborate ponderousness, undoubtedly reveals a certain detachment on his part, but it is not extreme, at least not so extreme that one can use the word "irony" to describe his view of it. Nor can we actually expect an extreme detachment by any writer whose creative talents do not exceed the standard shown in these poems, for without doubt, Müller to this time was a poet of modest rank.

Let us consider the openings of a few of his best poems: "Mit der Fiedel auf dem Rücken, mit dem Kappel in der Hand" [With my fiddle on my back, my cap in my hand], "Der Mai ist auf dem Wege, der Mai ist vor der Tür" [May is on its way, May is at the doorstep], "Vor der Türe meiner Lieben häng ich auf den Wanderstab" [Outside my beloved's door, I hang up my walking stick], "Im Krug zum grünen Kranze, da kehrt' ich durstig ein, da sass ein Wandrer drinnen" [Thirsty, I entered the (tavern); there sat a traveler within . . .] etc. We see a total preoccupation with traveling—indeed, he can only imagine being "on the road" in the month of May.

Closely associated with traveling is wine—wine is drunk almost incessantly. Müller composed several series of wining and dining songs. Certainly some of the poems are expressive, but the feelings expressed tend to be assumed rather than experienced feelings.

As a poet, Müller seems to exist in a vacuum; it almost appears as though he is unable to muster any emotion other than assumed feelings, but then he immerses himself in these feelings as if they were his own. Thus he is at his best when he is actually only playing a role.

Oddly enough, the role has a double meaning for him. On the one hand it is a game—for instance, the parlor game at Stägemann's home, where, following Goethe's model, the guests engage in writing and composing little song-playlets about the lovely miller maiden and her unlucky suitor, using the Romantic form as it was available to the educated person. On the other hand, Müller's poetic talent finds fulfillment in such roles; under the pressure of the role, he becomes free in a sense; so when he is role-playing, he is completely himself. Aside from his state when actually in love, which, as his diary shows, is in itself only a role, his love poems about the lovely miller maiden are perfectly genuine in some respects. He brackets them with prologue and epilogue in an amused way that can by no means be considered a detriment; rather, in his case this device works favorably.

One is certainly not far from the truth in assuming that young Heine was in a comparable position. But Heine differs from Müller in three ways: his soul is more adventuresome, his mind sharper, and his poetic talent greater. Where Müller comes across as sardonic like Heine, as in the closing lines of "Tränenregen" cited earlier, this must or may be understood as an almost inadvertent, possibly even completely unconscious step in the direction in which Heine has gone consciously under similar emotional circumstances, incurring much more discomfiture, yet at the same time more freely. In this respect, there is really no connection for Müller between the prologue and epilogue on the one hand and the lines between them on the other.

We have already seen that Müller's deliberate suspension of all emotion in that bracket of prologue and epilogue has nothing to do with true Romantic irony, unless we now want to call the social fashion of "playing the romantic" (however much it may be associated with late Romanticism) a late form of Romantic irony—but then this term would lose all its definable content. On the other hand, that subtle feeling that germinates in the closing lines of "Tränenregen" and then comes into full flower in Heine's *Buch der Lieder* well deserves the name irony. But this irony is anything but Romantic. In a way, it is long since finished with Romanticism and now turns on and attacks it. Not that this irony underestimates the beauty of Romantic moods; it is just that it no longer sees them as anything other than beautiful moods. One could almost say that these moods gain a new measure of truth, a first-hand rather than a mediated truth, only by being undermined. In fact it is often at those very places where he deals in irony that Heine is loving and suffering; but of course this is a thoroughly unromantic point of view.

So much for *Die Schöne Müllerin*. As far as Müller, independent of Schubert and Heine, is concerned, after the travel, wine, and love songs, he gained a reputation as the so called Greek Müller. On his occasional trips, Müller had come to know some of those who were leading the Greeks in their struggle for independence from the Turks in the 1820s. Müller, capable of new enthusiasms and politically quite aware, immediately took a stand for the Greeks, as did many other young people all over Europe. He published several booklets of *Lieder der Griechen* [Songs of the Greeks] in rapid succession. Müller could produce poems readily, a talent employed notably in this case. Thanks to this facility, his were the first poems devoted to the Greek cause, and hence the name Greek Müller.

The Greek poems have nothing to do with folk song. He used long rhyming lines, mostly hexameter; and all in all, like so much of Müller's work, especially his epigrams and poetic proverbs, the Greek poems show a striking similarity to Rückert's works. This is due first of all to native Greek poetry, including contemporary Greek folk songs which Müller used as a model. On the other hand, the similarity to Rückert goes deeper than this. But first, another word about Müller's *Lieder der Griechen*: Here, too, he is playing a role, and a dual one at that. First he imagines himself at the side of the fighting Greeks; yet he also speaks in his poems through the mouths of Greeks—slaves, warriers, children, women.

Turning now to Müller's similarity to Rückert, (whom Müller, incidentally, is purported to have once rescued from drowning in the Mediterranean), we note that both composed poetry continually, perpetually, without rest. Rückert's colossal lyric output is a commentary on everything that ever happened to him: he scarcely perceived anything without putting it into verse at once; in a way, writing poetry was life itself for him. That is not to derogate the quality of his poetry in the least. Rückert was an artist of high rank; he elicited almost unbelievable subtleties from 19th-century German poetic language. This quality has been forgotten, but unjustly so.

Müller, in this completely a non-Romantic, likewise never spared his muse. He rarely went anywhere without bringing home a bundle of poems. And as I have said of Rückert, this should not be considered a criticism of Müller's poems. Here the poet has found a new and different kind of existence. Müller's poems from the Isle of Rügen or from Franzensbad are lovely—at any rate, we cannot imagine that the poet could have produced any lovelier poems about Rügen or Franzensbad using a different style. But Müller has neither Rückert's substance nor his talent; so that those of his works which have been forgotten are justifiably forgotten. But it is understandable how, in his brief life of 33 years, he managed to leave behind 350 finely-printed pages of poems, without having been the kind of poet who simply "cranks them out."

But what is hard to comprehend, even upon careful reading of those 350 pages, is how this poet—not at the end of his life, for one often thinks one understands a great deal by that time, but right in the middle of his poetic career—was suddenly able to write *Winterreise*. The poems of this cycle were written in 1823; at that time, Heine was writing *Lyrisches Intermezzo* [Lyric intermezzo] and *Die Heimkehr* [Homecoming], the best-known and most characteristic poems of his *Buch der Lieder*—the ones that see the blossoming of Müller's 'Tränenregen" mood. But there is no longer a trace of this mood in Müller's work. Nor is there a trace of the pleasantly superficial tone of countless other Müller poems. *Winterreise* leaves us dumbfounded. Compounding our confusion is the fact that, from what we know of Müller's life, there was not the slightest cause for the tone of *Winterreise*, which is not the case with Rückert's similarly unexpected *Kindertotenlieder* [Children's death songs].

It is remarkable enough that one must look for a cause. These poems differ from all his others in that they actually seem to have a living, suffering subject. Not in the sense of the subjective lyric poetry that Germans call *Erlebnislyrik* [experiential poetry], for even the poems of *Winterreise* are role poems—Müller is true to himself in this respect. But the role is filled with such unique life that it seems tailormade for some living person, and yet it is hard to imagine anyone in this role, least of all Wilhelm Müller. Of his early motifs, only one is included, the main motif: traveling. But the nature of this travel is changed: it is now purely a state of being driven, and it is certainly no young lad who is being driven. It is a question of love—love for a girl who has been given to another—but the matter of love gradually sinks into the background, so that the real reason for the traveler's restlessness, his longing for aging and death, is not at all clear in the end.

A despair that no longer has anything poetic about it takes hold here. And it takes hold in a language that also seems to reject poetry, at least poetry as Müller understood it before and afterwards. The incredible thing about these poems is that Müller comes up with images and turns of phrase that simply never occurred to him previously, or, if they did occur to him—and this is almost more incredible—that he would without a doubt not have used. There are images and phrases that counter the style of Müller's other work so markedly that they must be labeled unpoetic. One can often find prosaic insertions, even images that hardly belong in the realm of the normal. But Müller ventures into territory that knows nothing yet of poetry—a truly unique turn of events, not only for him but for the whole body of lyric poetry of his time.

Let us now cite some of these images and turns of phrase: "Irre Hunde" [stray dogs] ("Gute Nacht"); "sie pfiff' den armen Flüchtling aus" [she was hissing the poor fugitive away] ("Die Wetterfahne"); "Mit harter, starrer Rinde hast du dich überdeckt, liegst kalt und unbeweglich im Sande ausgestreckt" [You have covered yourself with a hard, petrified crust and lie cold and motionless stretched out in the sand] ("Auf dem Flusse"); "Es brennt mir unter beiden Sohlen" [the soles of both my feet are burning] ("Rückblick'"); "möcht ich zurücke wieder wanken" [I would like to stagger back again] ("Rückblick'"); incidentally, the "runden Lindenbäume" [round linden trees] in this poem are also an astounding image, totally naive, almost childish, as if someone were seeing something for the first time and then expressing it as a banality; "Der Reif hatt' einen weissen Schein mir über's Haar gestreuet. Da meint' ich schon ein Greis zu sein und hab mich sehr gefreuet" [The frost had spread a white glow over my hair. I thought I was an old man already and was overjoyed.] ("Der greise Kopf'"); "Es bellen die Hunde . . ." [The dogs are barking . . .]—this whole poem ("Im Dorfe") is amazing, from the "schnarchenden Menschen" [snoring people] to the "säumenden Schläfern" [tarrying among the sleepers]; "Bin matt zum Niedersinken und tödlich schwer verletzt" [I am about to fall in fatigue and am mortally wounded] ("Das Wirtshaus'"); "Barfuss auf dem Eise schwankt er hin und her," [barefoot on the ice, he totters to and fro] and "und die Hunde brummen um den alten Mann" [and the dogs growl around the old man] ("Der Leiermann'").

What strikes us is the almost appalling childishness of these images and visions. To be able to say to a frozen river, "You lie cold and motionless, stretched out in the sand" requires an eye that still sees the ordinary as alien or that has alienated itself from all that is ordinary. This image is precise in every detail, yet presented as though the familiar sight of a river has, for the describer, never before consisted of all these details—one would wander far astray in literary interpretation in believing that the river is simply compared here to a man lying dead, cold, and motionless, stretched out in the sand. Childishness, but somehow a completely unnatural childishness, not as if someone were reverting to it or somehow regaining it, but more as if to say: here someone is afflicted with childishness.

The dismay that this childishness arouses is certainly due in part to the fact that the calm flow of the verses is almost completely unaffected by it. We discern a maddening "anything goes" attitude. "Je nun" [Oh, well], it says in the poem "Im Dorfe:" a flat, utterly prosaic expression, just as this whole stanza impresses us almost as "non-poetry;" but there is a kind of calmness about it that is so foreign as to make one shudder. Particularly in "Der Leiermann," the despair, or whatever emotion it is that has been reached at this point, has arrived at such a nerveless rest that any emotion is superfluous. The poem is stark description, without a single unnecessary word. In the first draft, even the word "ihm" [for him] in the eighth line is omitted, which is basically understood anyway; also the fourth line in the draft reads: "bleibet immer leer," and here, as with "gefreuet" in "Der greise Kopf," the inserted "e" has an almost alarming effect. Then the fourth stanza is so prosaic, with the almost clumsy "alles" inserted in the second line, that one wonders how this ever came to be viewed as a poem at all.

However and for whatever reason Müller may have come to write these verses (I am tempted to say: whoever may have written these verses), has little to do with the Romanticism that Heine describes, understandably with tongue in cheek. Of course it also has nothing at all to do with Heine's break with Romanticism. It is difficult to see the direction in which Müller moves as he distances himself from Romanticism. In the Romanticism of which Heine writes, time flows by and does not even know where it actually stands. In *Winterreise* it seems suddenly to pause in its roaring tempo, to stand still on the spot, and then, suddenly and hopelessly, to sink into an abyss. One could say this, but such pictures are certainly not very enlightening.

"Den uns der Tod in seiner heitersten Jugendfülle entrissen" [whom death snatched from us in the happiest fullness of youth] —Heine wrote when he was only slightly older than Müller was at the time of his death (1827), and Heine most certainly did not then consider himself to be "in the happiest fullness of youth." Happy, certainly; but to him Müller probably seemed rather like a happy youth, an overgrown child who could not grow up, who, unlike himself, could not become a man and perhaps did not want to. This was not just meant maliciously but also affectionately; and as time proved, it was certainly true as well.

But *Winterreise* is also true, and that is its double misfortune: for now its credibility is lost in the greater untruth. And here I would like to go one unprovable step further and say: it is this very feeling of being lost that prevails in *Winterreise*. If so, then Heine was still right, but not totally. And Schubert had greater insight.

# VIII. Notes

1  Cf. Arnold Feil: *Studien zu Schuberts Rhythmik* [Studies on Schubert's rhythmics] Munich 1966.

2  Also worthy of mention is a critical essay by Dieter Conrad, which seems to complement this book: "Schumanns Liedkomposition—von Schubert her gesehen" [Schumann's song composition—seen through Schubert eyes], in the magazine *Die Musikforschung* 24, 1971, pp. 135–163.

3  A detailed explanation of the method used here, with its premises, derivation, and possibilities, is presented in the first chapter of my *Studien zu Schuberts Rhythmik.*

3a Ed. Note: D = Abbreviation for Deutsch, *Thematic Catalogue.* See IX Editions and Literature.

4  Thus wrote Eusebius Mandyczewski, editor of the song series in the old complete edition of Schubert's works, on August 25, 1894, to his friend Johannes Brahms.

5  The manuscript in Schubert's hand bears this date, but it is a copy—that is, a fair copy rather than the original composition manuscript.

6  Quoted from Max Friedlaender: *Das deutsche Lied im 18. Jahrhundert. Quellen und Studien* [The German song in the 18th century. Sources and studies], I, 1, Stuttgart and Berlin 1902 (Reprint: Hildesheim 1962), p. 116.

7  Quoted from Friedlaender: op. cit. I, 1, p. 196.

8  The passages quoted are from the preface written by Johann Abraham Peter Schulz for the second printing of his celebrated collection *Lieder im Volkston* [Songs in the folk manner], Berlin, November 1784. (Quoted from Friedlaender: op. cit. I, 1, p. 256 f.).

9  Consider Reichardt's collection *Frohe Lieder für deutsche Männer* [Joyful songs for German men], that "experiment with songs in the folk manner, to be sung without accompaniment in simple gatherings," whose preface we quoted and discussed above, was published in 1781, the same year in which Haydn published his String Quartets op. 33 ("in a wholly new special way") and in which Mozart moved from Salzburg to Vienna at which time he was working on his *Entführung aus dem Serail* [Abduction from the Seraglio].

10 Cf. A. Feil: "Volksmusik und Trivialmusik. Bemerkungen eines Historikers zu ihrer Trennung" [Folk music and trivial music. A historian's comments on their separation], in: *Die Musikforschung* 26, 1973, pp. 159–166.

11 As formulated in Thr. G. Georgiades: *Schubert Musik und Lyrik,* Göttingen 1967, p. 17.

12 *Schubert. Die Erinnerungen seiner Freunde* [Schubert. The recollections of his friends], collected and published by Otto Erich Deutsch, Leipzig[2]1966, p. 94. (When cited hereinafter, this title is abbreviated: *Erinnerungen.*) Published in English as *Schubert: Memoirs by His Friends* (London, 1958)

13 Admittedly, another of Schubert's friends, the poet Johann Mayrhofer, reports (*Erinnerungen,* p. 18): "Without deeper knowledge of composition and thoroughbass, he actually remained a naturalist. A few months before his death, he began to take lessons from Sechter. Thus the celebrated Salieri

seems not to have put him through that strict school, even though he checked over Schubert's earlier efforts, and praised or corrected them."

14    *Schubert. Die Dokumente seines Lebens* [Schubert. The documents of his life], collected and annotated by Otto Erich Deutsch (*Neue Schubert-Ausgabe* [New Schubert edition] Series VIII, Vol. 5), Kassel etc. 1964, p. 430. (When cited hereinafter, this title is abbreviated: *Dokumente.*) Published in English as *The Schubert Reader, A Life of Franz Schubert in Letters and Documents*, London and New York, 1947

15    *Erinnerungen*, p. 163.

16    Quoted from: *Deutsche Reden* [German speeches], edited by Walter Hinderer, Stuttgart 1973, p. 440 (Reclam's Universal-Bibliothek No. 9672–78, 9679–85).

17    *Dokumente*, p. 235.

18    *Dokumente*, p. 229. Also cf. the foreword to: *Neue Schubert-Ausgabe: Oktette und Nonett* [New Schubert edition: octets and nonet], Series VI, Vol. 1, p. ix, edited by A. Feil, Kassel etc. 1969.

19    Reichardt wanted his 1781 collection of unison songs, mentioned earlier, to remain the only one of its kind, and typically, he later reprinted only an expanded version of the Foreword in his *Musikalisches Kunstmagazin.*

20    Quoted from Friedlaender: op. cit. I, 1, 1902, p. 203.

21    This declaration has been handed on by Friedrich Rochlitz, who visited Beethoven in Vienna in the summer of 1822.

22    Schubert's songs from 1810 to 1813, together with Zumsteeg's models, have recently been published in Vol. 6 of the *Lieder* series, *Neue Schubert-Ausgabe*, edited by Walther Dürr, Kassel etc. 1969. For the following, cf. Dürr's foreword to this volume.

23    It is quite astonishing how many poorly equipped writers blithely pass judgment on both Schubert and his works.

24    For example, cf. M. J. E. Brown: *Schubert. Eine kritische Biographie* [Schubert. A critical biography], Wiesbaden 1969, p. 16 f. (Publ. originally in English, London, 1958)

25    Cf. Schubert's letter of March 31, 1824, quoted on page 16.

26    Quoted from Friedlaender: *Schubert-Album Supplement*, Leipzig 1884, p. 1. The origin of the poem cycle is presented in detail by Max Friedlaender in: *'Die Schöne Müllerin'* . . . *von Franz Schubert. Kritische Ausgabe* . . . , Leipzig, n. d. (1922), p. 7 ff., and by F. V. Damian in: *Franz Schuberts Liederkreis 'Die Schöne Müllerin,'* Leipzig 1928, p. 88 ff. Also cf. Georgiades: *Schubert. Musik und Lyrik*, p. 215 ff.

27    Cf. W. Vetter: *Der Klassiker Schubert* [Schubert, the classic composer], Vol. 2, p. 180.

27a   Ed. Note: Vogl, 1768–1840, a baritone, sang opera in Vienna for many years. He met Schubert in 1817 and became the foremost interpreter of his songs.

28    Cf. R. Schollum: *Die Veränderungen in der Diabelliausgabe der Schönen Müllerin* [The changes in the Diabelli edition of "Die Schöne Müllerin"] and W. Dürr: " 'Manier' und 'Veränderung' in Kompositionen Franz Schuberts" [Style and change in compositions of Franz Schubert] in: *Zur Aufführungspraxis der Werke Franz Schuberts* [On the performance practice of Franz Schubert's works], Kongressbericht Wien [Vienna congress report] 1974 (= *Beiträge zur Aufführungspraxis* [Articles on performance practice]).

29  On the question of "changes" and "copies," cf. "Vorwort" [Foreword] and "Quellen und Lesarten" [Sources and versions] by W. Dürr in *Neue Schubert-Ausgabe: Lieder. Band 2.*

30  Also compare the excellent facsimile edition, Bärenreiter-Verlag, Kassel and Basel 1955.

31  Also compare the cited facsimile edition of Schubert's manuscript with the reduced-size facsimile first edition by H. Kralik, Verlag Steyrermühl, Vienna n.d.

32  Cf. Georgiades: *Schubert. Musik und Lyrik*, p. 194: "Exkurs. Zur Notierungsweise der Lieder" [Digression. On the notation of the songs].

33  Cf. W. Dürr: *Neue Schubert-Ausgabe, Lieder. Band 1*, "Vorwort".

34  In the solving of various analytical problems, Dr. K. Kos has been of great help to me.

35  W. Dürr, in the preface to the *Lieder* series of *Neue Schubert-Ausgabe*: "Schubert did not compose a piano introduction for a large number of his songs. However, this does not mean that the songs were performed without an introduction; the accompanist most likely improvised a short introduction. It can be assumed that many of the introductions in posthumous editions for which Schubert's authorship cannot be proved do in fact go back to improvisations by Schubert himself. Thus these introductions were not "forgeries" but necessary expansions for an edition intended primarily for amateurs." The best-known example is 'Die Forelle' [The trout]: Four copies of this song in Schubert's hand and two in another hand have been handed down; the latter are copies from the working manuscript. Only one, a copy by Schubert himself, includes the familiar piano introduction. Cf. M. J. E. Brown: "Die Handschriften und Frühausgaben von Schuberts 'Die Forelle' " [The manuscripts and early editions of Schubert's 'Die Forelle'], in: *Österreichische Musikzeitschrift* 20, 1965. pp 578–588. From May 1819 on though, all Schubert's songs have piano introductions.

36  Such attempts to find out how a piece "goes" by moving along with it in conducting gestures had been suggested by Leopold Mozart, the great teacher, in his *Gründliche Violinschule* [Basic violin method], which appeared in Augsburg in 1756, the year of his son's birth. "In instructing a beginner, one must make every effort to make him understand the time. To this end, it is expedient for the instructor to move the pupil's hand frequently in time to the music; but then to play for him several pieces with various times and motions, letting the pupil beat the time himself, in order to test whether he understands the division, the regularity, and finally the change of motion." Johann Philipp Kirnberger, one of the important theoreticians in the second half of the 18th century, offers similar advice (*Die Kunst des reinen Satzes in der Musik* [The art of pure composition in music], Part II, 1, Berlin 1776, quoted from a 1798 Vienna edition: "Therefore it is advisable for the inexperienced composer first to sing or play the melody that he has in mind and wants to write down, and to beat the time with his hand or foot; then if the melody is measured, he will not miss the main tones that fall on the downbeat." Also cf. A. Feil: *Studien zu Schuberts Rhythmik*, pp. 17–21.

37  In a review from the year 1814. Cf. E. T. A. Hoffmann: *Schriften zur Musik* [Writings on music], edited by F. Schnapp, Munich 1963.

38  The expression "Konstruktion," which has to do with architectural building,

may seem an unusual usage for musical analysis. It is taken from Adolf Bern-
hard Marx (1795–1866), who introduces it in his celebrated treatise on composition (1837 ff), which was widely admired.

39    Alfred Einstein's claim, in his book on Schubert, that Schubert never puts
dynamic marks in the voice part, therefore must be corrected.

40    In the transition from the middle to the third part, that is from the simple 3/4
time to the motion of quarter-note values outside the time, Schubert uses the
compositional device of repeating a single part of a measure, a single beat:
measure 47, third quarter is repeated as the first quarter of the following
measure.

41    The decrescendo mark from the forte at the beginning of the measure to the
piano on the fifth eighth-note beat should be read as an accent mark indicat-
ing the accentuation of the figure as a whole.

42    Measure 30 is the last in the preceding group of four measures, 27–30 ("ei
willkommen, ei willkommen, süsser Mühlengesang!"). Therefore the *pp,*
which belongs to the new group of measures, is moved from measure 30 to
measure 31; it has to be at the beginning of the new section of the composition (corresponding to the *p* in measure 23). Even the engraver of the first
edition inadvertently placed it one measure too early.

43    In Wilhelm Müller's version, the song was first entitled "Wanderlust" (1818),
then "Wanderschaft" (1820).

44    1800–1860; *Des Müllers Lust und Leid, 6 Gesänge aus der Schönen Müllerin von
Wilhelm Müller,* [The miller's joy and sorrow; six songs from "Die Schöne
Müllerin" by Wilhelm Müller], op. 6, 1844.

45    M. Friedlaender: *Die Schöne Müllerin,* p. 89: "As lightly and smoothly as the
melody flows, it is still hard to sing, with its sixteenth-note turns; a master of
[Julius] Stockhausen's rank considered the song almost a touchstone for
vocal technique. Despite its simplicity and beauty of line, the melody has not
become part of the folk tradition. The poem that Schubert fashioned into an
art song, Karl Zöllner recomposed as a marching song for male chorus,
thereby creating one of the best-known and most widespread German
hiking songs. His melody has also carried over into the treasury of school
and children's songs."

46    First act, No. 6. This whole march is a curious piece. Also cf.: Feil: *Studien zu
Schuberts Rhythmik,* p. 114 ff.

47    Dietrich Fischer-Dieskau and Gerald Moore, on a phonograph recording,
take the quarter note at about 88. Peter Pears and Benjamin Britten, also on a
phonograph recording, take it at about 96. Of course only outstanding
singers can achieve such tempos, which present difficulties not only in the
technical but even more so in the musical realm. For instance, when the
tempo is too fast and musically uncontrolled, causing the unit of reference to
shift from the quarter notes in the sprightly 2/4 time to whole measures, the
beat is slowed again, that is, in the sense of an *alla breve,* whereby the individual note values become faster, the units of reference slower; but the
system of metric relationships is altered and no longer corresponds to that of
the composition (with its constituent harmonic progressions from quarter to
quarter). Therefore let the amateur be content with more relaxed tempos,
rendering them in his own way; the effect will not be any the worse for it.

48    M. Friedlaender: *Die Schöne Müllerin,* p. 89.

49  *Schubert. Musik und Lyrik,* p. 224 f.

50  Descriptions of the song such as this: "The music follows the quietest stirring of his [the miller lad's] thoughts: the joyful, exultant beginning, where it sounds as if he is throwing his cap in the air—measures 2 and 6 of the voice part—, then the return to normal thought, to pensiveness and reflection, where the bass notes trudge along with the melody in thirds, only to fall back immediately into their old familiar uniform beat," (Friedlaender: *Die Schöne Müllerin,* p. 89). Descriptions like this seem inappropriate to me; of course they are as widespread today as ever and certainly not just limited to Friedlaender's time (1852–1934), which understood music primarily as the language of the heart, that is, as a medium for expressing what cannot be put into words, not as an autonomous conveyor of meaning.

51  First mentioned in Alfred Heuss: "Franz Schuberts und Friedrich Zöllners 'Das Wandern ist des Müllers Lust,' " in: *Zeitschrift für Musik* 96, 1929, pp. 5–10, 65–70.

52  Cf. the thorough analysis in Georgiades: *Schubert. Musik und Lyrik,* p. 231 f.

53  The compositional-technical premises for such an insertion are described in: A. Feil: *Satztechnische Fragen in den Kompositionslehren von F. E. Niedt, J. Riepel und H. Chr. Koch* [Compositional-technical questions in the composition theories of F. E. Niedt, J. Riepel, and H. Chr. Koch], Heidelberg 1955. This place p. 54 f.

54  Compare the related place in "Eifersucht und Stolz," measure 58: "*Hörst du, kein Wort'* [do you hear, not a word].

55  Cf. Feil: *Studien zu Schuberts Rhythmik,* p. 88 ff.: "Versuch über den 'Tonmechanismus' " [Essay on tone mechanism].

56  In many editions, "Mein!" is incorrectly printed in C time.

57  The performance instruction "Recit." actually appears in the Diabelli edition of *Die Schöne Müllerin* from the 1830s, which goes back to Johann Michael Vogl, Schubert's great singer friend. At "ullen eine gute Nacht" there is an additional "ad libitum."

58  Georgiades (*Schubert. Musik und Lyrik,* pp. 241–243) has described the linguistic-musical structure in detail.

59  D. Fischer-Dieskau: *Auf den Spuren der Schubert-Lieder* [On the trail of the Schubert songs], p. 206.

60  The transition after his conversation with himself takes place in the rest measure, 22. E. Schwarmath has described the function of rest measures in "turning points" of this and similar types in her dissertation: *Musikalischer Bau und Sprachvertonung in Schuberts Liedern* [Musical structure and the setting of speech to music in Schubert's songs], Tutzing 1969, p. 53 ff.

61  E. Schwarmath, *Musikalischer Bau und Sprachvertonung in Schuberts Liedern,* has described this nicely, p. 187 f, note 23.

62  On the differences in the types of 6/8 time, cf. A. Feil: "Mozarts Duett 'Bei Männern, welche Liebe fühlen.' Periodisch-metrische Fragen" [Mozart's duet 'Bei Männern . .': Periodic-metric problems in: *Festschrift Walther Gerstenberg zum 60. Geburtstag* [Festschrift for Walther Gerstenberg on his sixtieth birthday], Wolfenbüttel 1964, pp. 45–54.

63  Composition theory on the second half of the 18th century, still widely accepted during Schubert's time, has a binding stipulation that whenever a two-measure unit is expanded to three measures, it must be repeated. So

Schubert is simply following composition theory, giving it meaning in his composition at the same time. Cf. A. Feil: *Satztechnische Fragen in den Kompositionslehren von F. E. Niedt, J. Riepel und H. Chr. Koch,* Heidelberg 1955.

64    Cf. W. Dürr: *Neue Schubert-Ausgabe, Lieder. Band 2.*

65    It strikes me as typical that Schubert writes and composes ". . . durft' ich aushauchen in Lieder*schmerz*" [I could breathe out in painful song] whereas Wilhelm Müller used the rhyme "Lieder*scherz*" [jesting song]. Most Schubert editions fail to point out this change.

66    *Schubert,* p. 262.

67    Supporting this view is the fact that the fermata on the closing b-flat of the piano in the last measure, between the stanzas, (middle of the measure) is *not* to be held; it only denotes the end after the last stanza. Therefore the introduction should not be repeated as closing. Cf. W. Dürr: *Neue Schubert-Ausgabe, Lieder. Band 2.*

68    The declamation error in the second stanza: "und brechen in ihren Kohl-garten ein" [and break into her cabbage *patch*] can be traced back to an engraver's error in the first edition. It should be corrected as follows (cf. *Neue Schubert-Ausgabe, Lieder, Band 2*):

Example 88
und   bre-chen in   ih - ren   Kohlgar-ten ein,

69    *Schubert. Musik und Lyrik,* pp. 272–282.

70    The poem has no stanza division but falls easily into three groups of four lines.

71    Georgiades: *Schubert. Musik und Lyrik,* p. 277.

72    Compare the "Gelt" in "Danksagung an den Bach," measure 13.

73    D. Fischer-Dieskau: *Auf den Spuren der Schubert-Lieder,* p. 208.

74    Georgiades' (*Schubert. Musik und Lyrik,* p. 283, note 1) count: The tone sounds a total of 536 times!

75    The compositional method used here, the "scaffolding principle" (Georgiades), was developed from thoroughbass composition by the so-called pre-classical composers; the Viennese classical composers Haydn, Mozart, and Beethoven adopted and expanded it. It was first described by Thr. Georgiades in relation to parts of Mozart's operas ("Aus der Musiksprache des Mozart-Theaters" [From the musical language of the Mozart theater], in: *Mozart-Jahrbuch 1950,* pp. 76–98) and subsequently by A. Feil in relation to symphonic movements of Johann Stamitz and Beethoven (*Satztechnische Fragen in den Kompositionslehren von F. E. Niedt, J. Riepel und H. Chr. Koch,* Heidelberg 1955, pp. 93–99, and: "Zur Satztechnik in Beethovens Vierter Sinfonie" [On the compositional technique in Beethoven's Fourth Symphony] in: *Archiv für Musikwissenschaft* XVI, 1959, pp. 391–399). E. Schwarmath, following Georgiades (*Schubert. Musik und Lyrik,* p. 69), examined it more closely in connection with Schubert (*Musikalischer Bau und Sprachvertonung in Schuberts Liedern,* Tutzing 1969).

76    It is not by coincidence that the last of the eight variations on this song for flute and piano is a march (D 802—Op. post. 160; January 1824; cf. *Neue Schubert-Ausgabe, Werke für Klavier und ein Instrument* [New Schubert edition, works for piano and one instrument], edited by H. Wirth, Kassel 1970). To the best of my knowledge, the first person to point out how closely this song

conforms to a funeral march was F. V. Damian in his excellent booklet: *Franz Schuberts Liederkreis 'Die Schöne Müllerin''* [Franz Schubert's song cycle "Die Schöne Müllerin"], Leipzig 1928.

77   In current editions, accents and *fp* should be expanded in keeping with this example. Cf. *Neue Schubert-Ausgabe, Lieder. Band 2.*

78   *Schubert. Musik und Lyrik*, pp. 305–318.

79   Alpine yodeling, from whose melodies this part is derived, has been called "harmonisches Getön" [harmonic din].

80   On the previously noted recordings, one by Dietrich Fischer-Dieskau and Gerald Moore and the other by Peter Pears and Benjamin Britten, both take the quarter note at about 52.

81   In order to distinguish his *Pastorale* from his other symphonies, and also to indicate that it was not just part of the old tradition of naive program music, Beethoven wrote at the top of his score just this once: "Mehr Ausdruck der Empfindung als Malerei" [More an expression of feeling than tone painting].

82   Compare also the upper voice in "Erster Verlust" [First loss] from Robert Schumann's *Album für die Jugend* [Album for the young] Op. 68, 1848).

83   In the seventh and last chapter of *Der Zauberberg* [The magic mountain] (1926), in the section "Fülle des Wohllauts" [Fullness of harmony].

84   Georgiades: *Schubert. Musik und Lyrik*, p. 361.

85   Schubert also uses horn fifths motivically in the piano part in another place, when the memory of good times past is addressed in the text. Compare for example "Antigone und Oedip" (D 542; Op. 6, 2; March 1817; text by Johann Mayrhofer; *Neue Schubert-Ausgabe, Lieder. Band 2*, p. 50 ff.).

86   Commentators frequently fail to consider that Silcher was older than Schubert. He was born in 1789, but his life span extended far into the 19th century (he died in 1860), and so into another musical era. His folk songs and adaptations began to spread widely and rapidly after 1826 (!).

87   As we have noted before, dynamic markings are seldom provided in Schubert's voice parts.

88   By contrast, this is a fundamental characteristic of so-called Romantic music.

89   The question as to whether the third eighth note of the triplet in the right piano hand of "Wasserflut" and the sixteenth note of the left hand should be struck together or consecutively is probably best answered this way: If the song is performed alone, that is, outside the context of the cycle, one may prefer the rhythmic sharpening of the dotted eighth—it is more interesting. But *within* the cycle one should align them and otherwise (such as in measure 7) file down the dotted values rather than sharpen them, because only then are the triplets clearly distinguishable in their relationship to those of the preceding songs. Rhythmic sharpening, in addition, brings a certain activity to the flow, which contrasts with the weary resignation of the song.

In Schubert's manuscript, as well as in the first edition, the last sixteenth note of measure 3 appears directly beneath the third eighth of the triplet, as it does in the old complete edition, whereas most newer editions, probably going back to the Peters edition, set the sixteenth note *after* the eighth of the triplet. However, we should not hastily conclude from this that the notes are to be aligned rhythmically. In those days there were performance practices governing such cases that were taken for granted—and remain valid today, though to a more limited extent. The trained musician knew and applied them regardless of the notation in a given situation. However, one should also keep in mind that in the time of Beethoven and Schubert, the rigidity of such "rules of the game" in music and performance practice was on the decline, and new possibilities outside the traditional system were gaining acceptance. Cf. A. Feil and W. Dürr: "Die Neue Schubert-Ausgabe. Über einige Probleme des Herausgebens von Musik," in: *Österreichische Musikzeitschrift* 24, 1969, No. 10, pp. 553–563.

90    Experiment by singing the song from memory, and note whether the entrances fall as Schubert has composed them. Variations such as the one between the first "Ob's unter seiner Rinde..." (measure 48 with sixteenth-note pickup) and the second (measure 62 with eighth-note pickup) are certainly no accident. An alignment in this case would not mean that the performer had taken liberties with the text declamation.

91    Schubert changed the tempo mark for "Auf dem Flusse" from "Mässig" [moderately], which corresponds to the first song, "Gute Nacht," to "Langsam" [slowly], which we find here.

92    As in the folk song: "Drei Lilien, drei Lilien, die pflanzt' ich auf mein Grab. Da kam ein stolzer Reiter und brach sie ab.—Ach Reitersmann, ach Reitersmann, lass doch die Lilien stehn, sie soll ja mein feins Liebchen noch einmal sehn." [Three lilies, three lilies, I planted on my grave. Along came a proud horseman and picked them. Ah, horseman, ah, horseman, let the lilies be, for I want my sweetheart to see them once more."]

93    Georgiades: *Schubert. Musik und Lyrik,* p. 361.

94    Schubert forms the lines "der Rücken fühlte... mich wehen" and their repeat into two five-measure phrases (21–25, 26–30), which complement each other symmetrically—but only on the surface. They have different internal structures, and therefore, when the listener compares them, "subconsciously counting," they appear different in "content."

95    Georgiades: *Schubert. Musik und Lyrik,* p. 360.

96    On the problem of the tragic element in the music of the Viennese classic composers and Schubert, cf. Thr. G. Georgiades: *Musik und Sprache. Das Werden der abendländischen Musik dargestellt an der Vertonung der Messe* [Music and speech. The development of westen music illustrated in the musical setting of the mass], Heidelberg etc. ²1974 (= *Verständliche Wissenschaft* Vol. 50), Chapter 11 "Die Wiener Klassiker" [The Viennese classic composers] and Chapter 12 "Stufen musikalischer Wirklichkeit" [Levels of musical reality].

97    *Musikalischer Bau...,* p. 55.

98    This is why the frequent essays on Schubert's songs proceeding from such themes as the portrayal of nature in the piano accompaniment usually leave the reader unsatisfied.

99    Richard Benz: *Die Stunde der deutschen Musik* [The hour of German music], Jena 1923, ²1943, p. 373.

100    Cf. Paul Mies: "Die Bedeutung des Unisono im Schubertschen Liede" [The significance of unison in the Schubert song] in: *Zeitschrift für Musikwissenschaft* XI, 1928/29, pp. 96–108.

101    Schwarmath: *Musikalischer Bau...,* p. 145.

102    The decrescendo mark in measure 32 is to be interpreted as an accent applying to the measure as a whole; the *fz* in measure 33, as a repeat of this accent with the entry of the dissonant chord instead of the tonic. Not until

measure 33 does a decrescendo occur, leading to the piano of the next measure, where the repeat begins.

103 Georgiades offers a careful and detailed analytical interpretation in: *Schubert. Musik and Lyrik,* pp. 370–376. He concludes: "This perhaps somewhat fragile song is a great masterpiece."

104 Cf. Georgiades: *Schubert. Musik and Lyrik,* p. 360.

105 Cf. Feil: *Studien zu Schuberts Rhythmik,* p. 88 ff: "Versuch über den 'Tonmechanismus.' "

106 The introduction is described in detail and analyzed by E. Schwarmath in: *Musikalischer Bau . . . ,* p. 139 f.—Behind the noted C time, in which all conclusions fall in the middle of a measure, which is not at all what the listener hears, I perceive a 2/4 time. Then the introduction would not consist of 2 + 1 (C) measures, but of 4 + 2 (2/4) measures; that is, it would now be symmetrical—the way we actually hear it. The same thing holds for the other phrases in the song. Typically, there is an uncertainty about the time signature in Schubert's fair copy (the working manuscript is lost): 2/4 is crossed out and replaced by C. What might have caused Schubert to make this correction (and to change the tempo mark, which was originally "Nicht zu geschwind, doch kräftig" [not too fast, but forcefully]), and whether the original version was perhaps written in 2/4 time, are not discussed further here. Hugo Riemann, in his Steingräber edition of *Winterreise,* has shifted each of Schubert's bar lines one half measure, so that all final chords fall after the bar line. The unprejudiced musician, if told to write out the song from musical dictation, will either write it in 2/4 time from the beginning, or set the bar lines in C time as Riemann did in his edition, rather than as Schubert set them.

107 For rhythmic formations of this kind as hallmarks of Schubert's compositional technique and "style," cf. A. Feil: *Studien zu Schuberts Rhythmik,* Munich 1966, passim.

108 Schwarmath: *Musikalischer Bau . . . ,* p. 168.

109 Schwarmath: *Musikalischer Bau . . . ,* p. 55 f.

110 "'Das Wirtshaus' von Schubert und das Kyrie aus dem gregorianischen Requiem" ['Das Wirtshaus" by Schubert and the Kyrie from the Gregorian Requiem], in: *Gegenwart im Geiste, Festschrift für Richard Benz* [The present-day mind. Festschrift for Richard Benz], Hamburg 1954; then in: *Schubert. Musik und Lyrik,* p. 381.

111 *Schubert. Musik und Lyrik,* p. 379 f.

112 Cf. Georg Knepler: *Musikgeschichte des 19. Jahrhunderts* [Music history of the 19th century], Berlin 1961, Vol. II, p. 646 f.

113 For instance, cf. Richard Capell: *Schubert's Songs,* London 1928, and recapitulated in Alfred Einstein: *Schubert. Ein musikalisches Porträt* [Schubert. A musical portrait], Zürich 1952. (Engl. edition New York, 1951)

114 Tempo mark in the first version of the song: "Mässig, kräftig" [moderately, forcefully], that is, related to the motion of "Gute Nacht"; later: "Ziemlich geschwind, kräftig" [quite fast, forcefully], that is, related to 'Der stürmische Morgen."

115 The first version calls for an earlier return to the *forte,* at measures 8 and 15, rather than 10 and 17.

116 For the completely different understanding of song by the so-called

Romantic composers, compare the thought-provoking article by Moritz Bauer: "Zu Schuberts Gedächtnis" [In Schubert's memory], in: *Zeitschrift für Musikwissenschaft* XI, 1928/29, p. 129 ff., especially p. 133 ff.

117  "Toward the end of the song, there is usually a text repeat, as in all songs of *Winterreise* except 'Die Nebensonnen,' 'Täuschung,' and 'Der Leiermann.' In 'Der Leiermann,' the two last lines of the second and fourth stanzas are repeated in typical fashion, but not the closing, in which the old man is addressed directly."

118  Quoted from Georgiades: *Schubert. Musik und Lyrik*, p. 388 f.

119  The instrument is not a barrel organ, but rather a hurdy-gurdy, a folk music instrument used all over Europe since the Middle Ages, especially by street musicians. It consisted of a body shaped like a lute, guitar, or viol; one or two melody strings tuned in unison and stopped by springed keys; and two or four drone strings, which always produce the same two tones. All strings were struck simultaneously by a rotating wheel.

120  Georgiades: *Schubert. Musik und Lyrik*, p. 389, note 3.

121  Theodor W. Adorno: "Schubert," in: *Die Musik*, 21, 1928, No. 1 (reprinted in: *Moments musicaux*, Frankfurt a. M., 1964, pp. 18–36).

121a Ed. note: The teacher Friedrich Ludwig Jahn (1778–1852) established the first open-air gymnasium in 1811, stressing fitness as a patriotic virtue. He soon gained a large following and became known as "Turnvater Jahn" [Father of Gymnastics]. Gymnastics clubs sprang up throughout the land and were at the height of popularity between 1840 and 1914.

122  This was probably the edition from which Schubert worked. Except for the modernization of orthography and punctuation the text reprinted here is complete and true to the original—that is, it also includes the poems that Schubert did not set to music:

> Der Dichter, als Prolog
> Das Mühlenleben
> Erster Schmerz, letzter Scherz
> Blümlein Vergissmein
> Der Dichter, als Epilog

The numbers here are those of Schubert's cycle. Changes Schubert made in Wilhelm Müller's text are added in square brackets and distinguished by italic type. For details of the text form, compare: *Neue Schubert-Ausgabe, Lieder. Band 2.*

123  Schubert composed according to the text he was working from: "Und immer heller rauschte / Und immer heller der Bach." The change to "frischer," which has become established, goes back to a handwritten entry by Müller in a copy of the poems located in Dessau. Max Friedlaender adopted it for his Peters edition and it spread from there.

124  This edition of Müller's poems was probably what Schubert worked from for the first part. Except for the modernization of orthography and punctuation, the text reprinted here is complete and true to the original. The numbering is the same for Müller and Schubert. Changes that Schubert made in Wilhelm Müller's text are added in square brackets and distinguished by italic type.

125  This was probably the text Schubert used for his *Fortsetzung der Winterreise*

*von Wilh. Müller* (this heading appeared above "1. Die Post" in the autograph). Of the entire cycle (for the sequence, compare p. 24f), only the additional poems Schubert found in this edition and composed as a "continuation" are reprinted here. See the preceding note regarding text form. The poems are not numbered in Müller's version. The numbers here are from Schubert's first edition, in which the songs are numbered straight through; those in parentheses are from the autograph, in which Schubert numbered the second part beginning again with 1.

# IX. Editions and Literature

## 1. Editions

*Franz Schuberts Werke. Erste kritisch durchgesehene Gesamtausgabe* [Franz Schubert's works. First complete critical edition], Series XX, *Lieder und Gesänge* [Songs] (edited by Eusebius Mandyczewski), Vols. 7 and 9, Leipzig 1894–1895 Also pertaining to this: *Revisionsbericht* [Critical commentary], edited by E. Mandyzcewski, Leipzig 1897

*Franz Schubert. Lieder und Gesänge* [Franz Schubert. Songs]. Complete popular edition organized by voice range and chronology. Based on the critical edition edited by E. Mandyczewski, Vol. I, Song Cycles, Leipzig (Breitkopf & Hartel) n. d. (ca. 1900)

*Schubert-Album.* Collection of songs for one voice and piano accompaniment. Revision by Max Friedlaender based on the first editions, Vol. 1, Leipzig (Peters) 1884 Variants and critical commentary to Vol. 1, ed. by M. Friedlaender, Leipzig (Peters) 1884

*Die Schöne Müllerin. Ein Zyklus von Liedern, gedichtet von Wilhelm Müller, in Musik gesetzt von Franz Schubert. Kritische Ausgabe* [Die Schöne Müllerin. A cycle of songs written by Wilhelm Müller, set to music by Franz Schubert. Critical edition], introduction, notes, and text revision by M. Friedlaender, Leipzig (Peters) n. d. (1922)

*Franz Schubert. Neue Ausgabe sämtlicher Werke* [Franz Schubert. New edition of his complete works], Series IV: *Lieder. Band 2 und Band 4* [Songs. Volume 2 and Volume 4], presented by Walther Dürr, Kassel etc. (Bärenreiter) 1975 and 1979 (with a considerable number of corrections in respect to the widely used editions and those named)

*Franz Schubert. Lieder,* Urtext der Neuen Schubert-Ausgabe [Songs, original text of the new Schubert edition], edited by Walther Dürr, Kassel etc. (Bärenreiter) and München (Henle), Book 1: *Die Schöne Müllerin,* Book 2: *Winterreise* (each for high or mid-range voice). In process of publication.

*Franz Schubert. Die Winterreise.* Facsimile reprint of the original manuscript, published by Bärenreiter-Verlag, Kassel and Basel 1955

*Schuberts Liederzyklen. Die Schöne Müllerin, Winterreise und Schwanengesang* [Schubert's song cycles . . .]. Reduced facsimile of the original editions, edited and introduced by Heinrich Kralik, Verlag Steyrermühl, Vienna n. d. (= *Tagblatt-Bibliothek* No. 625/633)

Literature pertaining to the editions

Arnold Feil and Walther Dürr: "Kritische Gesamtausgaben von Werken Franz Schuberts im 19. Jahrhundert" [Complete critical editions of Franz Schubert's works in the 19th century], in: *Musik und Verlag, Festschrift für Karl Vötterle* [Music and the publishing house, Festschrift for Karl Vötterle], Kassel etc. 1968, pp. 268–278

Id.: "Die Neue Schubert-Ausgabe. Über einige Probleme des Herausgebens von Musik" [The new Schubert edition. Concerning a few problems in the publishing of music], in: *Österreichische Musikzeitschrift* 24, 1969, pp. 553–563

## 2. Source Works

Otto Erich Deutsch: *Schubert. Thematic Catalog of All His Works in Chronological Order*, London 1951

*Schubert. Die Dokumente seines Lebens* [Schubert. The documents of his life], collected and annotated by O. E. Deutsch, Kassel etc. 1964 (= *Neue Schubert-Ausgabe*, Series VIII: *Supplement. Vol. 5*) (See Note 14)

*Schubert. Die Erinnerungen seiner Freunde* [Schubert. The recollections of his friends] collected and edited by O. E. Deutsch. Leipzig ²1966 (See Note 12)

*Franz Schubert. Die Dokumente seines Lebens und Schaffens*, edited by O. E. Deutsch. Third volume: *Schubert. Sein Leben in Bildern* [His life in pictures], Munich and Leipzig 1913

*Franz Schubert. Die Texte seiner einstimmig komponierten Lieder und ihre Dichter* [Franz Schubert. The texts of his songs composed for one voice and the poets who wrote them], complete collection edited by Maximilian and Lilly Schochow, 2 Vols., Hildesheim and New York 1974

## 3. Literature

Willi Kahl: *Verzeichnis des Schrifttums über Franz Schubert 1828–1928* [Index of writings on Franz Schubert 1828–1928], Regensburg 1938 (= *Kölner Beiträge zur Musikforschung* [Cologne articles on music research] 1)

### a) Biographies

Maurice J. E. Brown: *Schubert. Eine kritische Biographie* [Schubert. A critical biography], Wiesbaden 1969 (English: London 1958)

Id. and Hans Redlich: "Schubert," in: *Die Musik in Geschichte und Gegenwart. Eine allgemeine Enzyklopädie der Musik* [Music in history and in the present. A general encyclopedia of music], edited by Friedrich Blume, Vol. 12, Kassel etc. 1965 (with a comprehensive index of works and literature)

Alfred Einstein: *Schubert. Ein musikalisches Porträt* [Schubert. A musical portrait], Zürich 1952 [English ed. New York 1951]

Harry Goldschmidt: *Franz Schubert. Ein Lebensbild* [Franz Schubert. A picture of his life], Berlin ⁴1962

Heinrich Kreissle von Hellborn: *Franz Schubert,* Vienna 1865

Ludwig Kusche: *Franz Schubert. Dichtung und Wahrheit* [Franz Schubert. Fiction and fact], Munich 1962

Walther Vetter: *Der Klassiker Schubert,* 2 Vols., Leipzig 1953

### b) Studies

On Schubert

Theodor W. Adorno: "Schubert," in: *Die Musik* 21, 1928, No. 1 (reprinted in: *Moments musicaux*, Frankfurt a. M. 1964, pp. 18–36)

Arnold Feil: *Studien zu Schuberts Rhythmik,* Munich 1966

Peter Gülke: "Die Verjährung der Meisterwerke," [The aging of master works] in: *Neue Zeitschrift für Musik,* 127, 1966, pp. 6–12

On the song genre

Max Friedlaender: *Das deutsche Lied im 18. Jahrhundert. Quellen und Studien* [The German song in the 18th century. Sources and studies], 2 Vols., Stuttgart and Berlin 1902 (Reprint: Hildesheim 1962)

Hans Joachim Moser: *Das deutsche Lied seit Mozart* [The German song since Mozart], 2 Vols., Zürich 1937 (Reprint: Tutzing 1966)

Heinrich W. Schwab: *Sangbarkeit, Popularität und Kunstlied. Studien zu Lied und Liedästhetik der mittleren Goethezeit 1770–1814* [Singability, popularity, and the art song. Studies on the song and song esthetics of the middle Goethe period 1770–1814], Regensburg 1965 (= *Studien zur Musikgeschichte des 19. Jahrhunderts* [Studies on the music history of the 19th century] Vol. 3)

Walter Wiora: *Das deutsche Lied. Zur Geschichte und Ästhetik einer musikalischen Gattung* [The German song. On the history and esthetics of a musical genre], Wolfenbüttel 1971

On Schubert's songs

Moritz Bauer: *Die Lieder Franz Schuberts* [The songs of Franz Schubert], Vol. 1 (no more were published), Leipzig 1915

Richard Capell: *Schubert's Songs*, London 1928 ($^2$1957)

Franz Valentin Damian: *Franz Schuberts Liederkreis 'Die Schöne Müllerin'* [Franz Schubert's song cycle 'Die Schöne Müllerin'], Leipzig 1928

Dietrich Fischer-Dieskau: *Auf den Spuren der Schubert-Lieder* [On the trail of the Schubert songs], Wiesbaden 1971

Thrasybulos G. Georgiades: *Schubert. Musik und Lyrik*, Göttingen 1967

Thrasybulos G. Georgiades: " 'Das Wirtshaus' von Schubert und das Kyrie aus dem gregorianischen Requiem" ['Das Wirtshaus" by Schubert and the Kyrie from the Gregorian Requiem], in: *Gegenwart im Geiste. Festschrift für Richard Benz* [The present as reflected in the intellect. Festschrift for Richard Benz], Hamburg 1954

Harry Goldschmidt: "Schuberts 'Winterreise,' " In: *Um die Sache der Musik* [On the subject of music], Leipzig 1970

Alfred Heuss: "Franz Schuberts und Friedrich Zöllners 'Das Wandern ist des Müllers Lust,' " in: *Zeitschrift für Musik* 96, 1929, pp. 5–10 and 65–70

Felicitas von Kraus: *Beiträge zur Erforschung des malenden und poetisierenden Wesens in der Begleitung von Franz Schuberts Liedern* [Research on the tone-painting and poetizing elements in the accompaniment of Franz Schubert's songs], Mainz 1928

Paul Mies: *Der Meister des Liedes*, Berlin 1928

Erdmute Schwarmath: *Musikalischer Bau und Sprachvertonung in Schuberts Liedern* [Musical structure and the setting of speech to music in Schubert's songs], Tutzing 1969 (= *Münchner Veröffentlichungen zur Musikgeschichte* [Munich publications on music history] Vol. 17)

Julian Armitage-Smith: "Schubert's 'Winterreise,' Part I: The sources of the musical text," in: *The Musical Quarterly* 60, 1974, pp. 20–36

Marc-André Souchay: "Zu Schuberts 'Winterreise' " [On Schubert's "Winterreise"], in: *Zeitschrift für Musikwissenschaft* 13, 1930/31, pp. 266–285